SHADOW WARRIORS

SHADOW WARRIORS
The Covert War in Korea

WILLIAM B. BREUER

John Wiley & Sons, Inc.
New York • Chichester • Brisbane • Toronto • Singapore

Copyright © 1996 by William B. Breuer
Published by John Wiley & Sons, Inc.

Library of Congress Cataloging-in-Publication Data:

Breuer, William B.
    Shadow warriors : the covert war in Korea / William B. Breuer.
        p.   cm.
    Includes bibliographical references and index.
    ISBN 0-471-14438-X (cloth : alk. paper)
    1. Korean War, 1950–1953—Military intelligence. 2. Korean War,
1950–1953—Korea (North)—Wonsan. 3. Subversive activities—Korea
(North)—Wonsan. 4. Korean War, 1950–1953—United States.
5. Korean War, 1950–1953—Great Britain. I. Title.
DS921.5.S7B74   1996
951.904'2—dc20   95-35856

Printed in the United States of America

10 9 8 7 6 5 4 3 2 1

Dedicated to

MAJOR GENERAL JOHN K. SINGLAUB
United States Army (Ret.),
a valiant warrior and patriot
whose covert exploits in
three major wars and many
global locales have been
equaled by few.

Undermine the enemy. Subvert him, attack his morale, strike at his economy, corrupt him. Sow internal discord among his leaders. Then his army will fall to you.

Sun Tzu
Chinese conqueror
550 B.C.

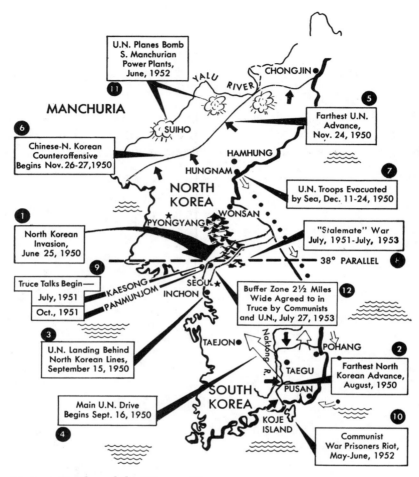

Major episodes of the Korean War

Contents

Acknowledgments

JOHN DONNE, the noted sixteenth-century poet and philosopher, wrote the often-quoted line: "No man is an island entire of himself." That time-honored truism most certainly applies to a nonfiction author who must diligently collect thousands of bits of information and painstakingly piece them together in a book such as this one. Had it not been for the invaluable assistance of many individuals, institutions, and organizations, creating this work would have been impossible.

I am especially indebted to the participants in the clandestine actions who related their experiences in person, by telephone and fax, and by correspondence. Although their recollections remain quite vivid, many of them conferred by mail or telephone with former comrades in Korea to double-check their own memories.

Special appreciation is expressed to Joseph C. Goulden, an acclaimed American historian and foremost authority on the Korean War era, who provided leads for tracking down participants and furnished significant research materials and photographs.

Others who were most helpful in a variety of ways include the following:

William Colby, former director of the Central Intelligence Agency (CIA); W. Raymond Wannall, former assistant director for intelligence of the Federal Bureau of Investigation (FBI); Richard A. Long, head, oral history, Marine Corps History Division and Museum, Washington, D.C.; Swanson D. Carter, unit chief, FBI Office of Public Affairs, Washington, D.C.; Michael P. Korton, unit chief, FBI Press Office, Washington, D.C.

Fred L. Schultz, editor-in-chief, U.S. Naval Institute, Annapolis, Maryland; James L. Gilbert, historian, U.S. Army Intelligence and Security Command, Fort Belvoir, Virginia; Benedict K. Zobrist, director, Harry S. Truman Library, Independence, Missouri; Archie DiFante, historian, Historical Research Center, Maxwell Air Force Base,

Alabama; Richard J. Sommers, historian and archivist, U.S. Army Military History Institute, Carlisle Barracks, Pennsylvania; Colonel Lyman H. Hammond (Ret.), director, Douglas MacArthur Memorial, Norfolk, Virginia; Dean Allard, Naval Historical Center, Washington, D.C.

Lieutenant General William P. Yarborough (Ret.); Vice Admiral John D. Bulkeley (Ret.); Don Lassen, publisher, airborne *Static Line,* Atlanta, Georgia; Colonel Morton N. Katz (Ret.); Lieutenant Colonel Michael Mark (Ret.), editor, *Military* magazine, Sacramento, California; Matt Matteson, executive director, Korean Rangers Association; Colonel Herman W. Dammer (Ret.), Korean Rangers; Lieutenant General Edward M. Flanagan (Ret.), and two former CIA officials who prefer to remain anonymous.

Also of immense importance in creating this book were the diligent and tireless efforts of my wife, Vivien. She conducted extensive and meticulous research, helped with the vast volume of correspondence that was generated, pursued slim clues to help locate participants, and performed many other literary chores.

A tip of my hat to the qualified persons who read various manuscript chapters or portions of them with the critical eye of experts and provided most helpful critiques and suggestions.

It was my good fortune to have working with me at John Wiley & Sons (publishers since 1807) exceptionally gifted professionals, Associate Managing Editor John K. Cook and Senior Editor Hana Umlauf Lane, and their skilled staff members.

William B. Breuer
Lookout Mountain, Tennessee

1

"Terminating" a Communist General

AN EARLY-MORNING MIST hovered over the bustling port of Sasebo, in southwestern Japan, as a cigar-shaped American submarine slipped out of the harbor and set a westward course across the Sea of Japan. Its destination was Wonsan, on the east coast of North Korea and nearly one hundred miles above the front lines where United Nations forces were locked in a death struggle with Chinese and North Korean Communist armies. It was late March, 1951.

On board the submarine were three men on a deadly secret mission: to seek out a certain top North Korean general and "terminate him with prejudice," cloak-and-dagger jargon for assassination. Two of the terminators were members of the elite U.S. navy underwater demolition teams (UDT), and the third was a British Royal Marine. All there were enlisted men who had been handpicked for their courage, physical stamina, and resourcefulness. None held any illusion that their task would be a simple one. Rather, it had the earmarks of a suicide sashay.

One of the Americans, Petty Officer Milt Von Mann, was a native of Alabama and had just turned twenty-one. Stocky, strong, and oozing with self-confidence, Von Mann had been a star fullback on his high school football team. Later he joined the UDTs because their hazardous function appealed to his venturesome nature. Six months earlier, he had been wounded while clearing underwater mines ahead of General Douglas MacArthur's amphibious assault at Inchon, an operation that caught the North Korean generals totally by surprise and halted their all-out offensive to drive the Americans into the sea.[1]

Boatswain Mate Harry Branson, at age thirty, was an old hand at war, having seen heavy fighting with one of the U.S. navy's first UDTs in the Pacific during World War II. A man of average height and

1

build, Branson was serious-minded, always focused intently upon the task at hand.

Sergeant Miles Gibbons, the third member of the team, was forty years old and powerfully built. As a teenager, Gibbons had joined the Royal Marines and was shipped halfway around the world to the British crown colony of Hong Kong. There he was assigned to a gunboat that cruised the coast in search of Chinese pirate vessels. During World War II, Gibbons fought as a guerrilla leader and secret agent behind Japanese lines in China and Burma.[2]

Milt Von Mann knew that the odds were stacked against the success of the mission. The Wonsan region was thick with Communist soldiers, and Westerners would be especially vulnerable because their Caucasian features set them apart from the North Korean civilians. There was a bright side, however. Von Mann was reassured to know that in a tight situation, he would have the help of stalwarts like Gibbons and Branson.[3]

The audacious scheme to terminate the North Korean general had its origins in London and was based on the knowledge that the two Communist superpowers, China and the Soviet Union, were deeply suspicious of one another despite their public pose of solidarity. In Korea, the two nations had joined in a marriage of convenience to try to crush the armed forces of the United States and its democratic allies. Chinese troops were fighting, and the Soviets had been and were clandestinely providing the North Koreans with weapons, ammunition, supplies, and large number of military "advisers."

Seeking to drive an even deeper wedge between the Chinese and the Soviets, British intelligence had targeted the North Korean general as the centerpiece of the stratagem. It was widely known that he was a "Stalinist general" who had close ties with and admiration for the leaders in Moscow, and only disdain for the Chinese. The idea was for him to be terminated in a way that would lead the Soviets to conclude that the Chinese had perpetrated the deed.

Once the concept had been hatched, London turned the detailed planning and implementation over to British intelligence officers in Japan. Through information culled from spies planted in the higher echelons of the North Korean government and military, the Brits knew that the target was a political general, and in that role carried great clout in army circles. Most combat commanders pandered to him because of his close friendship with key North Korean government leaders.

Tall for a Korean and heavyset, the general was much admired by junior officers and enlisted men because he seemed to care about their well-being and morale. His pattern was to tour North Korea in his plush private railroad coach, which had once belonged to a wealthy Japanese industrialist. The coach would be connected to the rear of a freight train, and when it reached his destination, the railcar would be cut loose and shunted onto a sidetrack. There it would remain for two or three days while the general called on army units in the region to indoctrinate them with heavy doses of Communist philosophy. When a visit was concluded, the coach would be hitched onto another freight train that would take the general to his next stop.

Traveling with the general on his railroad tours was his Russian-born wife, who reputedly was a major in the NKVD, the sinister Soviet secret police. She had met and married the North Korean when they were both studying Communism at Moscow University several years earlier. It was there that the general was introduced to Stalin, whom he greatly admired. In essence, the North Korean was a secret agent for the Soviets.

Again through secret sources in North Korea, British intelligence had learned that the general would be in Wonsan for three days during which his coach would be parked on a sidetrack. So it was decided that a three-man team, loaded with explosives, would sneak ashore and blow up the coach while the general was in it.

Now, thirty-six hours after the three terminators' submarine departed from Sasebo, it surfaced off Wonsan under a blanket of night. The three men, wearing black clothing, their hands and faces blackened with grease and charcoal, climbed out of the hatch and stood on the slippery deck, peering toward the shore. There were no lights or other signs of life.

Clutching submachine guns and toting backpacks crammed with dynamite sticks, putty, and timing devices, they edged into an inflated rubber dinghy and began to paddle. As they approached the beach, their tenseness heightened; at any moment they might be raked by bursts of gunfire. Minutes later, the dinghy crunched onto the sand, and the men paused to listen for any telltale noise that might indicate their arrival had been detected. There was only the sound of the gentle lapping of the surf.

Swiftly and silently, they hid the dinghy in the sand nearby and marked the spot with a circle of seashells so that it could be found easily upon their return. Then they began marching inland. All were acutely aware that they now were marooned in hostile territory; the submarine had cast off and would not return to pick them up until the evening of the third day.

Dawn, gray and foreboding, broke just as the intruders reached their destination. Hearts quickened. Fifty yards to the front stood the general's coach. So far, so good. After scanning the bleak landscape to make certain no hostile eyes were watching, they walked along the tracks for a half-mile to an abandoned water tower that would serve as their base. The structure had been selected after a study of aerial reconnaissance photos back in Japan. From the upper reaches of the tower, the three men, peering through high-powered binoculars, would be able to observe activities around the coach.

Just past ten o'clock that morning, the eyes in the tower caught their first glimpse of the general. Resplendent in a dress uniform, he emerged from his coach and, while his chauffeur and two aides bowed and fawned, he stepped into an olive-drab staff car and set out to make his rounds of the army units.

As soon as the general had departed, the terminators' focus fell on a man, dressed in the shabby garb of a railroad maintenance worker, who was sauntering leisurely back and forth near the coach as though inspecting the tracks. Then a curious scenario unfolded. A Chinese police car, with two occupants, drove up and parked behind a nearby building. It was precisely ten-fifteen. The maintenance worker walked to the vehicle, climbed inside, and remained for exactly twenty-five minutes.

The observers in the water tower concluded that the maintenance worker was actually a spy for the Chinese, and that he had been stationed near the coach to keep a close eye on the Stalinist general and any visitors he might have. No doubt the spy had gone to the police car to report his findings.

That night British Sergeant Miles Gibbons stood watch in the tower while the Americans, Milt Von Mann and Harry Branson, stole along the railroad tracks for several hundred yards to a point where they had seen a few legitimate maintenance workers leave a handcar. On arrival, the two intruders slipped into a nearby shack and stole garments that the crew apparently had left. Then the handcar was put onto the tracks and the two men hand-pumped it back to the water tower and hid it in some bushes.

In the morning, the identical routine that had played out twenty-four hours earlier around the railroad coach took place again. The general left, the Chinese police car appeared and parked in the same spot at exactly ten-fifteen, and the spy strolled over and got into the vehicle, again remaining for twenty-five minutes. It was as though the procedure had been timed almost to the second.

Now, the terminators concocted their tactical plan. Through secret sources, they knew that the general's coach would be hooked up to a freight train at two-forty the next afternoon, so the explosives would have to be planted in broad daylight. It would be exceptionally risky business and would require intricate timing. While Sergeant Miles Gibbons, a crack marksman, would be perched atop the water

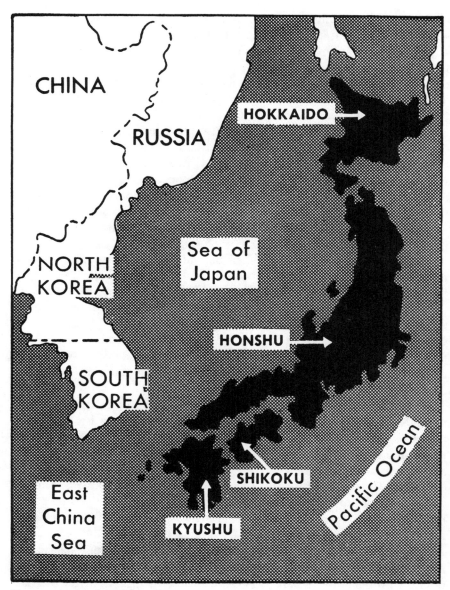

Korea geographical location

tower to provide cover with his sniper's rifle, Milt Von Mann and
Harry Branson would sneak up to the coach during the twenty-five
minutes the spy was out of sight in the parked police car. Success of
the mission would hang on a slim thread: a calculated assumption
that the identical scenario around the coach would unfold as it had
during the previous two mornings.

Dawn on the third day the intruders had spent on North Korean soil brought with it a spring snowfall. That was not all bad: The white stuff would help to mask their presence when Von Mann and Branson were sneaking up to the coach to do the dirty work. Outwardly, the three men were calm. Inside, their tension was growing. How much longer could three Caucasians escape detection in the midst of an Oriental civilian population and Chinese soldiers?

Promptly at ten o'clock, the Communist general rode away in a staff car for his final visits to army units. Moments later, Miles Gibbons scurried to the top of the water tower with his sniper's rifle, which was equipped with a scope, a silencer, and an infrared ray for night vision. Meanwhile, Milt Von Mann and Harry Branson had donned the workclothes pilfered the night before, climbed aboard the handcar, and started pumping it toward the coach. Now it was snowing much harder.

In the event enemy eyes might be watching, the two men halted the handcar a few times and pretended to be inspecting the track. Steadily, they edged closer to the target, feeling quite vulnerable in the daylight. Up ahead, the spy could be seen going through his customary ploy. Von Mann peeked at his watch: It was ten-fifteen. Where was the police car? What if it failed to appear? Moments later, the two Chinese drove up and parked behind the building. No doubt eager to get out of the cold and snow, the spy hurried over and climbed inside the vehicle.

Now the two Americans made their move, pumping the handcar to the rear of the coach where they could not be seen by the occupants of the police car. Crawling on hands and knees, their hearts thumping furiously, Von Mann and Branson slipped under the coach and began attaching the dynamite sticks to its bottom. They planted enough explosives to blow up two railcars that size. Then the timers were set for four-thirty. If their prior calculations proved to be accurate, the general's coach would be on the outskirts of Wonsan when the dynamite detonated.

Trying to act nonchalant, Von Mann and Branson got back on the handcar and returned to the water tower. Sergeant Gibbons scrambled down from his sniper's perch and spoke the obvious: "Let's get the hell out of here!" The three men clambered onto the handcar and pumped it furiously in the direction away from the ticking time bomb. Three miles down the track, they ditched the handcar and set off on a cross-country march of seven miles to link up with the submarine.

Onward they trudged over the bleak terrain. The snowfall had grown into a blizzard and visibility was limited. Suddenly, the terminators felt a jolt of alarm and halted abruptly. Barely discernible, less than forty yards to their front, a heavily armed, ten-man Chinese patrol was marching directly toward them.

Belly-flopping into a gully, the three men lay motionless, their faces pressed into the snow. The sound of marching boots drew closer. And closer. Now the heavy footsteps were just above their heads. Detection seemed certain. But the clumping sounds grew dimmer and finally faded away. The intruders peered cautiously above the rim of the gully and issued sighs of relief. The patrol was out of sight. "They came so close I could smell the garlic on their breaths!" Milt Von Mann whispered.[4]

Their lives had been spared because the providential blizzard snow-blinded the Chinese patrol.

The North Korean political general's private coach had been hooked onto a freight train and now was crossing a bridge over a river outside of Wonsan when . . . *Boom! Boom! Boom!* The railcar erupted in a huge ball of fire, and jagged chunks of metal and wood soared high into the snow-speckled sky.

Although marching far from the blast site, the terminators heard the muffled sound. "I believe a eulogy will be in order in the ancestral home of the general!" the Royal Marine remarked.[5]

At dusk, the men reached the beach and recovered their hidden inflatable dinghy. Von Mann picked up a few of the small seashells that had marked the spot and stuck them in a pocket. "I want to remember Wonsan," he explained.[6]

Night fell. Now the men were confronted by another haunting peril: The surf had been whipped into a frenzy by the blizzard, and paddling out to the submarine would be difficult, perhaps impossible. So they carried the dinghy out to sea until the water was almost up to their necks to get past the angry surf. Then Miles Gibbons got into the dinghy to steer, while Branson and Von Mann took hold of connecting lines and began swimming.

Perhaps a thousand yards from shore, Von Mann and Branson slithered into the dinghy, shaking violently from the strenuous exertion and so much time in icy water. Now they could make progress by paddling, but danger still lurked. It was pitch-black and the dinghy was a flyspeck on the vast sea. What if the submarine failed to return? Or if the underwater craft was hovering out there but the men would be unable to locate it?

Then . . . they saw it. Three green flashes of light—the submarine's code signal. Spirits soared. Von Mann responded with three green flashes—the countersign. Thirty minutes later, the men were inside the submarine. Exhausted, hungry, cold, but exultant, they were given dry clothing and a few shots of "medicinal" brandy.

When the submarine reached its base at Sasebo, Japan, Milt Von Mann was running a temperature of 104 degrees. Rushed to a U.S. naval hospital, he remained for three weeks while recovering from a bout with pneumonia. Finally, he was permitted to telephone his parents in Montgomery, Alabama, after being warned by U.S. security officers not to even hint that he had paid a secret visit to North Korea.

The spectacular mission to Wonsan long would be concealed in a cocoon of official secrecy. Even when Milt Von Mann eventually was awarded the Silver Star for valor, the citation was not phrased in the details of his achievement, as is customarily the case. Rather, the wording read: "For an action in Korea."[7]

There was ample reason for this tight secrecy. Intelligence officers knew that in the wake of the North Korean general's demise, the Communists would conduct an extensive investigation. Should word leak out that the British and Americans were involved, a finger might point to the spies high up in the North Korean hierarchy who had provided the intelligence on the Stalinist general and his travels.

By the time Milt Von Mann and his two companions had returned from their secret mission, the brutal war in Korea had been raging for nine months. But the origins of the bloody conflict traced back for nearly six years, to the conclusion of World War II.

2

A Tangled Web of Politics

TOKYO, A TEEMING CITY of seven million people, was a wasteland, a pit of glazed rubble. Over two million homes had been destroyed by U.S. B-29 Superfortresses. Here and there was the twisted skeleton of a roof or a charred structure with heavy, blackened iron shutters. There were few telephones, virtually no trains, and no power plants to generate electricity. People were living in shacks and huts built of salvaged corrugated strips and cardboard. It was August 15, 1945.

Twelve hours earlier, Japanese Emperor Hirohito, a myopic, absentminded, mild-mannered father of six, recorded a *kodo sempu* (dissemination of the royal way) for broadcast the next day. Most Japanese regarded him as a god, a figure so sacred that his subjects had never heard his voice.

When Hirohito's recording was broadcast by Radio Tokyo, millions of Japanese were dumbfounded. Women, frightened and emotional, knelt before the wireless sets. Children huddled close to their mesmerized parents. Citizens were shocked not only by the sound of their god's voice, but also by his message: The Japanese Empire was surrendering unconditionally to the Allies.

"The enemy has recently made use of an inhuman bomb, and the devastation is taking on incalculable proportions," the monarch told his subjects. "We must endure the unendurable and suffer the insufferable."

World War II was over.

Hirohito's stupefying pronouncement touched off a flurry of ceremonial hara-kiri suicides by generals and admirals, who felt disgraced and could not live in dishonor. At the same time, thirty-two die-hard Japanese junior officers broke into the emperor's palace grounds to seize the surrender recording. They claimed that the broadcast was a fake, a machination engineered by the Allies. All of the heavily armed militants were killed after a fierce firefight with bodyguards loyal to Hirohito.[1]

Three hundred fifty miles below the southern tip of Japan that day, a howling monsoon was lashing Okinawa, a large, bleak island where one of the bloodiest battles of the Pacific war had raged for months earlier in the year. The raging storm failed to dampen the jubilation of the soldiers of Major General John R. Hodge's U.S. XXIV Corps. The war was over; they would not have to take part in a looming invasion of Japan that had promised to result in a massacre such as mankind had not seen before.

Amidst this unbridled revelry, General Hodge received an urgent telephone call from five-star General Douglas MacArthur in Manila. MacArthur, who had been appointed to lead ground forces in Operation Downfall, the assault on Japan, ordered Hodge to rush his forty-five thousand men to Korea to counter an apparent effort by the Soviets to seize that ancient land.

Seven days earlier, Soviet leader Josef Stalin, the inscrutable dictator of the Soviet Union, had torn up the friendship pact he had signed with Japan in early 1941 and declared war on that nation. Within hours, Russian tank-tipped spearheads burst across the Siberian border into Korea and plunged southward for some three hundred miles, occupying the two largest cities of Seoul and Inchon.

Hodge's true mission was to keep the Soviets out of the southern half of Korea, but he would go there with the announced purpose of helping to disarm tens of thousands of Japanese soldiers, most of whom had been there since December 1941 when Tokyo had converted Korea into an important military base.

John Hodge, though a tough and capable combat leader, had no experience handling civic affairs. In the army he was known for his impatience and lack of tact, certainly not the character traits needed for a complex assignment that would be largely diplomatic. One of his staff members quipped: "General Hodge is the first man in history selected to wield executive power over a nation on the sole basis of his nearness to that nation."[2]

MacArthur, who was swamped by monumental postwar problems in the Far East, had given Hodge no specific instructions. Hodge's superior, General Joseph "Vinegar Joe" Stilwell, the hard-bitten Tenth Army commander, told him that the U.S. occupation should be considered "semi-friendly"—leaving Hodge to interpret that peculiar term.[3]

Hodge's bewilderment was compounded when he received terse instructions from the "cookie pushers," as military men called bureaucrats in the State Department, to "create a [Korean] government in harmony with United States policies." What were those policies? No one seemed to know.

Much of the mass confusion over how the United States should regard Korea, a peninsula 550 miles long hanging down from mainland Asia, lay in that land's ancient history. Korean legends say that Tangun, who lived in the 2300s B.C., was the father of Korean civilization. In 1122 B.C., Kija, an exile from China, led about five thousand followers to the mountainous, barren peninsula and founded a kingdom which he called *Chosen* (Land of the Morning Calm). Between the 100s B.C. and the A.D. 600s, there were three separate kingdoms. Finally, one kingdom conquered the weaker two, and the combined kingdom was called *Koryu*, from which came the name Korea.

In 1910, Korea was "annexed" at bayonet point by the Japanese, who coveted the country as a base for future conquests in the Far East. A succession of handpicked Koreans became kings, but the real rulers were Japanese military officers.

During World War II, thousands of young Korean men were dragooned into the Japanese army. Many others volunteered, including hundreds of bright junior officers. Thousands of Korean civilians, including many who sought to feather their own nests, collaborated with the Japanese authorities.

Halfway around the globe, meanwhile, President Harry S. Truman, the peppery, decisive "Man from Missouri," as he was known, and his administration were burdened with an array of gargantuan problems. Because nearly all of Washington's attention was now focused on postwar Europe, far-off Korea was virtually ignored.

Then the Pentagon, the nerve center of the armed forces, received an urgent order (presumably from the White House): Resolve the Korean political situation. That night, a group of high-ranking army and navy officers held an emergency session. "We have to divide Korea," a general declared. "But where can we divide it?"

"We can't do that!" protested a colonel who had had extensive experience in Asia. "Korea is one social and economic unit. There is no place to divide it."

A wrangle broke out, but the protesting colonel refused to budge.

"Well, it has to be divided," another general declared. "And it's got to be done by four o'clock this afternoon!"[4]

A young colonel, Dean Rusk (later U.S. secretary of state), offered a suggestion: "Why not make the permanent dividing line the 38th Parallel?" He pointed out that such an arrangement would include the Korean historic capital, Seoul, within the area of responsibility of U.S. troops.[5]

No doubt delighted to have the knotty, but seemingly inconsequential, Korean tangle settled, members of the panel promptly accepted Colonel Rusk's proposal. But how would the suspicious Soviet
dictator Josef Stalin regard the suggestion?

Much to the surprise of Washington, Stalin and his military
chiefs had no objection to the plan. As a result of the quickie conference in the Pentagon, ancient Korea, which had somehow survived
for twenty-one centuries, became two entities.

Although MacArthur had ordered John Hodge to rush forty-five thousand troops to Korea with all possible speed, lack of ships caused a
delay, so it was not until September 8, a full month after the Soviet
army had arrived, that a fourteen-man vanguard of the 7th Infantry
Division sailed into Inchon, a large port on the western coast. Before
the tiny group had left Okinawa, Hodge told the men to regard Korea
as "an enemy of the United States."

Operation Black Forty, the influx of American soldiers into Korea, was under way. Expecting to encounter a hostile reception, the
GIs were amazed to be engulfed by hordes of wildly cheering, applauding Korean civilians. Climbing into dilapidated Korean trucks,
the Americans headed for Seoul, thirty-five miles to the northeast. En
route they ran another gauntlet of deliriously happy natives who were
convinced, after decades of living under the Japanese yoke, that the
newcomers would give their country independence.

Two days later, General Hodge arrived in Seoul—and promptly
stuck his foot in his mouth. Japanese General Nobuyuki Abe, the
wartime governor-general of Korea, complained that large street
mobs were attacking his surrendering troops and Japanese civilians,
and he asked Hodge for authority to keep Japanese police armed to
protect them from bloody reprisals.

No problem, Hodge replied. But later he told the press, "These
Koreans are the same breed as the Japanese," and he intended to treat
the natives like conquered enemies. His inflammatory comments
were splashed across the front pages of newspapers in the United
States, and howls of outrage rang through the hallowed halls of Congress. General George C. Marshall, the army chief of staff who had
built America's powerful military juggernaut virtually from scratch
during World War II, promptly cabled Hodge to boot out General
Abe, disarm the Japanese police, and stop making insulting outbursts
about the Koreans.[6]

Hard on the heels of his first faux pas, Hodge stirred up another
hornet's nest in Washington and infuriated South Koreans by moving
into the mansion long occupied by the now defrocked General Abe.

To the Koreans, it appeared that they had been freed from one foreign tyrant only to inherit another one.

Succeeding elements of John Hodge's 6th, 7th, and 40th Infantry Divisions continued to pour ashore at Inchon and fan out across the southern portion of the peninsula. Soviet troops, at the same time, pulled back from Seoul and other locales to behind the 38th Parallel, a meaningless geographic marker that split Korea roughly in half. This dividing line had been selected to simplify the immensely complicated task of disarming thousands of Japanese soldiers and shipping them home.

Before departing, the Soviets had sown abundant seeds of mischief in southern Korea during the month before Hodge's troops arrived. Tens of thousands of pamphlets promoting Communism were distributed. "People's committees," headed by avowed Korean Communists, were organized to "redistribute" the properties of well-heeled Koreans. And a foundation was laid for the eventual creation of Communist-led guerrilla bands, whose leaders would be in deep cover until summoned by Moscow to do its bidding.

In the south of Korea, political parties and organizations were springing up like daisies after a summer shower. Most, like the Full Moon Mating Society, had little success, unless that faction had a role in the exploding population. It was a chaotic, and often brutal, struggle for power. Forty years of slavery and degradation under the Japanese boot could not be brushed aside in a month or a year. General Hodge and his military government had an almost unsolvable problem on their hands.

The situation in South Korea bordered on anarchy, with each Korean for himself. In the port of Pusan, U.S. Lieutenant Colonel William P. Jones, a stocky man with a mustache, had been assigned to supervise engineering operations in the region as well as firefighting. Noticing that there were a great number of blazes breaking out, Jones, a regular army officer, called in a Korean firefighter.

"Why are there so many fires?" Jones asked.

"Oh, it's just the different factions, setting each other's houses afire!" the Korean replied cheerfully.

On one occasion, Colonel Jones watched a roaring blaze; Korean firefighters were using antiquated Japanese equipment. Close by he heard screams. Rushing over, Jones saw a group of native police officers savagely beating a Korean. Just as the colonel started to intervene, an American major tugged at his sleeve. "Don't interfere with them, sir," the major advised. "They're merely trying to find out who set the fire!"[7]

Not only were the Americans frustrated in dealing with the South Koreans, they were in constant hassles with the Soviets in the North. In one instance, a crisis developed just across the 38th Parallel from Seoul Province. The extensive rice paddies on the southern side of the dividing line were irrigated by water that flowed down from the North. Suddenly, the Soviets dammed off the water.

Thinking that the turnoff had been caused by some mechanical difficulty, the American officer in charge of Seoul Province sent a private first class named Peavy to investigate. The Soviets were not offended by the dispatch of a lowly GI to discuss the matter; they had political officers masquerading as privates within their own forces, so they comprehended Peavy's desire not to appear conspicuous.

Presumably believing that Peavy was at least a lieutenant colonel and therefore could make decisions on the spot, the Soviets demanded half of the rice harvest in Seoul Province in return for the water. Most of Korea's agriculture lay in the South, where two-thirds of the people lived and toiled.

Peavy and the Soviet officers argued for a while; then, finally, the PFC figured, what the hell? He was going to rotate out of Korea within a few days and become a civilian again. He agreed to everything the Soviets wanted. Within forty-eight hours the water was flowing once more into the rice paddies in the South.

When he returned to Seoul, Peavy was greeted as a conquering hero by his colleagues. How had he managed to pull off such a coup when Americans at the highest rank in Europe and elsewhere were finding it impossible to negotiate with the Soviets? Peavy merely smiled. Within the week, he was on a ship bound for the United States.

With the arrival of fall, the Soviets demanded their share of the rice crops. Unaware of the deal Peavy had cut with them, U.S. officers refused to share the rice, declaring, truthfully, that they knew nothing about an arrangement the Soviets had worked out a few months earlier with a "Colonel Peavy."

Josef Stalin and his clique in Moscow wasted no time planting deep roots of Communism in North Korea. The Soviets proclaimed the Democratic People's Republic of Korea and held "free elections" to choose a premier. Thirty-seven-year-old Kim Il Sung, a protégé of Stalin, was elected in a landslide, garnering 99 percent of the votes. Since any voter casting a ballot for a Kim opponent did so at his own risk, the announced results were hardly surprising.

Kim Il Sung had left Korea at twenty-one years of age to fight against the Japanese army, which had invaded the neighboring Chinese province of Manchuria. Despite his relative youth, Kim raised a large guerrilla force that engaged in hit-and-run raids against the Japanese during the next ten years. His leadership and drive caught the eye of higher-ups in the Soviet Union, and he was brought to Moscow to absorb a course in Communism. Eventually, he rose to the rank of major in the Soviet army.

Now, after an absence of sixteen years, Kim was back home and holding the reins of power in the North Korean capital of Pyongyang. In exchange for gaining the exalted office, Kim would dance the Communist tune as choreographed by the Kremlin in Moscow.[8]

While Kim Il Sung and his hundreds of Soviet "advisers" constructed a satellite state in the Communist image, South Korea's murky political morass grew thicker with the arrival from Chungking, China, of the self-proclaimed Korean Provisional Government (KPG), a group that had been in exile for many years. The KPG was a hodgepodge of old-line Korean politicians and would-be caesars. General Hodge's Counterintelligence Corps (CIC) turned up evidence that some KPG members had been distributing Communist propaganda and were thought to be creatures of Moscow. Hodge's civilian political adviser, H. Merell Benninghoff, cabled Washington: "Communists [here] may be a threat to law and order. It is probable that well-trained agitators are attempting to bring about chaos in our area so as to cause the [South] Koreans to repudiate the United States in favor of Soviet 'freedom' and control."[9]

Benninghoff's alarming signal was not merely conjecture. Wild rioting in the streets of Seoul, Inchon, Taejon, and other cities in the South forced General Hodge to send troops to quell the violence.

In Tokyo, Douglas MacArthur, no doubt at the urging of Hodge, decided that the widespread unrest and political upheavals by warring factions in the south of Korea were intolerable. MacArthur wanted a national leader of prominence that he could trust. A logical choice was Dr. Syngman Rhee, who had been in exile for thirty years and was now living with his Austrian-born wife, Francesca, in Washington, D.C. Rhee had the required credentials: He was a staunch anti-Communist, a lifetime Korean patriot, and a converted Christian who spoke adequate English.

There was a major roadblock, however, to bringing Rhee back: So that the people of South Korea could eventually choose their own leaders, President Truman had issued a directive specifically forbidding U.S. officials from supporting or promoting an individual or faction. But would those leaders be advocates of democracy? Or would they be hard-core Communists who would take their marching orders from Moscow, as Merell Benninghoff feared?

Syngman Rhee had been a Korean patriot almost from boyhood when he and his parents lived in a shack on the heights overlooking Seoul. The family survived on a few handfuls of rice a day. When he was in his early twenties, Rhee led protests demanding the ouster of the Korean puppet king the Japanese had installed. Thrown into prison for these actions, he was brutally tortured for months. Upon his release six years later, Rhee, then thirty years of age, scraped up the money to travel to the United States, where he nagged Washington politicians to help Korea gain independence. In the meantime, he earned a master's degree at Harvard and a Ph.D. at Princeton—the first Korean to obtain a doctorate in the United States.

Six years after leaving Korea, yearning for his homeland, Rhee accepted a job at the International Young Men's Christian Association in Seoul. Because of his record as a "political agitator," Rhee was shadowed constantly by the Japanese secret police. When the puppet king arrested many of his colleagues, Rhee knew his days of freedom were numbered; so he slipped out of Korea one night and made his way back to the United States.

Over the years, the Old Patriot, as he came to be known, continued to badger Washington officials to support Korean independence. Most avoided him as they would have avoided a carrier of the bubonic plague. In early 1944, when World War II was raging and powerful cliques in Washington cherished delusions about friendly cooperation with Josef Stalin after the global conflict, Rhee warned: "The only possibility of avoiding an ultimate conflict between the United States and the Soviet Union is to build up democratic, non-Communistic [governments] in Korea and around the world."[10]

Rhee had spoken with incredible foresight. But the State Department branded the Old Patriot a crackpot and a troublemaker.

For six weeks after the Japanese surrender, Rhee fretted and fumed in Washington, a man without a country. Then, in October 1945, his fortunes soared. Only later he would learn that a conspiracy of sorts in Tokyo and Seoul involving Douglas MacArthur, John Hodge, and possibly political adviser Merell Benninghoff had been oiling the machinery to bring Rhee back to Korea, despite President Truman's order to the contrary. However, the State Department refused to grant Rhee a passport, even though he was a Korean citizen. Possibly through contacts with Hodge's men in Seoul, Preston Goodfellow, a former deputy director of the Office of Strategic Services (OSS), America's wartime cloak-and-dagger agency, got into the act.

Goodfellow and Rhee had reportedly become friends during the war when the Korean told the OSS leader that he could provide secret agents to conduct operations behind Japanese lines in China, Burma, and elsewhere in the Far East. It would be alleged that after he left the OSS, Goodfellow helped raise funds for Rhee.[11]

It appeared that Goodfellow prevailed upon a secret contact in the State Department and Rhee was granted a passport. Within hours, Rhee and his wife climbed aboard a U.S. military plane and flew to Tokyo, where he held long discussions with Douglas MacArthur. The general "endorsed" Rhee's return and provided his personal aircraft to fly the Korean to Seoul.

Hardly had Rhee reached his homeland after being in exile for thirty years than General Hodge and his staff began to foster doubts about the wisdom of the scheme to bring him back. During a rousing speech delivered at a welcome-home ceremony orchestrated by his followers in Seoul, Rhee lambasted both the Soviet Union and the United States, blaming them for conspiring to divide Korea into two states. Then the U.S. Counterintelligence Corps turned up compelling evidence that Rhee's political confederates were inciting mobs to riot in the streets. Rhee, in fact, became so untrustworthy that the CIC bugged his telephone and intercepted his mail.

Hodge and his staff grew frustrated in dealing with their acerbic, demanding, and uncompromising protégé. Rhee was a crafty politician, however, and soon became South Korea's most celebrated public figure. He made it plain to the Americans in Seoul that his ultimate goal was to be president of a unified Korea.

During the next two years, Syngman Rhee served as an "adviser" to the American military government in Seoul and clashed repeatedly with John Hodge. In one especially bitter verbal battle, Rhee charged the general with trying to put Communists in power in the South. Later, frustrated and furious, Hodge barked to his staff, "This is the worst job I ever had!"

Finally, on May 10, 1948, the United Nations sponsored an election to choose delegates to a South Korean national assembly that would form a government. It was a bloody affair. Seeking to scuttle the election, Communist agitators murdered more than one hundred civilians in and around the polling places. Despite the terror, four out of five registered voters cast their ballots.[12]

Syngman Rhee received 90 percent of the votes for a national assembly seat from Seoul. Within three weeks, the assembly convened, wrote a constitution for the Republic of Korea, and named Rhee to be the first president of the fledgling nation.

Eleven weeks later, on August 15, Douglas MacArthur flew from Tokyo to Seoul to deliver the principal address at the inauguration of seventy-three-year-old Syngman Rhee. Prior to the ceremony, the general confided to the new president, "I will defend [South] Korea as I would my own country, as though it were California!"[13]

3

A Conspiracy in Moscow

THE TENACIOUS SYNGMAN RHEE had scarcely taken the oath of office than he began bombarding Washington with demands for modern arms and equipment for a proposed Republic of Korea (ROK) army of a hundred thousand men, with another fifty thousand in reserve. Included in his exhaustive shopping list were thirty-five P-51 Mustang fighter planes, twelve B-25 bombers, two navy destroyers, two submarines, and five minesweepers.[1]

George Marshall, who had retired as U.S. army chief of staff and now was Harry Truman's secretary of state, strongly opposed these demands. Based on Rhee's ongoing bellicose outbursts against North Korean Premier Kim Il Sung, Marshall was concerned that the South might invade the North instead of the other way around. A decision was made by the Truman administration to limit Rhee to a lightly armed, sixty-five-thousand-man constabulary force, one designed mainly to keep order in his own volatile country.

Infuriated by what he considered to be a Washington snub, Rhee publicly accused the "weak-kneed Americans" of abandoning Korea to the global Communist apparatus. Were it not for Washington, he complained loudly, there would be no Communists in North Korea since they had been "invited in by Russian-American agreement."[2]

In the North, Kim Il Sung was rapidly building a keenly trained, well-equipped, and highly motivated army of 135,000 men with the help of 3,000 to 5,000 Soviet military advisers. This modern force was backed by more than one hundred Soviet-built T-34 tanks, nearly two hundred medium bombers and Yak fighter planes, and hundreds of heavy artillery pieces.

On January 1, 1949, in a propaganda ploy to capture favorable world opinion, Moscow trumpeted that all Soviet occupation forces were being pulled out of North Korea to "permit its people to govern themselves without interference from foreign powers." The United States was urged to follow the Soviet example. What Moscow had failed to disclose was that hundreds of Soviet military advisers would remain in North Korea.

In Washington, a dispute had erupted between the Joint Chiefs of Staff in the Pentagon and the State Department over the role the United States should play in the tangled Korean situation. W. Walton Butterworth, head of the Far Eastern Office at State, created a top-secret report that labeled the Communist threat to Korea as "ominous," adding that there was a "growing conviction" that the Soviet Union was determined to "bring about at the earliest possible moment the destruction of the new [ROK] government."[3]

Butterworth's views failed to impress the Pentagon. South Korea continued to be "of little strategic interest" to the United States, a Joint Chiefs document declared. "Leaving large numbers of American troops in the South would only invite trouble [with the Soviets]."

President Truman agreed with the Joint Chiefs. By June 30, 1949, the last GI in the U.S. occupation force had departed. Left behind for the South Korean army were a hundred thousand obsolete rifles, two thousand antiquated bazookas, and a few hundred jeeps and trucks. Much to the consternation of Syngman Rhee, the Americans did not leave a single tank, heavy artillery piece, or major naval vessel.

Not all Americans left South Korea. A Korean Military Advisory Group (KMAG, or Kay-Mag), commanded by Brigadier General William L. Roberts, was set up in Seoul. Roberts, a combat veteran of World War II, was on his last tour of duty before retirement. His mission was to train Syngman Rhee's forces to be able to repel an invasion from the North.

Almost at once, General Roberts and his 472 men were gripped by frustration. Most of the trainees were indifferent students at best. Neither Roberts nor the other Americans spoke Korean, so communication was a serious obstacle. Most of the ROK officers spent their time in political infighting. Lieutenant Colonel Thomas D. McDonald, a KMAG officer, wrote in a report: "This [ROK] force could be the American revolutionary army in 1775."

Roberts was even more pessimistic. Writing to Lieutenant General Charles Bolte, an aide to the Joint Chiefs in the Pentagon, the KMAG commander said he was going to "lay it all on the line." Citing intelligence sources, he pointed out that the South Koreans had no warplanes and the North Koreans had about two hundred Soviet-built fighters and bombers and an elaborate program for training pilots.

In essence, the combat-tested Roberts was telling the Pentagon that if war broke out, South Korea would be unable to defend itself. "You know and I know what two hundred planes can do to troops, to towns, and to transport on the roads," he declared in his letter. "So if South Korea were attacked today, I feel that [it] would get a bloody nose. . . . Knowing the Korean people somewhat, I feel they would follow the apparent winner, and the South would be gobbled up to be added to the rest of Communist Asia."[4]

Now that U.S. occupation troops had been withdrawn from South Korea, Douglas MacArthur no longer held direct responsibility for the defense of that nation. In a curious move, the striped-pants set in the State Department had been given that function. However, MacArthur instructed his G-2, Major General Charles A. Willoughby, to establish a secret Korean Liaison Office (KLO) in Seoul. Manned by a handful of intelligence operatives, the KLO was to monitor Communist troop movements above the 38th Parallel and to keep a watchful eye on the thousands of Kim Il Sung's guerrillas operating in the South.

Tall and hulking, Charles Willoughby had been born Adolf Karl Weidenbach in Germany and was now fifty-six years of age. He had emigrated to the United States as a boy, changed his name, and joined the army as a private when he was still a teenager. Known to subordinates as "Sir Charles" or the "Prussian Drillmaster," Willoughby spoke with a thick Teutonic accent. He had been a member of MacArthur's palace guard since the beginning of America's involvement in World War II.

Late in 1949, a North Korea radio propaganda broadcast claimed that there were seventy thousand Communist guerrillas in the South. Although that figure was grossly exaggerated, Willoughby's KLO concluded that there were thousands of them operating below the 38th Parallel and that this irregular force was a serious threat to the security of South Korea. Then Willoughby learned a shocking fact: Hundreds of men enrolled at the Kangdon Police School, the main guerrilla training center in the North, were South Koreans who reputedly had fled after Syngman Rhee became president in 1948.[5]

After intensive training in guerrilla warfare techniques, graduates of the Kangdon Police School infiltrated into the South. Willoughby estimated that 60 percent of Kim Il Sung's entire guerrilla force was living in the South. Often these men returned to the same towns and even the same houses that they had lived in before heading to the North a year earlier. During the day, these guerrillas would till the soil or work at jobs. At night, they would take their weapons from hiding places and join with other guerrillas to wreak havoc on their own South Korean people—pillaging, burning, and shooting innocents.[6]

In a report to Major General Alexander Bolling, the army's intelligence chief in the Pentagon, Willoughby said that many guerrillas trained at the Kangdon Police School were skirting ROK defenses along the 38th Parallel by traveling in small boats. "The South Korean navy is of little value in stopping these infiltrators," Willoughby told Bolling, "because ROK patrol boats allow the [guerrillas'] boats to pass in return for bribes."[7]

Also late in 1949, General Willoughby claimed that he had sixteen spies operating in North Korea, although KLO officers held serious doubts about their competence, motivation, and loyalty. At least a few of them were suspected of being double agents, meaning they pretended to be spying for the Americans, whereas their true fidelity was to Kim Il Sung and his Communist regime.

If Willoughby indeed had sixteen secret agents in the North, Kim perhaps had ten times that number of spies operating in the South. In the battle of the spies, Kim held a distinct advantage. So ironfisted was his control of the North Korean people that a spy for the South most likely would be quickly recognized as a stranger and reported to the secret police. In Communist North Korea, informers were everywhere.

Although Kim Il Sung held a huge numerical lead in the competing espionage operations between North and South, his own armed forces high command and key government agencies had been penetrated by high-grade secret agents recruited and trained by a gung-ho young U.S. army captain, John K. Singlaub. His intricate scheme to plant spies in North Korea's upper echelons of military and government had its origins three years earlier, in March 1946.

At that time, Jack Singlaub was twenty-five years old. He arrived in Mukden, a Manchurian city of a million and a quarter people, as station chief for Secret Intelligence (SI), the army's covert branch. His cover was commander of the U.S. Army Liaison Group, which ostensibly was to coordinate information with the commanders of Chiang Kai-shek's Nationalist Army, then battling the Chinese Communist forces of Mao Tse-tung.[8]

The chief city and capital of Liaoning Province, Mukden lay on the bank of the Hun River in the most thickly populated region of Manchuria. A few miles north of Mukden was a park containing the tombs of the Manchu emperors who once ruled the vast Chinese empire. Mukden, as Captain Singlaub soon found out, was a hotbed of intrigue. He was plunged into a murky climate of espionage and counterespionage, plot and counterplot, where layers of deception concealed other layers of deceptions, where physical courage was most helpful but cunning and guile were crucial to survival.

Intrigue, secret missions, and danger were no strangers to Singlaub. After obtaining a lieutenant's commission in the ROTC at the University of California–Los Angeles (UCLA), he joined the fledgling Office of Strategic Services (OSS) during World War II. When the Allies were preparing to invade southern France in August 1944, Singlaub parachuted into that Nazi-held country with a three-man team known as a Jedburgh. It was composed of three officers—American, French, and British—and its mission was to organize, train, and eventually command groups of French Maquis (resistance fighters).

Now, less than two years after Singlaub had jumped into the midst of German armed forces in France, he was in Mukden and scouring the city for a suitable headquarters building for his U.S. Army Liaison Group, which consisted mainly of himself and several intelligence case officers. His eye fell on a compound that was said to have been owned and used by Americans prior to World War II and now was occupied by a contingent of Soviet army officers, who were actually secret service operatives.

Singlaub's jeep charged up to the front gate of the compound. He leaped out, strode up to the guards, demanded to see the Soviet colonel in charge, and ordered the Soviets to get out within twenty-four hours. They were poaching on an American preserve, he declared. Actually, he did not know to whom the compound belonged, but then again, neither did the Soviets.

Howls of outrage erupted. The Soviet colonel, indignant at being kicked out by a lowly captain, rushed to the U.S. consulate to complain. Consequently, for one of the few times in his life, Singlaub relented. Instead of twenty-four hours, he allowed the Soviets forty-eight hours to clear out.[9]

Late in 1946, Singlaub began focusing on a project to slip spies into North Korea, which was Manchuria's neighbor to the south, across the Yalu River. With the covert help of Kim Hong Il, a Korean who was a major general in the Chinese Nationalist Army, Singlaub and his case officers began to covertly contact young Korean men who had been living in Manchuria for several years. General Kim had identified these men as ones who were angry because the Soviet army was occupying the northern half of their homeland and imposing Communism on the people through strong-arm tactics. Nearly all the potential espionage recruits leaped at the offer to engage in secret and perilous missions in their homeland.

In the months ahead, Scott Miler, one of Singlaub's more enterprising young officers, whose specialty was counterintelligence, taught the Korean recruits the techniques and nuances of the spycraft trade. By the time the Soviets had installed their puppet, Kim Il Sung, as premier of the new North Korean government in 1948, Singlaub was ready to infiltrate the spies he had recruited and tutored. Each espionage recruit was instructed to seek a job in Kim's military or government and to work hard in an effort to be promoted to even more responsible duties.

Scott Miler escorted the Koreans to Antung, a city on the Manchurian side of the Yalu River. Time and again, each agent rehearsed his cover story. They were to report to Captain Singlaub by dead-letter drops, which would be set up in the near future. Or they could cross into South Korea and make their reports in safe houses that would be established in Seoul. Then, alone or in pairs, the agents slipped across the Yalu back to their homeland and began leading a hazardous double life.[10]

In November 1948, the long and bloody civil war in China was going badly for Chiang Kai-shek's Nationalist army. Captain Singlaub was elsewhere in China on a covert activity when he received news that Mukden had fallen to Mao Tse-tung's army. Soon all of Manchuria was in the hands of the Communists.

Two months after Mukden was captured, Singlaub, then a major, received orders to report to Washington for a new assignment. There he was infuriated to learn that the Chinese Communists had arrested Angus Ward, the U.S. consul in Mukden, his staff, and their families. Ward was a close friend of Singlaub, who admired the diplomat for his dedication and courage.

Singlaub felt that the U.S. State Department should make a violent protest over this breach of international law, thereby securing freedom for Ward and the others. But State remained virtually mute, and it would be many months before the American captives were released by the Communists.

On April 4, 1949, a Chinese Communist general named Chu Teh began massing one million Communist troops on the north bank of the Yangtze River, the final natural barrier between Mao and the relatively few southern provinces still loyal to Chiang. Chu's combat veterans plunged across the Yangtze on April 24, meeting only token resistance. In the first week of May, Chiang fled to Formosa (later Taiwan), a mountainous island rising from the South China Sea one hundred miles across the stormy Formosa Strait, taking as many of his Nationalist troops as he could with him.

Mao proclaimed the sovereignty of the Communist Chinese People's Republic on September 24. And on December 8, Chiang announced the formation of his new government, whose capital was Taipei. Now there were two Chinas.

With the arrival of New Year's Day 1950, tension between Kim Il Sung's Communist regime in North Korea and Syngman Rhee's democratic government in the South reached fever pitch. Along the 38th Parallel, opposing forces confronted one another like two American football teams on the fifty-yard line. Firefights became common. In each one, a few men would be killed or wounded. In the wake of the shootouts, both adversaries loudly blamed the other side. Outrageous claims were made. In one week alone, March 3–10, there were eighteen armed clashes. During that same period, Kim Il Sung's guerrillas launched twenty-nine bloody attacks throughout South Korea.

One experienced British observer in Seoul, Major J. R. Ferguson Innes, sent a candid report to the War Office in London concerning the true meaning of this rash of violence. "There can be no doubt whatever that [North Korea's] ultimate objective is to overrun the South. . . . There is no doubt that they will do so, in which case the Americans will have made a rather handsome contribution of equipment to the military strength of Asiatic Communism. . . . I think they are adopting the well-tried tactics of preparing the [South] from within."[11]

Early in 1950, Kim Il Sung was ready to convert the skirmishing along the parallel to an invasion of the South, ridding Korea of his hated rival, Syngman Rhee. Climbing into a four-engine aircraft at Pyongyang, the North Korean capital, he flew to Moscow to seek the approval of his mentor, Josef Stalin.

Moscow was characteristically cold, gray, and bleak when Kim and Stalin conferred in the Kremlin, a bewildering maze of complex buildings from different eras in history and fortified by high walls a mile and a half around. "I want to prod the South with the point of a bayonet!" Kim explained. Such an action, he stressed, would "ignite an internal explosion and topple Syngman Rhee from power."[12]

Stalin reacted cautiously, wanting to make certain the invasion of South Korea would succeed. He counseled Kim to return to Pyongyang, review his operational plan, and then bring it back to Moscow for Stalin's final approval.

As instructed, Kim returned to the Kremlin seven weeks later and told Stalin that he was "absolutely sure" the invasion would be a success. Stalin still was far from convinced, fearful that the Americans might "jump in." Kim had an immediate answer: Rhee's forces were so weak and lightly armed that they would be crushed before General Douglas MacArthur in Tokyo could intervene.[13]

Kim soon discovered that he had a booster who happened to be a guest in the Kremlin: Mao Tse-tung, the Chinese People's Republic dictator. Mao, who was fifty-six years of age at the time, had founded the Chinese Communist Party in 1921. During the period of 1937 to 1945, Mao commanded a large guerrilla army in northwest China and alternately fought the Japanese and Chiang's Nationalist forces.

Stalin suggested that Mao talk with Kim Il Sung, and the Chinese leader staunchly supported an invasion of South Korea. Mao agreed with Kim that Syngman Rhee's army was so poorly armed that it could be defeated rapidly before the United States could rush troops to Korea.[14]

That night, at a vodka-drenched banquet at Stalin's estate outside Moscow, the deal to invade South Korea was clinched. Speaking in an emotional tone, Kim Il Sung ticked off the enormous benefits that could accrue to the Korean people if the nation were unified under Communist rule.

Among those present was a loquacious extrovert, Nikita Sergeyevich Khrushchev, who had been a three-star general in the Soviet army in World War II and now held one of the Soviet Union's most powerful posts, first secretary of the Communist Party. Greatly impressed by Kim's impassioned oratory, Khrushchev led a toast to the North Korean premier, declaring that he looked forward to the day when Kim's struggle to unify Korea would be won.[15]

Shortly thereafter, early in the spring of 1950, Syngman Rhee's intelligence scored an exceptional feat: It destroyed two major North Korean espionage and sabotage rings operating in the South. Caught in the dragnet were Communist agents in the ROK army, the national police, and the government, along with numerous prominent citizens. Seized were a large amount of radio equipment, secret codes, weapons, and ten thousand U.S. dollars.

Among those arrested were Kim Sam-yong and Yi Chu-la, two of North Korea's most important spies. Also taken into custody, and quickly released, was the man largely responsible for smashing the two espionage rings, a courier who had regularly risked his life as a double agent by sneaking messages and funds between Seoul and Pyongyang for the past six months.[16]

4

A Ruse to Mask an Invasion

A BRIGHT SUN WAS ASCENDING into the cloudless heavens above Seoul as Harold J. Noble, first secretary of the U.S. embassy, tuned his set to Radio Pyongyang, a practice he had been following each morning for the past two years. Noble's title was camouflage. His true role was intelligence officer for the State Department, and he was eager to gain any clue that might shed light on Kim Il Sung's rumored plan to invade the South. It was June 2, 1950.[1]

Born in Pyongyang of American parents who had been Presbyterian missionaries in Korea and China, Noble was long accustomed to hearing Radio Pyongyang, Kim's broadcast mouthpiece, haranguing against the United States and Syngman Rhee and vowing that the North Korean army, the In Min Gun, would "liberate" the South from "American imperialists."

On this day, however, Noble was flabbergasted: Radio Pyongyang was conciliatory. It said Kim was calling for the immediate peaceful reunification of Korea under the auspices of the Fatherland Front, an entity unknown to Noble. All political parties in the North and South were invited to join in the undertaking.

Noble was convinced that Kim was hatching some sort of devious mischief, but he could not deduce his precise goal. He had no way of knowing that Radio Pyongyang had launched Phase One of a clever *ruse de guerre* (war trick) whose purpose was to sucker South Korean and American leaders in Seoul into benevolent apathy on the eve of Kim Il Sung's invasion.

For six consecutive days, the Radio Pyongyang unification appeals were broadcast. Even anti-Communist newspapers in the South published stories about Kim's proposal. As intended by the deception

26

artists in the North, nearly all leaders in the South gave their full attention to the startling developments.

Then Phase Two began. Radio Pyongyang announced that three leaders of the Fatherland Front would be at a specified railroad station, a few hundred yards above the 38th Parallel near Kaesong, on the following morning. All political parties in the South interested in a peaceful reunification were invited to send emissaries to meet with the Fatherland Front people.

Again, the focus of officials in the South was upon this latest Communist overture. But only one person, John Gaillard, decided to go. He was an American member of the United Nations Mission to Korea, whose tricky task it was to try to keep peace between the North and South.

Shortly after dawn, Gaillard drove to Kaesong, thirty-five miles northwest of Seoul and just below the 38th Parallel, and set off on foot to cover the one mile to the designated railroad station. His trek took him through the no-man's-land between the North and South armed forces. Twinges of anxiety gripped him because of the greatly increased number of shootouts between the two sides in recent weeks.

Suddenly, automatic weapons erupted and bullets hissed past Gaillard's head. Diving into a roadside ditch, he lay flat for ten minutes until the firing ceased. It was small solace to him to know that he had not been the target. Rather, he found himself in the center of a fierce shootout. Brushing off his dust-caked clothes, he resumed walking.

Arriving at the dilapidated railroad station an hour later, Gaillard was met on the platform by the three Fatherland Front representatives. Coldly formal, they gave the American a document that called for the peaceful reunification of Korea. Gaillard tried to draw out the North Koreans on the background of the Fatherland Front, but they refused to discuss it.

The powwow lasted only about ten minutes, and then Gaillard retraced his route to Seoul. There he was questioned at length by South Korean military intelligence about the Fatherland Front, an all-consuming topic in the capital, but he could provide no enlightenment.

From a global perspective, a lone American civilian crossing the 38th Parallel into the North for a brief discussion with three Communist functionaries was of no significance. But nearly every military and political leader in Seoul and Tokyo closely monitored Gaillard's strange odyssey. What was the true meaning of this bizarre scenario, one in which Kim Il Sung had replaced his sword with an olive branch?

Had Kim and his Soviet mentor, Josef Stalin, for whatever their reasons, actually decided that Korea should be peacefully united?

That night Phase Three of the Communists' deception strategy began when Radio Pyongyang blared more sensational news. Since the "reactionary Syngman Rhee" had refused to permit representatives of the political parties in the South to meet with the Fatherland Front delegation, these same three men would cross the 38th Parallel by walking down the railroad track and continue on to Seoul, beginning at ten o'clock the next morning.

This unexpected shock triggered a renewed flap in Seoul. For the past two years, Kim Il Sung had not permitted a single civilian to cross the dividing line. What was the significance of this new connivance?

As advertised, the three Fatherland Front emissaries walked across the 38th Parallel. Alerted in advance, South Korean soldiers withheld fire, then pounced on the intruders and took them to a nearby guard shack.

An hour later in Seoul, an American officer telephoned the U.S. embassy to tell about the arrests. Ambassador John J. Muccio and his deputy, Everett F. Drumright, were out on business matters, so Harold Noble, the State Department intelligence chief, took the call.

After a brief conversation, Noble telephoned Captain Sinh Sung Mo, the South Korean defense minister, and asked what he intended to do with the Fatherland Front captives. Sinh was both embarrassed and angry. His ego had been bruised; he had not been told of the episode until Noble, an American, broke the news.

Sinh ranted about the "impudence" of the three Communists who had "brazenly penetrated our defensive positions." Since they had been caught in a military zone and were obviously agents of a state bent on conquering South Korea, Sinh snapped, he would order the captives to be given a fair court-martial and shot.[2]

Alarmed, Noble urged the defense minister not to take such a drastic action. "I don't know what [Kim Il Sung] is planning," he said, "but certainly he wishes in some manner to use these men to confuse public opinion in the South."[3]

Apart from serious questions of international law, Noble added, executing the men would hurt South Korea in the court of world opinion, which did not understand the long-time efforts of Pyongyang to overthrow Syngman Rhee's regime. He pleaded with Sinh to send the intruders back across the parallel—immediately.

Sinh was unimpressed, saying he would have the North Korean captives shot the next day. Later, he had a change of heart and ordered the Fatherland Front men brought to Seoul, blindfolded and handcuffed, for grilling by South Korean intelligence. Precisely as the deception planners in Pyongyang had anticipated, all eyes and ears in

Seoul were directed toward the interrogation—and away from North Korean troop movements above the 38th Parallel.

For four days, the Fatherland Front envoys played their role to the hilt, sticking doggedly to the claim that their only goal was the peaceful reunification of Korea. Their purpose in striving for unity was that Syngman Rhee and his "American overlords" were forcing the South Korean people to live in poverty and hunger, they stressed.

How did they know economic conditions were so brutal in the South Korean democracy? Because Kim Il Sung had told them that was the case.

Time and again the captives harped on the deplorable conditions in the South, claiming that Seoul itself was a huge ghetto filled with beggars, thieves, and women forced to prostitute themselves to survive. Bent on proving that Kim had lied to his own people, the South Koreans took the three Communists on a jeep tour of Seoul. On their return, the prisoners voiced amazement at seeing that the citizens were relatively well dressed, that many of them had cars and trucks, and that food was plentiful.[4]

Feigning disillusionment with Kim Il Sung and Communism, the men confessed that the Fatherland Front was a fraud, and that the entire peaceful reunification scenario of the past two weeks was merely a machination hatched by leaders in Pyongyang to stir up trouble in the South in the hope that the people would rise up and boot out Syngman Rhee.

So angry were the three North Koreans at having been duped by their leaders that they volunteered to speak on Radio Seoul to inform the people in the North about the true economic conditions in the South and disclose how Kim Il Sung and his Communist clique had been lying to the citizens. The South Korean intelligence officers were delighted and swallowed the bait. A broadcast by repentant hard-core Communists would be a major coup in the ongoing propaganda war between North and South. That reaction was precisely the one that deception planners in Pyongyang had anticipated.

One after the other, the apparent converts to democracy sat before the microphone and blasted Kim, his henchmen, and Communism. As the three men knew, their broadcasts caused no harm in the North. Few people there had radios, and those who had sets and tuned in would peg the diatribes as merely a Syngman Rhee hoax.

So sincerely had the "repentants" admitted that the Fatherland Front was a hoax, so bitterly had they denounced Kim and Communism, that they gained the total confidence of South Korean leaders as reliable sources of intelligence. When they were questioned at length about any troop concentration behind the 38th Parallel, they were believed when they denied seeing any heavy military activity.[5]

Harold Noble, the State Department intelligence chief, would recall: "These were slick operatives, Trojan Horsemen whose undercover mission was to get inside our 'gate' and attract our total attention away from the 38th Parallel. They had nearly everyone [in Seoul] believing what we wanted to believe: that having seen the free South, they had chosen democracy over Communism. Once that was believed by us, their testimony on North Korean military subjects was also believed. They did their job of confusing the South Korean army, government, and foreign observers, like us at the embassy, magnificently."[6]

On June 11, at the same time the three Communists were hoodwinking leaders in the South, twenty-four high-ranking officers of the North Korean People's Army (NKPA) were holding a conference in the offices of Lieutenant General Yu Suncheol, chief of operations, in Pyongyang. Until now, the People's Army had conducted only small-scale field exercises, General Yu said. "Now all divisions will take part in a major maneuver, the largest and most significant one since the founding of the In Min Gun," he said. All officers should take along enough socks, underwear, and personal gear for several weeks, he added. "The coming exercise is a top-secret matter," Yu stressed. "So you must not talk about it to your wives, relatives, or friends."[7]

No doubt the North Korean commanders present were astute enough to recognize that the large-scale field exercise designation was but a security gambit to keep tongues from wagging about a looming invasion of the South.

While the In Min Gun was secretly massing just above the 38th Parallel, Radio Pyongyang commenced Phase Five of the intricate deception ruse. Kim Il Sung was willing to release a revered Korean patriot, Cho Man Sik, in exchange for the two top Communist spies who had been caught in the South Korean counterintelligence dragnet a few weeks earlier and were under sentence to be executed, the broadcast announced.

Cho Man Sik had been jailed by the Communists four years earlier and had not been heard from since. South Korean leaders had presumed he was dead. Syngman Rhee, an old friend of Cho's, was eager to secure Cho's freedom and appoint him to a cabinet post, but Rhee refused to negotiate openly with the Communists. Therefore, behind-the-scenes bargaining over the prisoners' swap began.

South Korean intelligence, meanwhile, was concentrating intently upon these negotiations at a time when it should have been painstakingly scrutinizing every scrap of information that could be gleaned about North Korean troop movements.

Had South Korean leaders and U.S. officials in Seoul not been lulled into a false sense of security by the hocus-pocus of the North Korean deception scheme, perhaps they would have paid much greater attention to the abundance of telltale signs pointing to invasion preparations above the 38th Parallel. Hundreds of North Korean families along a two-mile-wide belt just above the dividing line recently had been relocated. This mass movement could mean that a secure strip of land was being prepared for assembling an invasion force. South Korean intelligence, however, discerned no hostile intent, taking the view that most of these border dwellers had left voluntarily to avoid land mines planted by the In Min Gun as a defensive measure and from fear of getting caught in the firefights that had become more frequent along the parallel.

There were other blatant clues known to leaders in Seoul. North Korean women were being drafted for administration and nursing duty. There was a sudden conscription of teenage boys into the army. The railroad track southward from Pyongyang to the 38th Parallel was closed to all but military traffic. And a large new factory was opened to produce small-arms ammunition and shells.

Meanwhile, in the South, key military men were out of the country. Both the ROK army deputy chief of staff and the adjutant general were in the United States, the navy chief was on a ship in the mid-Pacific, and fifty of the keenest junior army officers were training with the U.S. Eighth Army in Japan, seven hundred miles away.

On Saturday night, June 24, the streets of Seoul, a city of a million and a half people, were jammed as usual with hordes of white-clad natives. Slowly, the two-thousand-person American colony came to life. From the roof gardens of the Naija to the plush lounge of the Traymore Hotel, stylishly dressed women and men soaked up tax-free liquor. Many laughed uproariously over the plight of the high-level American civilian official who had become involved romantically with North Korea's top female spy.

No doubt unaware of her covert activities, the man had been so enamored of the beautiful young Korean that he showered her with gifts, including one that she had specifically requested—a two-way shortwave radio that was ideal for relaying intelligence to Pyongyang. The couple even had a love child, the American wives on the nightclub circuit whispered to one another.

Eventually, the local Mata Hari had been arrested by South Korean secret police and, it was said, the Rhee government was going to have her shot. And her boyfriend? Of course Rhee would not execute an American; instead, he probably would just have him slapped on the wrist and sent back to the United States.

Elegant cocktail parties were in full swing at the Banto and the Chisan hotels, and there was the regular Saturday night swingfest at the palatial symbol of midcentury Occidental culture, the Korean Military Assistance Group's mess hall. By three o'clock in the morning, the bar was closing, and only a few inebriated young American officers lingered in the hope of picking up a woman.

At the same time that the last barflies were being shooed away from the bar at the KMAG mess hall, forty miles to the north, just beyond the 38th Parallel, thirty-year-old Senior Colonel Lee Hak Ku, operations officer of II Corps of the In Min Gun, was seated at a desk in his headquarters in a town called Hwach'on. He met the eyes of the booted and blue-trousered officers standing before him. They were all quite young, tough, and disciplined. Nearly all of their adult lives had been spent at war, fighting with the Chinese Communists and then with the Soviets. They had battled the Japanese in Manchuria and Chiang Kai-shek's Nationalists on the Chinese mainland. Now they were ready to fight "the dirty dogs of the American imperialists" (the South Koreans) or anyone else who stood in their way.

Only now could Colonel Lee begin to relax and reflect on the monumental events of the past few days in which he had played a key role. Ninety thousand combat-tested soldiers, shielded by night and the Fatherland Front contrivance, had moved southward, many of them coming down from the distant Yalu River. Everything had gone smoothly.

Around Colonel Lee's headquarters, shadowy figures in mustard-colored uniforms were moving up to the line of departure. A day earlier, their officers had been provided with detailed maps that had South Korean defenses, gun positions, and unit deployments clearly marked—information that came from the hundreds of Communist spies in the South.

The In Min Gun assault divisions would be supported by 152 T-34 tanks, 1,643 pieces of heavy artillery and self-propelled guns, and 203 Yak fighter planes and medium bombers. H-hour was less than two hours away—at dawn on Sunday, June 25.

5

Search for a Scapegoat

S TORM DEMONS WERE SHRIEKING along the 38th Parallel in the pre-dawn darkness of Sunday. South of the dividing line, only three understrength ROK divisions were deployed. Nearly a third of the enlisted men were on fifteen-day leaves, back home helping with the rice crops. Most of the remaining ROK soldiers were asleep in billets.

Suddenly, at 4:00 A.M., the black sky was illuminated by a yellowish glow from the muzzle blasts of hundreds of North Korean artillery pieces whose roar could be heard above the monsoon almost to Seoul, thirty miles to the south. Twenty minutes later, the deluge of shells lifted, and the quaint tone of bugles rang out, the signal for In Min Gun infantry to advance. Hard on the heels of the foot soldiers, scores of low-slung T-34 tanks crunched forward through oceans of thick mud.

ROK forces were taken completely by surprise. Without tanks, heavy artillery, antitank guns, or warplanes, they began to fall back. A few ROK soldiers tied explosives to their bodies and crawled under the tanks, blowing up the iron monsters and themselves. Others rushed forward with dynamite attached to the tips of poles, which they thrust into the tanks' machinery. Some ROKs leaped onto the armored vehicles, pried open hatches with bare hands, and dropped in grenades.

These suicide attacks were in vain. Within two hours, the ROK withdrawal had turned into a rout. It was every man for himself.

In Tokyo shortly after daybreak, the telephone jangled impatiently in Douglas MacArthur's bedroom at his residence on the grounds of the U.S. embassy. A duty officer at the Far East Command blurted out: "General, we have just received a dispatch from Seoul, advising that the North Koreans have struck in great strength across the 38th Parallel."

33

MacArthur felt the chill of a nightmare. It couldn't be, he told himself. Not again! It had been nine years before, on another Sunday morning at the same hour, that a telephone call with the same tone of urgency had awakened him in his penthouse atop the Manila Hotel to tell him that the Japanese had struck at Pearl Harbor.[1]

How, MacArthur asked himself, could the United States have allowed such a deplorable situation to develop?[2] A few years earlier, America had been more militarily powerful than any nation on earth, he reflected. But Washington politicians had frittered away that heavy clout. Had only a significant portion of that power been retained, Kim Il Sung would not have dared to launch an invasion, MacArthur was convinced.

There was no doubt in the five-star general's mind about whose devious hand was behind the North Korean operation—Josef Stalin's. A cold war had been raging between the democracies and the Communist bloc even before World War II had ended five years earlier. Now it was in godforsaken Korea that Stalin had hurled the first challenge of a shooting war against the free world, a challenge the United States was ill prepared militarily to confront.[3]

At almost the same time MacArthur was awakened, the telephone rang in the bedroom of Ambassador John J. Muccio at the U.S. Embassy in Seoul. Sleepily, the fifty-year-old diplomat picked up the receiver and heard the excited voice of his deputy, Everett Drumright: "Brace yourself for a shocker! The Commies are hitting all along the front!"[4]

Indeed it was a shocker. Italian-born Muccio was wise in the ways of international intrigue, but he had been lulled into complacency by the Fatherland Front machination. Through a series of telephone calls, he scraped up bits and pieces of information and then fired off a telegram to Tokyo for transmission to the State Department in Washington: "Kim Il Sung's invasion has been launched."[5]

A few hours later, after the skies had cleared, four Yak fighters swept over Seoul at treetop level and sent bursts of fire into the Blue House, Syngman Rhee's residence. The Old Patriot escaped being hit, but the strafing impressed on him that Seoul might fall soon.

Rhee immediately assembled his cabinet. The members were so terrified that they infected the president, a man of great personal courage, and the entire group decided to flee. Ambassador Muccio heard about the proposed departure and rushed to see Rhee. Speaking bluntly, he told the president that if he fled, "There won't be a single South Korean soldier facing north. The entire ROK army will quit fighting!"[6]

Muccio's steadfastness gave Rhee pause to reflect and he agreed to remain in Seoul—at least until the next morning.

Six hours after the In Min Gun plunged across the 38th Parallel, Radio Pyongyang broadcast an astonishing version of what had happened. According to this account, Syngman Rhee and his "corrupt regime," doing the bidding of President Truman and General MacArthur, had launched the conflict by sending large forces into North Korea and capturing several towns. As a result of Rhee's "flagrant aggression," the North Korean army had liberated those towns by the dozen, then opened a counteroffensive to drive the South Korean invaders back into their own country, the broadcast explained.

Halfway around the globe in Independence, Missouri, President Harry Truman, his wife, Bess, and his daughter, Margaret, had finished their evening meal at the family home. They were engaged in idle conversation when the telephone rang. Secretary of State Dean Acheson was calling from his residence in the countryside near Washington. "Mr. President," he said, "I have very serious news. The North Koreans have invaded South Korea!"[7]

Truman replied that he would fly back to Washington immediately, but Acheson urged him to remain in Independence until the situation in Korea clarified. Besides, the secretary added, if Truman were to race across the continent in the middle of the night, the entire nation might panic. Truman agreed. Grimly, the president told his wife and daughter: "This is the opening round of World War Three!"[8]

Dean Gooderham Acheson, then fifty-six years of age, could have been Hollywood's version of a U.S. secretary of state—a foppish, mustachioed career diplomat whose arrogant mannerisms, clipped accent, and condescending demeanor often annoyed Washington government and military leaders as well as foreign dignitaries. He was never overburdened with humility, nor did he know when to remain silent.

Despite his annoying personality, Acheson had brains and energy. During his telephone conversation with Truman, he had suggested that the United Nations Security Council be called into emergency session and urged to pass a resolution (written by Acheson) branding North Korea an aggressor and demanding that it pull back behind the 38th Parallel. Truman gave him the green light.

Since Acheson was out of the capital, he promptly telephoned John D. Hickerson, the assistant secretary of state, at his Washington home and told him to rush to the State Department and set the United Nations wheels in motion. Hickerson contacted UN Secretary-General Trygve Lie at his home outside New York City.

"Mr. Secretary," Hickerson said, "the Communists have just invaded South Korea!" Lie, a Norwegian, gasped audibly and replied in disbelief, "My God, Jack, that's against the charter of the United Nations!"[9]

Lie swung into action. At two o'clock that afternoon, the Security Council convened. Ernest Green, the U.S. assistant delegate to the UN, was elated to notice that the seat for Yakov Malik, the Soviet delegate, was vacant. Six months earlier, Josef Stalin had boycotted the Security Council sessions after a dispute over Chiang Kai-shek's Nationalist government. A single dissenting vote could kill a resolution, and Malik most certainly would have opposed any measure branding Communist North Korea an aggressor.

As the delegates listened intently, Green read aloud the resolution that Acheson and his staff had drawn up: North Korea was ordered to cease fighting and withdraw to its own country. After two hours of debate, the resolution was adopted unanimously. Yugoslavia, a Communist nation but one not tied closely to Moscow, abstained.

It was a resounding diplomatic victory for the United States and the democracies—albeit a hollow one. Few in the upper echelons in Washington were naive enough to believe that the North Korean Communists were going to slam on the brakes of their surging war machine and put it into reverse gear.

Kim Il Sung's response to the United Nations edict was to thumb his nose at it. Taking to Radio Pyongyang, he launched a propaganda spiel: "Great danger threatens our fatherland and its people. What is needed to liquidate this menace? . . . Under the banner of the Korean People's Democratic Republic, we must complete the unification of the fatherland and create a single, independent, democratic state. The war which we are now forced to wage is a just war for the unification of our [country] and for freedom and democracy."[10]

Just past 7:00 P.M. on Monday, June 26 (U.S. time), Harry Truman's plane, *Independence*, landed at Washington National Airport. After a short limousine ride, the president reached Blair House, a stately mansion diagonally across Pennsylvania Avenue from the White House. Truman and his family were living in Blair House while the executive mansion was being renovated.

Truman went upstairs to telephone his wife to report that he had arrived safely; then he entered the downstairs living room, where thirteen top defense and diplomatic leaders had congregated. There were Secretary of State Dean Acheson and three of his key officials, along with Secretary of Defense Louis Johnson, the secretaries of the army, navy, and air force, and the Joint Chiefs.

Grim faces on Truman and his advisers reflected the critical situation: The United States was confronted by as great a crisis as it had known. World War III was at stake. General Omar N. Bradley, chairman of the Joint Chiefs, was hawkish. "We must draw a line [against global Communism] somewhere," he declared in his high-pitched voice. "We might as well draw it here and now!"[11]

The specter of Soviet armed intervention in Korea haunted the conference room. General Hoyt S. Vandenberg, the air force chief of staff, pointed out that Russian jets, if they jumped into the fray, would be operating from bases far closer to the scene of action than were U.S. bases in Japan.

Truman asked if Soviet airfields in the Far East could be knocked out. "It can be done," Vandenberg replied solemnly, "if we use A-bombs."[12]

An atomic-bomb assault on Soviet installations could trigger nuclear war, those present realized. A year earlier, the Soviets had exploded their first atomic bomb, and since that time the two superpowers had been competing to develop even heavier nuclear explosives.

All agreed that the United States had to take a tough stand at this critical stage. But get tough with what? As a result of Truman's determination to achieve the first peacetime "economy budget" in ten years, he had ordered Secretary of Defense Johnson to "cut away the fat" in the armed forces. Johnson complied. But he also hacked off bone and sinew along with the blubber. Now the U.S. Army had been pruned to only 592,000 poorly trained men armed largely with weapons that were relics from World War II. In the face of the Cold War tension and Communist saber-rattling around the world, the army's strength was less than half what it had been nine years earlier at the time of an epic American disaster—Pearl Harbor.

Finally, after each conferee at Blair House had expressed his views, Truman authorized several actions. Douglas MacArthur was to send weapons and equipment to Syngman Rhee's forces. A group of U.S. officers in Japan was to be sent to Korea to reconnoiter the confused situation on the battlefields. The U.S. Air Force would be used to fly cover for an evacuation of American civilians with orders to shoot down any Communist aircraft that might try to interfere with the operation.

Then, turning to General Vandenberg, the president said, "The air force should prepare to wipe out all Soviet bases in the Far East." However, Truman stressed, this was "not an order for action but an order to make plans."

Before the conference broke up, Truman warned that nothing was to be said about these decisions to the media for twelve hours. Dean Acheson and Louis Johnson were to testify before a congressional appropriations committee the next morning, and they were not to even hint that actions had been taken to counter the North Korean invasion.

Strangely, when Harry Truman and his top leaders needed every scrap of information they could get on the situation in Korea and the Far East, Rear Admiral Roscoe H. Hillenkoetter, the director of the Central Intelligence Agency (CIA), had not been invited to the Blair House conference. This omission reflected the total lack of confidence that the Washington elite had in the global sleuthing organization.

Created by Congress in 1947 to give the United States eyes and ears around the globe in the midst of the cold war, the CIA was an offshoot of the Office of Strategic Services (OSS), which had been formed shortly before the United States was bombed into war at Pearl Harbor in December 1941. Starting from scratch, William J. "Wild Bill" Donovan, a Wall Street lawyer and World War I Medal of Honor recipient, had built the OSS into an exceptional clandestine agency. Only in the Southwest Pacific was the OSS barred. There General MacArthur preferred to rely on General Charles Willoughby's conventional intelligence techniques.

Soon after the guns had fallen silent in World War II, many politicians in Washington decided there was no need for a global spy apparatus, that the United States could work in friendship and harmony with the Soviet Union to assure world peace. The OSS was abolished.

Since its inception, the CIA had been unwanted, undermanned, and underfunded—the ugly duckling in the Truman administration. Army, navy, and air force intelligence chiefs, tenaciously guarding their own turf and perquisites, ignored cooperation overtures by the CIA.

The agency's lowly status may have resulted in part from the nature of the appointments of the first three directors. Sidney Souers, the original head, was a reserve rear admiral who in civilian life was an executive in the Piggly Wiggly grocery chain based in St. Louis. Souers had no intelligence background, but he was a long-time crony of fellow Missourian Harry Truman.

Air Force General Hoyt Vandenberg, who succeeded Souers, had a distinguished record in World War II, but minimal intelligence know-how. Washington insiders felt that he had been appointed to the post because he was a nephew of Senator Arthur Vandenberg, an influential Republican senator whose favor Truman sought to curry. In less than a year, the general found a means for bailing out of a job he had never wanted: Truman named him air force chief of staff.

Admiral Hillenkoetter then got the CIA post. He had been on the battleship *West Virginia* when it was plastered by Japanese bombs at Pearl Harbor, and later he was naval attaché in Vichy, France, where Adolf Hitler had established a puppet French government. Washington insiders claimed that Hillenkoetter had been appointed because it was the navy's turn to head the CIA.

As a result of the CIA's lowly status, its intelligence reports had been largely ignored by the Washington power brokers. The frustration of Ray S. Cline, whose job was to conduct research and analysis of strategic factors affecting U.S. security, was a case in point. Formerly an analyst for the OSS, he joined the CIA in mid-1949. Each month, Cline produced a report of four or five printed pages with a fancy cover and the title "Estimate of the World Situation." Most of his analytical comments were based on a few scraps of intelligence from agents in the field and on newspaper and magazine articles.

Throughout early 1950, Cline's reports carried much information under a heading "North Korea's Menacing Preparations for War." After being cleared by two superiors and Admiral Hillenkoetter, the secret document was hand-carried to a prestigious clientele—President Truman, his cabinet secretaries, and the Joint Chiefs. "I doubt if anyone paid much attention to my contribution to [national security] each month," Cline would declare.[13]

Like most of official Washington, Congress was shocked and outraged at what appeared to be a massive failure of U.S. intelligence to detect Kim Il Sung's war preparations. A search for a scapegoat began. Republican Styles Bridges, a senator with no noticeable aversion to personal media recognition, called for a closed-door session of the Senate Appropriations Committee, chaired by an elderly, cantankerous Democrat from Tennessee, Kenneth McKellar. Top U.S. policymakers and intelligence chiefs were to be hauled before the panel and grilled about why Uncle Sam had been hoodwinked by "a bunch of Oriental rabble."

Dean Acheson was the leadoff witness. When responsibility for South Korea had been taken from General MacArthur a year earlier, the State Department was charged with the task. Wise in the workings of Washington intrigue, Acheson knew that the senators were trying to isolate a scapegoat. In his testimony he attempted to shift the blame to the CIA, the despised ugly duckling.

Louis Johnson, a West Virginia lawyer who had hacked the armed forces into near impotency in the name of government economy, testified later that morning and absolved himself and his Defense Department from culpability.

During the noontime break, news faucets began leaking. An unidentified senator told a media correspondent that there had been "a shocking intelligence failure."

At the time the often heated hearings were being held on Capitol Hill, Major Jack Singlaub, who had been the CIA station chief in

Manchuria before being called back to the United States, was taking an advanced infantry course at Fort Benning, Georgia. Singlaub was shocked to read the blaring newspaper headline: *Intelligence Failure in Korea.*

How could that be? Singlaub mused. He and his case officers in Mukden had dispatched a few dozen bright, dedicated, anti-Communist spies from Manchuria into North Korea between late 1946 and early 1949. Their primary mission was to provide advance warning if Kim Il Sung were preparing to invade South Korea. It seemed incomprehensible to Singlaub that not a single one of these secret agents had sounded the alarm.[14]

As the committee hearings continued in Washington, Roscoe Hillenkoetter, already being measured for scapegoat horns, was put on the hot seat. Undaunted, the CIA chief dropped a bombshell. Less than three weeks before the North Koreans struck, Hillenkoetter testified, the CIA had compiled an intelligence estimate, based largely on "field agents' reports" (meaning Singlaub's spies) that told in detail about alarming North Korean activity. Repairs were being made to North Korean railroads leading to the South, there were extensive troop movements, roads were being strengthened (in anticipation of heavy traffic), and civilian travel had been halted on railroads and roads near the 38th Parallel. The intelligence estimate concluded that Kim Il Sung was in a position to launch an invasion at any time of his choosing.[15]

On June 20, only five days before the North Korean offensive had been launched, Hillenkoetter had copies of this intelligence estimate hand-carried to President Truman, Secretary of State Dean Acheson, and Secretary of Defense Louis Johnson, the CIA boss testified.

Crusty old Senator McKellar lifted his eyebrows in disbelief. Dean Acheson had testified that he had received no warnings from the CIA. McKellar demanded proof. Hillenkoetter promised to produce three signed receipts from those who had received the intelligence estimate.

On the following day, Walter Pforzheimer, the CIA legal counsel, appeared before the committee and presented the three signed receipts. Glancing at the signatures, McKellar barked, "These are forgeries!"

Pforzheimer, a veteran of Washington infighting, held his ground. "They are genuine, sir," he responded evenly. McKellar painstakingly examined each signature and matched the handwriting with authentic signatures on other documents. Eventually, the senator admitted that the receipt signatures were authentic.[16]

6

Reign of Terror in Seoul

CONVINCED THAT THE SOVIET UNION was the chief instigator of the North Korean invasion, Harry Truman decided to put Josef Stalin on notice that the United States was aware that Moscow was not merely a spectator. Consequently, he directed Secretary of State Dean Acheson to draft a sharply worded message, just short of an ultimatum, and cable it to Ambassador Alan G. Kirk in Moscow. Kirk would be told to present the note immediately to Andrei Vishinsky, the Soviet commissar of foreign affairs.[1] In part, the note stated:

> In view of the universally known fact of the close relations between the [Soviet Union] and the North Korean regime, the United States Government asks assurances that the [Soviet Union] disavows responsibility for this unprovoked and unwarranted invasion, and that it will use its influence with the North Korean authorities to withdraw their invading forces immediately.[2]

Despite the urgency, the Kremlin took two days to reply. Syngman Rhee's government and "those who stand behind their back [meaning the United States] are to blame for provoking the war," the Soviets stated. The events in Korea are a civil conflict, the reply added, and the Soviet Union was opposed to "foreign intervention in the domestic concerns of other nations."[3]

In the meantime, Dean Acheson was being peppered with cables from Ambassador John Muccio in Seoul. All the messages were dismal. The North Korean army appeared to be unstoppable. Syngman Rhee and his key leaders had fled south to Taejon, ninety miles below Seoul.

41

One ROK general had suggested that Rhee continue to Japan and set up a government-in-exile.

Early Tuesday morning, June 27, Acheson telephoned President Truman to suggest that another high-level meeting was crucial. Truman agreed and told Acheson to instruct the same group that had convened the night before to be at Blair House at 9:00 P.M.

Acheson dominated the conference. As war clouds were gathering over Washington, a diplomat, not the generals and admirals, was, in essence, calling the shots. Acheson proposed that all previous restrictions on the U.S. armed forces be scrapped, and that the air force and navy go all-out to attack In Min Gun tanks, convoys, and guns to give the disorganized ROKs time to regroup. Truman concurred, but stressed that no actions would be taken north of the 38th Parallel. "Not yet, anyhow," the president added grimly.

Now that Truman had reached a decision to send in U.S. air and naval forces to defend South Korea, he ordered the news to be withheld from the American public for twelve hours. Needing bipartisan congressional support for his action, he did not want to irritate lawmakers by having them read about it in the *New York Times* and the *Washington Post*, the two journalistic bibles on Capitol Hill.

In Tokyo, Douglas MacArthur was infuriated by this seemingly political maneuver of blacking out news that the Yanks were coming. In cables to the Pentagon, he stressed that the ROK army was in disarray, demoralized, and fleeing. Unless he could give the ROKs an incentive to hold on, the war would be over within a matter of hours, the general declared.

MacArthur's plea was rejected by the White House; political expediency won out over military reality.

Just past 9:00 A.M. on Wednesday, fourteen prominent members of Congress were seated with Harry Truman around a huge mahogany table in the conference room of the White House to hear about unfolding events in the Far East. The cabinet secretaries were also present. Typically, Dean Acheson led off the briefing.

"If the Communists are permitted to get by with their aggression," Acheson declared in his clipped accent, "it will certainly be the beginning of World War III."[4]

Then Truman spoke for about ten minutes and told the grim legislators, "I have ordered United States air and sea forces to give the [South] Korean troops cover and support."[5]

This drastic action was necessary, the president stressed, because the United States "cannot let this matter go by default." Surprisingly, the congressional leaders had few questions, implying general agreement with Truman's decision.

Minutes after the conference broke up, the White House press secretary distributed news releases that told of Truman's action. In the release, the president took a few healthy swipes at North Korean Premier Kim Il Sung for his "bald-faced aggression," and he warned Mao Tse-tung of dire consequences if the Chinese Communists were to attack Taiwan, the island where Chiang Kai-shek had established his Nationalist government.[6]

Known to his admirers as "Give-'em-Hell Harry," Truman, now in his mid-sixties, had been regarded by the Washington elite as merely a caretaker president when he succeeded to the presidency on Franklin D. Roosevelt's death in April 1945. He had been the butt of countless jokes—a weak-kneed, weak-eyed, failed haberdasher from a small city in Missouri. Then came the election of November 1948, when most of the pundits had "conceded" the presidency to New York's Republican governor, Thomas E. Dewey. When the votes were counted, however, the spunky Truman had won the biggest presidential upset in U.S. history.

Having dramatically shed the label of "accidental president," Truman was his own man and proceeded to call the shots as he saw them, trusting to his own instincts and knowledge gained as a self-taught student of world history. Despite his smashing victory at the polls, "Give-'em-Hell" Harry refused to change his modest lifestyle; he still washed his own socks in a White House sink at night. Outwardly mild-mannered, Truman also refused to tone down his mule skinner's vocabulary when away from the public.

Truman's stern warning to the Chinese Communists to keep their hands off Taiwan triggered howls of outrage from Mao Tse-tung's capital of Peking. Forty-six Communist leaders congregated there to hear Foreign Minister Chou En-lai launch a diatribe against the United States in general and Truman in particular. Chou claimed that Truman had ordered the "Korean puppet army of Syngman Rhee to attack peaceful North Korea." This "unprovoked attack," he declared, was just a "fabricated pretext" for aggression by U.S. warmongers against Korea, Indochina, and the Philippines—part of America's dastardly "secret plan" to seize all of Asia.[7] Chou branded Truman a hypocrite, and he called on the "people of China and the people of the world" to arise and "defeat every provocation of American imperialism!"[8]

Late on June 27, Douglas MacArthur, who had held the title of Supreme Commander, Allied Powers (SCAP) since near the end of

World War II, was notified by the Joint Chiefs that he now was in command of all U.S. forces in Asia and that his new title, in addition to the current one, was Commander in Chief, Far East (CINCFE).

Although MacArthur was in total agreement with Truman's decision to intervene, he told aides that it had been a great surprise to him. The general had qualms about Washington's approach to the crisis. He was convinced that State Department functionaries were calling the shots and that they understood "little about the Pacific and practically nothing about Korea."

"They are certain to blunder," MacArthur told aides, "because errors are inescapable when a diplomat attempts to exercise military judgment."[9]

In the meantime, MacArthur had been receiving so many contradictory reports from the battlefield that on the fourth day of the war, he decided to fly to Korea to reconnoiter the situation. It would be a perilous trip. The lumbering, unarmed *Bataan* would take off from Tokyo without the pilot knowing where he would land. Kimpo, the airfield closest to Seoul, had been overrun by the invaders, and Suwon, twenty miles south of the capital, was under attack. In essence, MacArthur and his entourage would be winging into the battle scene blindfolded.

On the morning of MacArthur's departure, the Tokyo airport was socked in by fog and heavy rain. Ceiling was zero. Lieutenant General George E. Stratemeyer, chief of the Far East Air Force, was the first of the brass to arrive. He promptly told Colonel Tony Story, MacArthur's pilot going back to World War II days, that the *Bataan* was grounded.

Minutes later, MacArthur drove up in his limousine, its windshield wipers struggling to keep ahead of the rain. Climbing from the vehicle, the supreme commander, wearing faded khaki shirt and trousers, a leather jacket, and his famed gold-embroidered hat, strode up to the *Bataan* and overruled Stratemeyer. Turning to Colonel Story, MacArthur said simply: "We go!"[10]

For the flight, Stratemeyer had four P-51 Mustangs, fighter-plane relics from World War II, flying cover for the *Bataan*. Hovering overhead like mother hens watching over their brood, the Mustangs were soon needed. As the *Bataan* began gliding to a landing at Suwon airport, a Soviet-built Yak fighter dove toward it.

"Bandit at three o'clock!" an excited voice called out in the *Bataan*. Everybody ducked or flopped to the floor—all except MacArthur. He calmly strolled to a window and watched a Mustang peel off and head for the Yak.

"We've got him cold!" the general said evenly. However, Story began taking wild evasive action, so the fate of the Yak was left in doubt.[11]

Suwon's runway was pockmarked with bomb craters, and the *Bataan* made a rough landing. John Muccio, the American ambassador, greeted the general and escorted him to a nearby school. There Brigadier General John H. Church, whom MacArthur had sent to Korea a day earlier to evaluate the situation, painted a gloomy, even hopeless, picture. "Well," MacArthur declared, "let's go up front and have a look."[12]

Riding in a Dodge staff car and trailed by a caravan of jeeps loaded with military brass and a few American reporters, MacArthur headed north toward Seoul. Progress was snail-like. The tiny convoy had to weave its way through and around thousands of terrified, bewildered South Korean civilians trudging away from Seoul. Interspersed with the refugees were ragtag bands of ROK soldiers fleeing southward.[13]

A mile south of the broad Han River, which flows east to west through Seoul, the caravan halted and MacArthur strolled to a hill at a pace belying his seventy-one years of age. There the general, his hands thrust in rear trouser pockets and puffing on a corncob pipe, stood silhouetted against the sky and peered at the disaster unfolding before him. Seoul was in the hands of the North Koreans, and columns of thick black smoke spiraled into the sky over the ancient city.

After spending twenty minutes on the hill, MacArthur and his party got into their vehicles and headed back to Suwon airport, which by now might be in North Korean hands. It was not, and the supreme commander took off in the *Bataan* and flew back to Tokyo.

It was 5:00 P.M. in Tokyo when MacArthur reached the Dai Ichi building. All the while, since his stop on the hill overlooking tortured Seoul, he had been mulling over an audacious operation designed to alter the course of the war—an amphibious landing halfway up the west coast of Korea and deep behind Communist lines. Confronted by the specter of a large force to their rear, the invaders would have to pull back rapidly or be cut off and destroyed. MacArthur told his staff to get to work on such a plan, which was code-named Bluehearts.[14]

MacArthur teleconned a message to General J. Lawton "Lightning Joe" Collins, the army chief of staff in the Pentagon. It arrived at 3:00 A.M.. (Washington time) and stated: "The only assurance for holding the present line and the ability to regain later the lost ground is through the introduction of United States combat forces into the Korean battle area."

In conclusion, MacArthur asked for authorization to immediately fly a U.S. regimental combat team to provide protection for a possible heavy buildup of American ground forces. Collins, who had distinguished himself as a corps commander in Europe in World War II, replied that the request was too momentous for his decision, that it would be presented to President Truman later in the morning.

MacArthur was not happy. Time was Kim Il Sung's ally. Within hours, the North Korean tanks could be racing toward Pusan, a port at the southern tip of Korea.

Collins telephoned Secretary of the Army Frank Pace, rousting him out of bed at 4:30 A.M. Reluctantly, Pace telephoned the White House and was relieved to find that Truman already had shaved, dressed, and breakfasted and was in the Oval Office, primed and ready to make crucial decisions. On the president's desk was the sign "The buck stops here."[15]

Truman, a decisive man, told Pace he felt no obligation to consult Congress but would seek the views of a few confidants. Within two hours, Truman had granted MacArthur authority to commit U.S. ground troops. For the first time in history, a U.S. president, single-handedly, had taken the nation into a shooting war.

Later that day, Truman released another bombshell to the media: He had authorized the U.S. Air Force to strike at specific military targets above the 38th Parallel in North Korea and had "ordered a naval blockade of the entire Korean coast."[16]

Close behind the first North Korean tanks to burst into Seoul, a large psychological warfare contingent arrived and launched a massive propaganda blitz. A platoon of soldiers fanned out in the city and placed on the sides of buildings huge posters of Kim Il Sung and Josef Stalin. Tens of thousands of pamphlets were distributed; they appealed for South Koreans to join with the "glorious People's Army of North Korea in its noble struggle to unify the nation and throw out the white devils."

Americans despise the Korean people and look on them as an inferior race, the pamphlets proclaimed. "Who had set Korea free from forty years of brutal Japanese occupation? Certainly not the Americans. They are now close allies with the Japanese, our enemies." Rather, it had been the "gallant Soviet army that had swept down from Manchuria and freed us," the pamphlets stated.

Control of Seoul's newspapers was seized by the Communists, and the editors were forced to publish stories quoting Kim Il Sung and his desire for peace and the unification of the two Koreas. Other articles blasted Syngman Rhee and the "greedy Wall Street warmongers" in the United States for triggering the conflict.

North Korean soldiers were portrayed as peaceful, gentle souls who had volunteered to liberate the enslaved people of the South. Over Radio Seoul, now in Communist hands, North Korean correspondent Kim Sin-gyo said that the people of Seoul were frightened when the first "liberators" arrived. "But one civilian told me," Kim declared, "that Syngman Rhee's propaganda had painted North Korean Communist soldiers as monstrous rabble with the horns and tails of red devils. But now you can see that the gangster Rhee lied. The North Korean soldiers do not have horns and tails; they are young, brave, and handsome."

Almost daily, Communist commentators used Radio Seoul to castigate President Truman as an evil warmonger whose vicious goal was to gobble up all of Asia. Truman, they stressed, "hates brown people."

Plastered across the front pages of the Seoul newspapers were photographs of smiling children being given rides on tanks by their "liberators." Another picture showed an elderly woman bowing and presenting a bouquet of flowers to a group of grinning North Korean soldiers. The caption said: "Women of Seoul Thank Their Saviors."

Among the South Koreans who had a score to settle with Syngman Rhee was General Song Ho Song, whom Rhee had sacked as commander of the ROK 2nd Division for incompetence. Still bitter, Song joined in the propaganda offensive. Over Radio Seoul, he announced that he had been appointed to command the South Korean People's Volunteer Corps, whose ranks would be filled by South Koreans who wanted to fight alongside Kim Il Sung's soldiers to rid the country of Syngman Rhee.[17]

While the North Korean propaganda machine was functioning on all cylinders, a reign of terror gripped Seoul. Some six thousand South Korean murderers, rapists, thugs, and political prisoners were released from jails. They spilled out into the streets shouting, "Long live the fatherland!" and calling for revenge. Scores of ROK government officials, along with wealthy private citizens fingered by Communist sympathizers as "landowners," were immediately shot or dispatched by bayonets. Seoul's streets ran red with blood.

Hundreds of other South Koreans were hurled into filthy jails to await trial as "enemies of the people" before a Communist-appointed tribunal called the People's Court. Wearing white civilian suits, the South Korean judges were among those the invaders had freed from Seoul jails. Alone or in small groups, the terrified, bewildered suspects, bound at the wrists with strips of white cloth, were herded before the tribunal. In most instances, the verdict was immediate execution.

One of the prisoners was an American bishop, Patrick Byrne, the Catholic apostolic delegate in Korea. When other U.S. civilians had been evacuated from Kimpo airport prior to the entry of the North Koreans into Seoul, Byrne had decided it was his duty to remain. A tall, slim, soft-spoken man with gray hair and a dignified demeanor, Bishop Byrne was packed with scores of other prisoners in a damp basement only twenty feet square. Also in the suffocating enclosure were Father Paul Villemot, an eighty-two-year-old French priest, and eighty-six-year-old Mother Béatrix, the superior of the Sisters of St. Paul of Chartres and five of her nuns. Byrne was accused of being a CIA spy.

North Korean soldiers came to the basement, ordered the twelve or so priests, nuns, and missionaries (including a blind Frenchman) outside, and took them in front of the South Korean judges of the People's Court. Five hundred Seoul civilians sympathetic to Kim Il Sung jammed the room to watch the spectacle. All day the suspects were harangued by the judges and prosecutor. When aged Father Villemot, exhausted, trembling, and confused, asked for a cup of water, the mob hooted and jeered, shouting, "Don't help the white devil!"

Time after time, one especially belligerent judge demanded that Bishop Byrne confess that the CIA had sent him to Korea as a spy. Each time he replied that he had come on his own volition to teach religion and gain converts to Christianity. The crowd screamed, "Kill the American!"

When the "trial" was over, the People's Court pronounced sentence on Bishop Byrne: "You will broadcast by radio a denunciation of the United States, the United Nations, and the Vatican or you must die." If the cleric were to comply, the broadcast would be a propaganda coup for the Communists—a Catholic bishop condemning his own country and the seat of his faith in Rome.

Speaking in a calm, firm voice, Byrne replied, "There remains only one course for me—that I die."[18]

Clearly, the judges had not been programmed for such an unexpected response. Looking bewildered, they fell silent for several seconds. Then they suspended Byrne's death sentence.

A few days later, the bishop and other religious "enemies of the people" were crowded into old railroad freight cars and taken to an internment camp in North Korea. There, four months later, Bishop Byrne would die, a victim of Communist brutality.[19]

7

A Deception to Confuse the Invaders

U NLESS KIM IL SUNG AND HIS GENERALS could be coerced into believing the American ground forces were much stronger than was actually the case, Douglas MacArthur knew the invaders would overrun South Korea in a week. Unbeknownst to him, that timeframe coincided with that of the In Min Gun operations plan. Consequently, MacArthur would create "an arrogant display of strength" by hurling his units into battle piecemeal as they arrived from Japan, thereby causing the North Korean commanders to pause and then make faulty battlefield decisions.[1]

MacArthur's deception scheme would violate long-accepted military doctrine: mass, not driblets. But he was confronted by a desperate situation, and his initial troops would have to buy time—time to bring in more soldiers, heavy weapons, tanks, ammunition, and supplies.

All of the ground formations would be drawn from the spit-and-polish U.S. Eighth Army, which for five years had been stationed in Japan and was guarding that former enemy nation from Soviet invasion. A new Japanese constitution, created at the insistence of Douglas MacArthur, had gone into effect on May 3, 1947, and it abolished the army and navy, stating that Japan would give up war forever.

Commander of the Eighth Army was Lieutenant General Walton H. Walker, known to fellow officers as Johnnie, after his favorite brand of whiskey. During World War II, he had been a corps commander under General George S. Patton, who had dubbed him "my fightingest son of a bitch."

Walker's units were at only 70 percent strength and armed with World War II–era rifles, tommy guns, carbines, and machine guns. Most of these weapons were unfit for combat. Mortar mounts were broken; there were no spare barrels for automatic weapons; shells and grenades had corroded from age. Communications radios were in short supply, and many of those available would not function.

Eighth Army's greatest weakness, however, resulted from demands by Washington politicians that America's armed forces be "civilized." Army captains and lieutenants were ordered not to be too harsh on their men, or to discipline them for misdeeds, because the offended soldier might write his mother about the mean old officer and mother would complain to her congressman. As a result, most of the men in the ranks were a new breed of regular, who, even though wearing uniforms, were psychologically and physically unready for combat.

Thirty-seven-year-old Colonel John "Iron Mike" Michaelis, who had been wounded twice while a paratroop commander in World War II, minced no words in putting the Eighth Army's combat readiness— or lack of it—into perspective:

"In peacetime training, we've gone for too damned much falderal. We've put too much stress on Information and Education and not enough stress on rifle marksmanship, scouting, patrolling, and the organizing of a defensive position. These kids have all the guts in the world and I can count on them to fight. But they can't shoot. They don't know their weapons.

"They have spent far too much time listening to lectures on the difference between Communism and Americanism and not enough time crawling on their bellies on maneuvers with live ammunition hissing over them. They've been nursed and coddled, told to buy War Bonds, to give to the Red Cross, to avoid venereal diseases, and to write home to mother—when somebody ought to have been telling them how to clear a machine gun when it jams.

"The U.S. Army is so damned roadbound," Michaelis continued, "that the soldiers have almost lost the use of their legs. [If a] patrol were to be sent out on a scouting mission, they would load up in a three-quarter-ton truck and start riding down the highway."[2]

Rain was pelting the airport near Pusan on Friday morning, the fifth day of the invasion, as six huge C-54 cargo planes touched down and rolled to a halt. Rapidly disembarking were GIs of a 24th Infantry Division battalion commanded by thirty-four-year-old Lieutenant Colonel Charles B. "Brad" Smith. The soldiers were young, averaging nineteen years of age. This was the vanguard of Eighth Army.

West Pointer Smith knew that he had been handed a suicide mission: to stall the entire In Min Gun that was charging hell-bent for Pusan. He and his greenhorn GIs were to be sacrificed on the altar of strategy to buy time for MacArthur. They were expendable.

Smith's understrength battalion, grandiosely named Task Force Smith, climbed aboard a wheezing, huffing old train and headed for

Taejon, 120 miles to the northwest. On arrival, Smith rushed to see General John Church, MacArthur's liaison with the ROKs. Two days earlier, Church had remarked, "I would trade the entire ROK army for one hundred armed New York City policemen!"

Now Church pointed to a wall map and singled out the village of Osan, eight miles to the north. "There's a little action up there," he said airily. "All we need up there is some men who won't run when they see tanks." The implication was clear: The ROKs had "run"; Americans would not "run."

Night fell, and Task Force Smith moved northward in rickety Korean trucks. By dawn on July 5, the outfit was deployed at a road crossing near Osan. It was raining hard. Just before 7:00 A.M., Brad Smith detected a column of thirty-one North Korean tanks clanking toward the grim Americans. Out of sight behind the armor was a five-mile-long convoy of trucks loaded with troops. Smith's secret fear had come true: He and his tiny band were directly in the path of Kim Il Sung's major spearhead.

For six hours, a bloody clash raged. Task Force Smith, out-manned, outgunned, with no tanks, and most of its men hearing shots fired in anger for the first time, was chopped to pieces by the battle-hardened North Koreans. Survivors had to pull back, leaving behind scores of dead and wounded Americans. A lieutenant came upon five wounded and frightened GIs lying on the ground. "What's going to happen to us?" one of the teenagers asked pleadingly. Handing him a grenade, the officer replied, "This is the best I can do for you."[3]

The implication was not lost on the youngster: When the North Koreans neared, he could pull the grenade pin and blow himself up. Brad Smith and his men were the first Americans to learn that the North Korean soldier was tough, tenacious, dedicated, and utterly ruthless. Hard-muscled, uncomplaining, accustomed to brutal discipline, he scurried up and over steep ridges like a mountain goat. He could march for days with only a few pocketfuls of rice to eat. Lugging a heavy combat load, he was a beast of burden as well as a skilled fighter.

Task Force Smith had paid a horrendous price in blood, but its presence on the battlefield, as MacArthur had predicted, caused North Korean generals to halt their surging forces and bring their artillery across the Han River to counter this new American threat to speedy victory.

During the next few days, the U.S. 24th and 25th Infantry Divisions from Japan poured ashore at Pusan and deployed northward to meet the oncoming In Min Gun. Thrown against a battle-tested foe that often outnumbered them ten to one, the inexperienced U.S. units began to crumble as rapidly as had their ROK allies. Correspondents in Tokyo began writing ominously about an "American Dunkirk."[4]

Marguerite Higgins, a comely, thirtyish correspondent for the *New York Herald Tribune*, was covering the fighting after winning a verbal brawl with the U.S. brass, who felt the combat zone was no place for a woman. "I saw young GIs turn and bolt in battle," she wrote, "or throw down their weapons, cursing their government for what they thought was embroilment in a hopeless cause."[5]

"Bugout fever," the GIs called it.

Douglas MacArthur, perhaps for the first time in his career, had vastly misjudged the power and skill of an enemy force. Kim Il Sung's Soviet-trained and -equipped tank columns maneuvered in a style like that of the Russians during World War II, and his foot soldiers were adept at skirting American and ROK units and assaulting them from the rear. MacArthur cabled the Pentagon to send him four more divisions, but his request was rejected.

Forty-eight hours later, MacArthur again cabled the Pentagon, saying that even the four divisions he had asked for earlier would not be sufficient to halt the In Min Gun offensive. Now he wanted eight divisions to be sent to Korea "without delay and by every means of transportation possible." Should his latest request be denied, disaster loomed, MacArthur implied.

The power brokers in Washington were shaken by MacArthur's bombshell. For the first time, they faced the reality that a bloody, brutal war was raging in Korea and that the "hordes of illiterate Oriental rabble" from the North were not going to flee merely by a confrontation with a few Caucasian soldiers. It was decided that more troops for MacArthur would have to be scraped from a military cupboard that was nearly bare.

Harry Truman called into federal service selected National Guard units. Recruiting drives were intensified and draft quotas increased, with a goal of putting six hundred thousand would-be soldiers in uniform as rapidly as possible. There were few protests. Patriotism was still strong, and the nation's pride had been stung by the rout of the GIs by Kim Il Sung's forces.

A day after MacArthur sent his jolting cable, the United Nations General Assembly convened at Lake Success, outside New York City, to decide on the military control of the Korean conflict. Numerous countries had agreed to send troops, ships, or support units. Secretary-General Trygve Lie proposed that a "Committee on Coordination for the Assistance of Korea" be created. England, France, and Norway agreed. Since the United States would be bearing the heaviest burden, including most of the cost, Ambassador Warren Austin, speaking for

President Truman, insisted that Douglas MacArthur be appointed supreme commander of the United Nations forces. The motion carried unanimously. MacArthur would now wear a third command hat to go with his SCAP and CINCFE ones.

With the ROK army stumbling southward in disarray, the North Korean propaganda machine launched a campaign designed to destroy whatever remained of the South Korean soldiers morale and to crush the spirit of the civilian population. Radio Pyongyang kicked off the psychological warfare attack by broadcasting the contents of a document alleged to have been signed by forty-eight ROK National Assembly members who had remained in Seoul. The statement pleaded for officials in Syngman Rhee's government (which had been relocated to Taejon) to publicly denounce the South Korean president and "come over to the side of the people."

Later, Charles Willoughby, MacArthur's G-2, would learn that the Communist propaganda experts had pulled off quite a miraculous achievement, because at least half of the forty-eight members were dead when they affixed their signatures.

Two of the stars of the Radio Pyongyang propaganda broadcasts were North Korean pilots, identified as "Hero Ong" and "Hero Kim." In their stirring accounts of their triumphs over U.S. airmen, the American pilots came across as cowards, trying vainly to flee before Hero Kim and Hero Ong caught up with and blasted them from the sky. Radio Pyongyang credited these two North Koreans, along with other "hero pilots," with shooting down so many airplanes that the total eventually exceeded the number of planes in the entire Far East Air Force—several times over.

North Korean propagandists also took aim at world opinion. Correspondents from Communist newspapers in China, England, France, Australia, and other nations were brought in to provide "objective reporting" to counter the "lying American press." Alan Winnington, a reporter for the London *Daily Worker*, dispatched a story claiming, from everything he had seen and heard with his own eyes and ears, that Syngman Rhee and his clique, nudged by President Harry Truman and General Douglas MacArthur, had deliberately started the war. Moreover, Winnington wrote, the South Koreans were guilty of a huge slaughter of political prisoners near Taejon.

Winnington and other European and Australian Communist correspondents focused on American "terror bombing designed specifically to slaughter innocent civilians." Winnington told in vivid detail how he had seen a low-flying P-51 Mustang "deliberately race toward a mass of refugees and mercilessly rake them with machine guns."

Incredibly, these stories by Communist correspondents were often picked up and published by non-Communist newspapers around the world.

In Washington, meanwhile, President Truman and Pentagon officials had been gripped by a haunting specter since the North Korean invasion. Was the In Min Gun offensive, as powerful as it was, merely a strategic feint to draw U.S. attention away from other locales in the world where the Soviet Union might launch heavy military operations? Seeking answers, Truman directed Admiral Hillenkoetter and his CIA, along with J. Edgar Hoover's Federal Bureau of Investigation, to search for clues indicating how the Soviets were reacting to the U.S. involvement in Korea.

There are key indications that a nation is preparing for war: the destruction of files in a foreign embassy, the sudden evacuation of top officials and their dependents, and unusual flurries of activity in diplomatic circles around the world.

On July 8, Hillenkoetter sent President Truman the requested report, titled "Some Recent Developments with Regard to Soviet Personnel Abroad." Its main points were alarming:

- On July 2, Soviet personnel assigned to the consular and cultural-relations sections of the embassy in Tokyo were observed packing their personal effects.
- At 10:30 P.M. on July 4, agents noted a large amount of smoke and burning paper at the Soviet legation in Havana.
- On July 7, FBI agents reported that women at the Soviet embassy's camp at Woodland Beach, Maryland, across Chesapeake Bay from Washington, had hurriedly been summoned back to the embassy.
- Informant stated that hammering sounds, possibly indicating packing or crating, have been heard at the home of Boris K. Sokolov, first secretary of the Soviet embassy, at his home in northwest Washington.[6]

When Harry Truman read the CIA report, he grew angry because there had been no effort made to analyze the significance of these events. "I thought the CIA was an intelligence agency, not a bulletin board!" the feisty president snapped to an aide.[7]

Hillenkoetter's days as CIA director were numbered.

In Tokyo, Douglas MacArthur was involved in an ongoing hassle with Major General A. P. Kislenko, the Soviet delegate on the Allied Council, a four-nation panel created a few years earlier, at the insistence of Josef Stalin, to provide guidance to MacArthur on his stewardship of Japan. But the supreme commander had attended only one session and long had ignored its recommendations. Now, Kislenko's main function was to do everything possible to hurl the proverbial monkey wrench into MacArthur's command machinery.

Kislenko's current complaint was the covert involvement of Japanese manpower, professional skills, and facilities in the armed conflict. Despite the prevailing antiwar sentiment throughout *Dai Nippon* (Great Japan, as in Great Britain), 99 percent of the people supported the UN's action to halt North Korean aggression, Ichiro Ohno, Japan's vice-minister of foreign affairs, told the U.S. ambassador in Tokyo.

Airfields built by Japanese were of enormous benefit to George Stratemeyer's Far East Air Force. Japanese ships were ferrying U.S. troops to Korea. Japanese stevedores volunteered to go to Korea and unload freighters at the ports. And Japanese minesweepers were offered to sweep Korean coasts and ports.

Sensing an opportunity to stir up enormous unrest in Japan, the base of United Nations operations in the Far East, General Kislenko drew up a long list of these and other Japanese "violations" of the World War II peace treaty with the Allies and distributed the document to the Japanese media and to foreign embassies in Tokyo. Clearly, his intention was to generate such outrage that the Japanese government would withdraw from active involvement in the war.

Kislenko's machination collapsed like a house of cards in a windstorm. Neither the Japanese people nor the press raised an iota of protest.[8]

8

A Clandestine Organization Is Born

DURING HIS EXCEPTIONAL CAREER as a combat leader in two world conflicts, Douglas MacArthur had abided by a favorite expression: "Wars are not won by arms alone." In addition to skilled battle strategy, a victorious general must utilize deceptions, propaganda, secret missions, spies, guerrillas, sabotage, and trickery to confound and confuse the enemy commanders. Now, with his third war under way, MacArthur ordered Charles Willoughby, his G-2, to organize the super-secret Joint Services Operation (JSO).

It was the function of the JSO to initiate and coordinate covert activities. Operating under its general guidance would be all U.S. intelligence and counterintelligence agencies in Japan and South Korea, and a few ROK organizations. Although these groups would combine their talents and resources when the occasion demanded, each entity would have wide autonomy in conducting its own specific missions.

General Willoughby had had long experience in clandestine operations. Although smaller, the JSO would be almost a carbon copy of a cloak-and-dagger operation known as the Allied Intelligence Bureau (AIB) that he had created and directed in the Southwest Pacific in World War II. AIB's largely successful activities had fanned out like octopus tentacles throughout a vast oceanic area.[1]

Heading the day-to-day planning of the JSO was Major General Holmes E. Dager, who had compiled a splendid record as an armored force leader in Europe during World War II. Willoughby appointed the two-star officer because he felt, with much justification, that high rank would be vital in hassles with intransigent U.S. and South Korean civil and military agencies.[2]

MacArthur wanted the JSO to insert scores of spies and saboteurs into North Korea and behind enemy lines in the South. Commando-type units were to conduct hit-and-run raids, keeping North Korean commanders jittery and off balance. Escape-and-evasion (E & E) networks were to be established in hostile territory to rescue downed pilots. South Koreans were to be recruited as guerrillas, trained and armed by American officers and noncoms, and infiltrated into North Korea and behind Communist lines. A small fleet of tiny vessels was to be assembled for sneaking guerrillas to their destinations.

Along with these direct-action operations, a sophisticated psychological campaign would be designed to weaken the morale of the In Min Gun and to stir up unrest and doubt among the North Korean civilian population. Propaganda techniques would include dissemination of leaflets and newspapers, radio broadcasts, and the use of battlefront loudspeakers, phony documents, and assorted lies and conundrums.

Among those designated to play a key role in the covert war against the Communists was Hans V. Tofte, an OSS veteran of World War II, who arrived in Tokyo on July 16, three weeks after the North Korean invasion. Tofte belonged to the Office of Policy Coordination (OPC), a deliberately vague title intended to mask the agency's true clandestine function.

OPC occupied a freakish perch in the tangled maze of Washington bureaucracy. Its funding and personnel were assigned within the CIA, but the secretary of state appointed its director. Compounding this confusing mix of authority, guidance was provided by a committee consisting of officials in the State and Defense departments.

OPC's origins traced back three years to 1947, a time when the United States had no global cloak-and-dagger organization following the disbanding of "Wild Bill" Donovan's OSS in 1945. With the cold war steadily heating up and Josef Stalin mounting serious threats around the world, there had been an outcry in Congress for expanded covert activities.

Initially, Congress assigned responsibility for conducting clandestine actions to the State Department, which was without the needed know-how, experience, or personnel. Soon, George Marshall, the secretary of state, raised objections, pointing out that U.S. foreign policy could be seriously discredited if his department's covert missions were unmasked.[3]

So the State Department was relieved of its clandestine function, and, in June 1948, the National Security Council (NSC) created the Office of Policy Coordination to handle covert actions. On September

1, Frank G. Wisner, an OSS alumnus, was appointed chief of the new OPC.

Shrewd, energetic, and personable, Wisner landed in Washington with both feet running. He was in his element. Wealthy, a former member of a prestigious New York City law firm, the Virginia native had many contacts in the capital and the bureaucratic expertise to deal effectively with the bloated egos and idiosyncrasies of the high and the mighty in Washington.

Wisner plunged into the task of creating a global network to conduct the seemingly endless covert operations being thrust upon him by Congress and the Defense Department. His staff was rapidly expanded with OSS veterans who rushed to get back into harness, and Wisner conducted himself with the panache of a knight on a white horse fighting to save Western civilization from Communism.[4]

Hans Tofte, one of Wisner's prized recruits, was the ideal secret operative. He had a keen wit, nerves of steel, and seemed to thrive on danger. Moreover, he led a charmed life, a crucial trait for one in his hazardous trade. An enormous asset in his current assignment in the Far East was that he had lived in Manchuria as a representative of a Danish shipping firm for eight years in the 1930s. In that job, he traveled extensively throughout Korea and gained an intimate knowledge of all major roads and railroads.

When Nazi dictator Adolf Hitler's armed legions overran his native Denmark early in World War II, Tofte, then twenty-seven years of age, rushed back home and joined the underground. Soon he realized that his raids were mere pinpricks against the German war machine, so he cooked up bogus papers and escaped to Spain.

From Madrid, a hotbed of international intrigue, the Dane made his way to New York, where he contacted William Stephenson, chief of British intelligence in the United States and South America. Knowing a secret-agent gold nugget when he saw one, Stephenson sent Tofte to the British crown colony of Singapore. There Tofte organized guerrilla bands of native Chinese and led them in fights against the Japanese army.[5]

When the Japanese captured Singapore early in 1942, Hans Tofte escaped to the United States, volunteered as a private in the army, and was assigned to the OSS. Soon he was bound for Italy, where he organized a flotilla of old vessels to run arms across the Adriatic Sea to the hard-pressed guerrillas of Josip Broz (who went by the code name Tito) in mountainous Yugoslavia.

After the war, Tofte married an American woman, settled down to a peaceful life in Mason City, Iowa, and rose to the rank of lieutenant colonel in the U.S. Army reserve. When war erupted in Korea, Tofte was on two weeks of summer training at Fort Riley, Kansas, where he received an urgent telephone call from his old friend Frank Wisner, the OPC chief. Could Tofte get to Washington immediately?

A day later, Tofte was in OPC headquarters listening to Wisner's spiel about the need for someone to go to the Far East on an important undercover assignment. Would Tofte accept the mission? He would. How much time would he have before departing? the Dane asked. Three hours.

Before accepting the task, Tofte insisted on resigning his commission as a reserve lieutenant colonel and functioning in the Far East as a civilian with an OCP rank equivalent to that of a major general in the army. He knew that Charles Willoughby, MacArthur's intelligence chief, had been antagonistic toward a six-man CIA team that had been in Tokyo since May, shortly before the North Korean invasion. So, anticipating a clash with Willoughby, Tofte wanted a civilian rank that would permit him to tell Willoughby to go to hell.[6]

Tofte had arrived in Tokyo with vague orders. Wisner had instructed him to establish an escape-and-evasion network for downed pilots and a stay-behind spy apparatus in Korea and Japan in the event that those two nations were overrun by the Communists. He had been told to choose a building complex large enough to eventually handle a thousand people, to organize independent communications, and to take it from there on his own.

While prowling the Japanese countryside for a location on which to establish his base, Tofte and his deputy, Colwell Beers, sighted an isolated patch of ground near the Atsugi Air Force Base, south of Tokyo. Within forty-eight hours, U.S. army engineers and a construction company were busy erecting buildings. When the complex was completed, Beers would be in charge of the headquarters.

Escape-and-evasion operations were high on Tofte's priority list, so he called at the U.S. Air Force Office of Special Investigations (OSI). Working hand in glove with Major Julian M. Niemczk, chief of the OSI's counterintelligence division, he laid initial plans for creating a network of secret agents to spirit downed airmen out of North Korea.[7]

In the meantime, on the battlefield, General Johnnie Walker, leader of the Eighth Army, was hurling battalions, companies, and even platoons piecemeal into the paths of the In Min Gun spearheads. There was no continuous frontline as there had been during World War II in Europe. Rather, an endless series of skirmishes erupted. Throughout July, the U.S. and ROK forces were steadily pushed back, often under chaotic circumstances. Again American correspondents were writing dolefully about the looming "United Nations Dunkirk."

Johnnie Walker, like a demon possessed, roared around the battle fronts in a jeep. In addition to his .45 Colt, he gripped a repeating shotgun. "I don't mind being shot at," he rasped to an aide, "but those bastards aren't going to ambush me!"

Walker was hardly the fair-haired boy of the media reporters. Making it plain that he considered the scribes a necessary evil foisted on him by the higher-ups, he received a poor press. Nor was the general a genial man, one loved by his officers and troops. But MacArthur had not been seeking a combat leader graced with charisma and tact. Rather, in Johnnie Walker, he had a fighter who would draw a line and defend it with every fiber in his body.

From the opening shot in the invasion, the In Min Gun had been inflicting horrendous casualties on the disorganized and bewildered ROK units. Consequently, Syngman Rhee, to fill the gaping holes in their ranks, sent roving bands of his National Police to scour towns, villages, and countryside to collar any male who appeared reasonably capable of holding a rifle. Boys, teenagers, fathers, and even grandfathers were caught in the net and given a few hours of "training."

On a given day, the typical "volunteer" (as these dragooned civilians were called) might be working in a rice paddy or a store. A week later, he would be confronting battle-hardened North Korean soldiers. By sundown, he would be a veteran or a corpse.

In a desperate effort to slow the surging North Korean avalanche, Douglas MacArthur employed all available means, including his Psychological Warfare Section (PsyWar), which he had had the foresight to establish three years earlier in Tokyo. Chief of PsyWar was J. Woodall Greene, a retired army colonel with wide experience during World War II conducting psychological warfare against the Japanese.

A dynamic man who understood the Oriental mind-set, Greene had combed the Far East for experts in the field, and soon he had gathered a team of six persons. Although tiny, the unit drafted detailed plans to meet any contingency, including an attack by North Korea against its neighbor to the south. So in less than twenty-four hours after President Truman had reached the decision to send GIs to Korea, Greene's group in Tokyo had designed and printed tens of thousands of leaflets that called on North Korean soldiers to surrender. Native Koreans in the PsyWar headquarters made certain that the correct idiom was used in the wording.[8]

In Japan, Colonel Swampy Crawford's 374th Troop Carrier Wing, based at Tachikawa Air Base, was given the responsibility of dropping the PsyWar leaflets. Piloting the first C-46 was Captain Howard Secord, who would fly at five hundred feet while crewmen in the cabin pitched out the leaflets over the North Korean forces. Gremlins, as the airmen called unexpected difficulties, got into the act. Secord's men opened the bundles, grabbed stacks of leaflets, and pitched them out the open door. But wind gusts caught most of the paper sheets and blew them back inside.

Soon this problem was remedied by the use of blasting caps with delayed fuses attached to the leaflet bundles. When the intact bundles were pitched out of the open door of the aircraft, the minor explosion caused the bundles to burst open halfway to the ground, scattering the leaflets.

As their advance continued, Kim Il Sung's soldiers were regularly "bombed" with leaflets that urged them to surrender and receive good food, humane treatment, medical care, and shelter from the perils of war. Because the North Koreans had suffered relatively few casualties and clearly were winning the war at this point, Colonel Crawford's airmen seemingly were risking their lives futilely each time the lumbering, unarmed C-46s flew in low through antiaircraft gunfire to release the bundles. However, the impact of surrender leaflets is cumulative, and many soldiers in the In Min Gun tucked away the sheets of paper for possible use when in a tight situation.

As July faded into August, Johnnie Walker's beleaguered Eighth Army had been pushed back into a relatively small enclave that came to be known as the Pusan Perimeter. GIs arriving on the peninsula had been told that they were fighting to hold back Communism at the gate of the Pacific. Few, if any, grasped that lofty viewpoint; rather, each GI was desperately intent on defending himself against the swarm of enemy soldiers sneaking up to his position or the T-34 tanks clanking down a valley toward him.

On the night of July 31, Walker called in his division commanders. "There will be no more retreating, withdrawal, readjustment of lines, or whatever you might call it," the scrappy general barked. "There are no lines behind which we can retreat. This is *not* going to be a Dunkirk or a Bataan. A retreat to Pusan would result in one of the greatest butcheries in history. We must fight to the end. If some of us die, we will die fighting together!"[9]

Within the Pusan arc, which was small enough to be quickly crossed by jeep, troops and weapons were arriving daily. In response to Washington's urgent plea (or, perhaps, to "gray mail") the British 27 Brigade, two thousand men strong, was rushed from Hong Kong to join in the struggle. Brigadier Basil Coad, a skilled and dedicated professional who commanded the brigade, was met at the Pusan dock by an American colonel who greeted him cheerfully: "Glad you British have arrived—you're the real experts at retreating!"[10]

Coad, a no-nonsense, battle-hardened veteran of World War II, was escorted on a tour of the perimeter. He was appalled: His every movement was being orchestrated by American public relations officers, and moving-picture and still cameramen dogged his heels. Washington, it appeared, had sent orders to play up the arrival of the British, a tactic designed for propaganda purposes to convince the world that the United Nations, not just Uncle Sam, was battling against Communist expansion in Korea.

Also landing within the perimeter were the U.S. 1st Cavalry Division from Japan and the U.S. 5th Marines and the U.S. 2nd Infantry Division from home. Then came Turks, Frenchmen, Filipinos, and Dutchmen—the vanguard of small supporting units from thirteen more United Nations members. Steadily, almost imperceptibly, Johnnie Walker's army numbered as many as or more than that of the Communist forces fighting savagely to break through to Pusan.

Pusan and its outskirts had become a gigantic arsenal and supply depot. Tanks, trucks, ammunition, jeeps, weapons carriers, fuel, shells, artillery pieces, food—and five large crates filled with Ping-Pong balls and paddles. Within the confines of the port area were masses of fearful, confused, and hungry refugees mingled with beggars, whores, black marketers, gangsters, and an untold number of Kim Il Sung's spies.

Brigadier Coad was shocked by the casual style in which the U.S. Army was functioning in Pusan. He was amazed by the freedom with which GIs were permitted to use civilian circuits to telephone the Japanese girlfriends they had left behind. Some American noncombat officers had refused to abandon the comfortable lifestyle to which they had grown accustomed, so they brought their Japanese houseboys, cooks, and other servants with them to Pusan.

Correspondents got wind of the presence of the servants and filed stories indicating that MacArthur had secretly brought in Japanese troops to fight against the Communists. Newspapers around the world latched onto this incredible nonsense and published it.

Radio Pyongyang and Radio Peking seized upon the stories to howl that Japan, which had fought Chinese troops for fourteen years and had occupied Korea for four decades, was now "joining with the war criminal MacArthur" in an effort to thwart the will of the Korean people.

Alarmed by the uproar over Japanese "combat troops" in Pusan, U.S. authorities directed the newly arrived 704th Counterintelligence Detachment to investigate. Through intense sleuthing, the army's "detectives" located the source of the embarrassment, collared the Japanese servants, and shipped them back home.[11]

Meanwhile, in Tokyo, Douglas MacArthur was preparing to take the greatest calculated risk of his long military career. With Johnnie Walker's Eighth Army battling desperately to keep from being driven into the sea, MacArthur was preparing to launch Operation Chromite (formerly Bluehearts), a large amphibious assault deep behind enemy lines at Inchon. Chromite would saddle Kim Il Sung with a two-front war, seize a vital port, trap much of the In Min Gun fighting against Walker's Eighth Army, and deal the North Koreans a staggering psychological blow. This was the identical strategic concept that MacArthur had envisioned back on July 4 when he stood on a hill overlooking chaotic Seoul and watched in dismay as the disintegrating ROK army fled over the Han River and rushed on to the south.

If Chromite were successful, it would be MacArthur's most spectacular triumph. Should it fail, the general would forever be remembered for his stupidity in sending thousands of young Americans to their deaths and causing the United Nations to lose the war in Korea.

9

Spying on the Enemy

DOUGLAS MACARTHUR'S AUDACIOUS Chromite operation was opposed almost unanimously by his staff and battle commanders. U.S. Navy Lieutenant Commander Arlie G. Capps set the tone: "We drew up a list of every conceivable and natural handicap—and Inchon has them all."[1]

Undaunted, MacArthur began bombarding the Pentagon with arguments supporting Chromite and requesting more troops for the operation. "They'll give in," the general assured confidants. "They know that a great victory is essential at this moment."[2]

On July 25, 1950, precisely one month after the In Min Gun charged across the 38th Parallel, the Joint Chiefs (no doubt with the approval of President Truman) reluctantly agreed to Chromite—just as MacArthur had prophesied.

In keeping with MacArthur's request, the 1st Marine Division, then at Camp Pendleton, California, would be rushed to South Korea to spearhead the Inchon assault. Getting the leatherneck division to the Far East in time for D-day, September 15, would be a herculean task, not only because of the nine-thousand-mile distance involved, but also because the division had only regimental strength. Its ranks would have to be filled by a crash call to a few thousand reservists peacefully engaged in civilian pursuits across the nation.

Once the Joint Chiefs had given Chromite the green light, they became angered because MacArthur was sending the Pentagon only sketchy details of the operation. In one cable, MacArthur said that he thought it "unwise" for him to go into greater detail. His implication stunned the Joint Chiefs. Did the UN commander mean that the generals and admirals in the Pentagon could not be trusted to keep secrets?

Again in an enigmatic tone, MacArthur warned the Joint Chiefs to be extremely careful what the army spokesman in the Pentagon revealed in his routine briefings of media reporters: "He should not even hint [about our] grand strategy [at Inchon] in the slightest degree."

The Joint Chiefs felt that he was engaged in what his critics called "theatrics." Actually, MacArthur felt certain that there was a serious security leak in the higher echelons in Washington. His dark suspicions later would prove to be well founded.

Plans for Chromite proceeded at a feverish pitch. Then, on the morning of August 23, Army Chief of Staff General J. Lawton Collins and Navy Chief of Operations Admiral Forrest P. Sherman stepped out of a four-engine Constellation at Tokyo's bustling Haneda airport after a grueling twelve-thousand-mile flight from Washington. MacArthur had no doubt about why the two service chiefs had come. Although Washington had given lukewarm approval to Chromite, Collins and Sherman had been sent to talk MacArthur out of launching the operation.

Late that afternoon, a glittering galaxy of U.S. brass congregated in the sixth-floor conference room of the Dai Ichi building. Among those present, in addition to MacArthur, Collins, and Sherman, were three admirals, four generals, and two air force commanders. Tension was thick. D-day for Chromite was only three weeks away.

Douglas MacArthur puffed serenely on his corncob pipe and listened without comment as a series of navy lieutenant commanders, one at a time, entered the room and recited a litany of reasons why Chromite could turn into a monumental American debacle. The navy had many deep-rooted concerns, especially about Inchon's treacherous tides, among the highest in the world, ranging up to thirty-two feet. When the tide was low, the port had wide, oozing mud flats, which could strand ships and landing craft.

There were other equally daunting obstacles. Inchon had no beaches, only piers and seawalls, so the assault force would have to strike at the heart of the city. In World War II, a similar frontal attack from the sea directly against the port of Dieppe, France, had been carried out mainly by Canadian troops, nearly all of whom had been wiped out on the first day by German soldiers barricaded in shorefront buildings.

Rear Admiral James H. Doyle, a stouthearted old sea dog who would command the amphibious fleet, pointed out that the waters around Inchon might be mined. Were they? No one knew.

Doyle spoke grimly of other hazards. Steaming toward Inchon in the pre-dawn darkness of D-day, invasion ships would have to gingerly maneuver around the rocks and shoals of narrow Flying Fish Channel. Should two vessels collide, the channel could be blocked, preventing following ships to proceed.

Another potential peril, Doyle said, was that the invasion fleet would be confronted by North Korean guns on Wolmi-do (Moon Tip

Island), which jutted into Flying Fish Channel. If these guns were to sink or disable a ship, the water approach to Inchon also could be blocked.[3]

General Collins, who had led the U.S. VII Corps in the assault on Utah Beach in Normandy in World War II, described an Inchon landing as an "impossibility." He proposed Kunsan, a port a hundred miles to the south, as a site for the operation. Kunsan lacked the drawbacks of Inchon and was much closer to Johnnie Walker's Eighth Army, which would break out of the Pusan perimeter and link up with the invading force, Collins declared.

Finally, nine critics finished an eighty-minute presentation. No one spoke in favor of Chromite. "I waited a moment or two to collect my thoughts," MacArthur would write. "I could feel the tension rising in the room. If ever a silence was pregnant, this was it."[4]

Rising to his feet, MacArthur gave a thirty-minute performance that one admiral later called "masterful." He began by telling the brass that "the very arguments you have made as to the impracticabilities involved" confirmed his faith in Chromite, "for the enemy commander will reason that no one would be so brash as to make such an attempt."

Pausing briefly, MacArthur added that an amphibious landing "is the most powerful tool we have." To utilize it fully, "we must strike hard and deep." Looking squarely at Admiral Sherman, he said, "My confidence in the navy is complete, and in fact, I seem to have more confidence in the navy than the navy has in itself. The navy has never let me down [through eighty-seven amphibious landings in World War II], and it will not let me down this time."[5]

If he was wrong, MacArthur said, "I will be there personally and will immediately withdraw our force." Admiral Doyle spoke out: "No, general, we don't know how to do that. Once our [marines] start ashore, we'll keep going." When another admiral said that North Korean shore batteries could rake Flying Fish Channel, Forrest Sherman, silent until now, declared firmly, "I wouldn't hesitate to take a ship in there!"

Douglas MacArthur had won over his critics. In his sonorous tone, he concluded: "Inchon will succeed, and it will save a hundred thousand lives!"[6]

Later, Admiral Sherman told Marine General Lem Shepherd that MacArthur had been "spellbinding." By the next morning, however, MacArthur's mystique had begun to wear off, and one general remarked gloomily, "Inchon is a five-thousand-to-one shot!"

Within hours, MacArthur called in Major General Edward M. "Ned" Almond, chief of staff of the Far East Command, and told him he was creating a new X Corps as the Inchon spearhead and that Almond would be the commander. X Corps would consist of Major General Oliver P. Smith's 1st Marine Division (when it arrived from California) and Major General David G. Barr's 7th Infantry Division, which had suffered heavy casualties fighting against the In Min Gun. Barr's ranks were filled with eight thousand young Koreans who had been yanked off the streets of Pusan by Syngman Rhee's National Police. They were hustled into ships and taken to Japan. A bewildered lot of confused civilians, few could speak English. In Japan, they were decked out in ill-fitting fatigues, handed rifles, and told they now were soldiers.

Army General Ned Almond and Marine General Oliver Smith were psychological opposites with different ideas about how battles should be fought and won. Almond, fifty-eight years of age, had been a much-decorated combat leader in two wars. Shrewd, incisive, impatient, he had a sharp tongue and was both feared and obeyed by his subordinates.[7]

Texas-born Oliver Smith was tall and thin with a shock of snow-white hair that made him look older than his fifty-seven years. Like Almond, Smith had fought with great courage in two wars. Mild-mannered and soft-spoken, he had a reputation as an intellectual. Despite his outwardly gentle demeanor, however, Smith could be as tough as a boot when the situation demanded.

Soon after General Almond had taken command of X Corps, he came up with what Oliver Smith disparagingly labeled "an incredible brainstorm." Almond planned to form a "special action company" to launch a commando-type operation at Inchon. Smith was asked to contribute one hundred of his best marines to the elite unit. "I want no part of that!" Smith told aides. "I need all the marines I have!"

Almond's scheme proposed piling the "special action company" into a British frigate and sailing from Pusan to Inchon at the same time the assault fleet made the trek. While the 1st Marine Division was storming the port, the special unit would transfer into rubber boats, row ashore near Inchon, and march rapidly inland to capture Kimpo airport, twenty miles to the northeast.

On hearing of the commando operation, Smith called it a "wild idea." He told an aide, "It never occurred to those jokers [Almond's staff] to figure out what would happen when the tide was going out and they tried to row ashore against the [swift] waters! It's a lot of foolishness!"[8]

In a tense showdown with General Almond, Oliver Smith shot holes into the Kimpo airport scheme. He pointed out that radios to be carried by the special outfit had a range of only four miles, so the commandos could not contact warships offshore for gunfire support in case heavy resistance was encountered. Again because of limited radio range, U.S. commanders would not know the location of the "special action company" at any given time, so the unit might be attacked by friendly planes whose pilots mistook it for a North Korean unit. Moreover, Smith added, intelligence reports indicated that there were far more North Korean soldiers defending Kimpo than the commando outfit could handle.

Neither man was impressed by the other's arguments. And the heated confab broke up with no decision reached.

Back at his headquarters, the marine general fumed to his staff, "We can seize Kimpo in a short time, if we are just left alone!"[9]

Although Almond clung tenaciously to his "special action company" scheme, Oliver Smith succeeded in hanging onto his one hundred marines, and, only twenty-four hours before the Inchon assault, the X Corps commander would quietly cancel the Kimpo operation.

Meanwhile, in Tokyo, a joint planning staff produced a detailed Chromite operational plan by the first week in September. Heavy warship bombardments and poundings by airplanes in and around Inchon would precede the assault. Then Wolmi-do, the fortified island guarding the entrance to Flying Fish Channel, would be assaulted by a battalion of marines early on the morning of D-day.

As soon as the battalion was put ashore, the fleet would have to pull back because of the swiftly falling tide. If the marines on Wolmi-do ran into serious trouble, there would be no way that reinforcements could be rushed to their aid for many hours.

In late afternoon, the fleet would surge back in on the rising tide, and the bulk of the 1st Marine Division would storm the seawalls and charge into Inchon. David Barr's 7th Infantry Division, its ranks loaded with the bewildered instant-soldiers snatched off the streets of Pusan, would follow the marines ashore.

After wiping out the North Koreans in and around Inchon, the invading force would advance and capture Kimpo airport, cross the Han River, seize Seoul, and set up defensive positions in an arc north of the capital. Meanwhile, Johnnie Walker's Eighth Army would launch an offensive, drive to the northwest, and link up with Ned Almond's X Corps east of Inchon.

MacArthur's planners were haunted by a raft of unknown or uncertain factors. How many North Korean troops were in the Inchon region? How many big guns were there on Wolmi-do and along the Inchon seawalls? Where were the enemy artillery pieces located? Were the sea approaches to Inchon mined? Had the In Min Gun placed underwater obstacles in Flying Fish Channel? Aerial photos produced only limited information. Hard, on-site intelligence was crucial, but ROK secret agents in Inchon had vanished. A U.S. intelligence officer explained: "By this time, ROK commanders were having trouble in getting people to go into the front lines, much less behind them!"[10]

Douglas MacArthur had no intention of striking "blind." So late in August, nineteen days before D-day, U.S. Navy Lieutenant Commander Eugene F. Clark was summoned by a high-ranking intelligence officer in Tokyo. Speaking in conspiratorial tones as though Kim Il Sung were hovering at the keyhole, the officer asked Clark if he would lead a team of secret agents to the Inchon region to collect vital information. Sensing excitement, Clark promptly accepted. His secret mission was code-named Trudy Jackson.

During World War II, Eugene Clark had been a skipper of a craft that prowled the China coast for the OSS. Now thirty-nine years old, he had seen duty with the navy in the Far East for nineteen years. One U.S. clandestine operative who had known Clark in the past war said that he "had the nerves of a burglar and the flair of a Barbary Coast pirate."[11]

After the Pacific conflict, Clark had been chief interpreter-translator for the war crimes trials on Guam, and in 1949, he was assigned to MacArthur's intelligence staff in Tokyo. He spoke fluent Japanese and passable Chinese.

Clark began preparing for his secret mission at Inchon, where he would be amidst North Korean troops and a hundred miles from the nearest American soldiers. His first action was to seek the assistance of another daredevil, Hans Tofte, the OPC special operations chief in the Far East.

Working together, Clark and Tofte recruited qualified agents, including Youn Joung, a young, bright ROK navy lieutenant who spoke several Asiatic languages, and middle-aged South Korean Colonel Ke In-ju, Syngman Rhee's former counterintelligence officer, whom Rhee had sacked for failing to predict the North Korean invasion.

Tofte arranged to fly Clark and his two Koreans on a CIA airplane to Sasebo, the U.S. naval base in southwestern Japan. There Clark picked his three-man communications team of Koreans—a major, a lieutenant, and a corporal—and ten Korean civilians to round out the Trudy Jackson espionage team.[12]

On August 31, D-day minus 16, Clark and his entourage sailed for the Inchon region aboard the British destroyer *Charity*. With the intruders went a mountain of supplies—fish, rice, DDT, communications radio, whiskey, halazone tablets, medical gear, two .50-caliber machine guns, a squad tent and cots, and a million South Korean won (about fifty thousand U.S. dollars). Clark quipped that he was disappointed because his group had no wardroom steward.

In the meantime, a tiny ROK task force of small vessels, under Rear Admiral Sohn Won Yil, had been conducting hit-and-run raids along the western, North Korean–occupied coast of the peninsula. In one of these actions, Sohn sent Commander Lee Sung and a landing party ashore on the four-mile-square island of Yonghung, twelve miles south of Inchon. Instead of finding North Korean soldiers, Lee discovered that the civilian population of several hundred people was loyal to Syngman Rhee.

Before departing, Commander Lee left behind a platoon of ROK soldiers and sailors with Lieutenant Commander Ham Myong Su in charge. An energetic type, Ham began to mobilize the teenage boys and young men of Yonghung into his private army. It was to this island that the *Charity* was taking Eugene Clark and his espionage team.

Shielded by darkness, the *Charity* sailed to the entrance of Flying Fish Channel, where Clark and his men, along with their heavy gear and supplies, transferred to a small Korean vessel that carried the team to Yonghung.

Clark was delighted to have such a secure base, one protected by Lieutenant Commander Ham and his ROK platoon. However, Ham had disturbing news. Only a few days earlier, the Communists's West Coast Regiment had moved onto the island of Taebu-do, only a half-mile to the east—almost within shouting distance.

Ham's "private army" of Yonghung natives—christened "The Young Men's Association" by Clark—was assigned to observation and listening posts to spread the alarm if the North Korean troops on nearby Taebu-do were to head for Yonghung. At night, these eager youngsters, alone or in pairs, paddled silently across the water and sneaked ashore on Taebu-do. After reconnoitering the island, they returned to Yonghung and reported to Clark on enemy troop and gun positions.

Yonghung proved to be an excellent place for spying on Inchon and vicinity. Peering through high-powered binoculars from a perch atop a hill that crowned the island, Eugene Clark could see most of the activities in the harbor and along the waterfront in Inchon.

Two days after the espionage team arrived, Clark discovered an engine-powered sampan (a small native boat). He called it "my warship" and armed it with a .50-caliber machine gun for the "main battery" and his men holding tommy guns as the "secondary battery." Then Clark began raiding adjacent islands in the warship and captured a few In Min Gun soldiers. Valuable intelligence was gleaned from these POWs and from members of the Young Men's Association who were reconnoitering other islands in the region.

In the nights ahead, several of the South Koreans that Clark had brought from Japan sneaked ashore at Inchon and meandered around the waterfront, noting North Korean gun positions and other intelligence that would be valuable for the Chromite assault force. On another occasion, one South Korean slipped onto heavily defended Wolmi-do and returned with a wealth of information.

During several nights, a few of Clark's team rowed sampans to the peninsula and infiltrated In Min Gun positions to Seoul, thirty-five miles inland. Their mission was to watch for any sign of major North Korean troop movements that might indicate Chromite had become known to the enemy.

Each night, the intelligence gained from these nocturnal forays was radioed back to a designated post near Pusan, from where it was relayed to MacArthur's headquarters in Tokyo.

All the while, Commander Clark had a heavy personal concern: He knew many details of Chromite, so if he were captured this information would be of enormous value to the North Koreans and could conceivably result in a major debacle for the Inchon assault force. Therefore, he kept a grenade strapped to his pistol belt at all times. If capture were imminent, he would merely have to pull the safety pin to destroy himself.[13]

During his briefing before leaving Japan, Clark had been told that the U.S. Navy was especially concerned about conflicting figures for the tides at Inchon. A depth of twenty-five feet was required to navigate Flying Fish Channel and Inchon Harbor, and LSTs (landing ship, tank) needed twenty-nine feet to land assault troops. Because the U.S. Navy's tide tables differed from those of the Japanese, it was up to Clark to find out which were accurate.

On the sixth night, Clark and his twenty-two-year-old ROK navy lieutenant, Youn Joung, climbed into a sampan and paddled all the way to blacked-out Inchon. As silently as possible, they edged the craft up to the seawall, right where Oliver Smith's marines were to storm ashore. They paused and listened. There were no unusual sounds. The two men could discern shadowy figures walking about in the dark streets.

Now all the intruders could do was to sit and wait for the tide to ebb so they could use primitive measuring techniques to gauge the harbor's depth at high tide. At any moment a searchlight beam might shine on them, sealing their doom. Clark felt for the grenade on his pistol belt to make certain it was secure.

After what seemed to the two men an eternity, the tide ebbed and the sampan rested on the mud flat. Rapidly, Clark took his measurements. It was guesswork at best. Without sophisticated devices, and working in the darkness, it was impossible to obtain precise figures.

Then Clark and Youn removed their clothes, climbed onto the mud flat—and sank up to their knees. Even while naked, they found it almost impossible to walk. A marine burdened with heavy boots and combat gear most certainly would sink to his waist. Clark envisioned hundreds of marines unable to proceed, sitting ducks for North Korean machine gunners, if an assault were attempted across the mud flat.

During the next two nights, Clark and Youn returned to Inchon and again measured the tide and the height of the seawall. On his return to Yonghung, Clark radioed that the Japanese tide tables seemed to be accurate, that the seawall was twelve to fourteen feet high, and that the mud flats were virtually impossible to walk through.

10

Machinations to "Hide" a Landing

MUCH TO THE DISMAY of Douglas MacArthur's security officers, media correspondents in Tokyo were calling the looming Inchon invasion Operation Common Knowledge. Censorship was voluntary because the Korean violence was not an official war. So it was left to the judgment of reporters and their editors in the United States whether a story might jeopardize battle plans and cost lives if published or broadcast.

Even while Ned Almond's X Corps was preparing to board ships for Inchon, the *New York Times* ran an article saying: "An amphibious landing on the Korean coast well behind the enemy's lines is an obvious and possible strategy."[1]

Perhaps that tactical conclusion had been reached by a *Times* reporter while hoisting a few with colleagues in a Tokyo bar. But the publication of the story sent chills up the spines of MacArthur's officers responsible for Chromite security.

President Syngman Rhee, who should have been more security conscious, delivered a rousing speech in which he declared: "We are about ready to go!"

In Tokyo, MacArthur's headquarters was jolted by an alarming report from the U.S. Counterintelligence Corps. Its agents had collared a North Korean–Japanese spy ringleader named Yoshimatsu Iwamura. On him, CIC sleuths reported, were the top-secret plans for the Inchon operation. How many copies of the plan were floating around Tokyo? Had the Communist spy ring had the opportunity to smuggle the plan to Pyongyang?

From the conception of the Inchon operation, Douglas MacArthur and his chief planner, Major General Edwin K. Wright, had recognized that it would be impossible to conceal preparations from

Kim Il Sung and his generals. Unlike the World War II army and marine invasions, which were launched from lonely island bases where all plans could be kept secure, Inchon was to be staged out of Japan—a nation saturated with Communist spies and sympathizers—and South Korea.

Although the North Koreans did not have the sophisticated electronic devices the Germans and Japanese used to eavesdrop on wireless traffic during World War II, they did have an untold number of spies who had reached Pusan with the masses of genuine refugees. So no doubt North Korean intelligence would be provided with the identity of UN units as they prepared to sail for Inchon.

To counter these Communist espionage sources in Japan and South Korea, MacArthur's planners, two weeks before D-day at Inchon, had launched an intricate deception scheme to mask the true target of the operation. The idea was for North Korean intelligence to collect numerous bits and pieces of information and to fit them into a mosaic that would point to the wrong invasion target—Kunsan, one hundred miles south of Inchon and an ideal location for an amphibious landing. Kunsan was such an obvious site to the military eye that it had been the primary choice of General Lightning Joe Collins, the army chief of staff, and Admiral Forrest Sherman, the chief of naval operations—and every top officer on MacArthur's staff.

Reinforcing the deception scheme was the fact that Inchon presented so many obstacles to a landing from the sea that North Korean commanders, almost by knee-jerk reaction, would reject that location as an invasion target.

Kicking off the deception, two GIs, wearing dark clothing and with faces blackened, paddled a rubber raft ashore just below Kunsan on an especially dark night. Taking a standard U.S. army shovel and two pails, they stole along the beach and left the three items. Then they scrambled silently back into the raft and returned to a boat that had been hovering offshore.

Hopefully, from the deception artists' view, North Korean patrols would find the American shovel and pails (which had been put in plain sight) and turn them over to intelligence officers. It was intended that the North Koreans would deduce that Americans had visited the beach at night to collect sand samples but had been frightened off, leaving the shovel and pails behind. This scenario was designed to imply that the sand samples were to be evaluated by scientists to determine if their texture was strong enough to support invading tanks and heavy vehicles.

In Tokyo and Pusan, junior officers of the U.S. Counterintelligence Corps went barhopping. Feigning intoxication, they struck up conversations at random with civilian patrons, swore them to secrecy, then disclosed in conspiratorial tones that a large amphibious force was preparing to hit far behind North Korean lines—at Kunsan. It was hoped that the "secret" eventually would reach the ears of Communist agents.

During the second week of September, the deception spotlight focused even more brightly on Kunsan. For several straight days, the British cruiser *Triumph* bolted into Kunsan Harbor and blasted the town and docks with her big guns. At the same time, General Stratemeyer's Far East Air Force pounded railroads, bridges, and roads in a thirty-mile arc around Kunsan, a standard tactic prior to an amphibious landing. Then, on D-day minus 4, Kunsan was hit hard from the air.

Two nights after the air assault on Kunsan, the British frigate *Whitesand Bay* dropped anchor off Kunsan. On board were Royal Marines of 41 Commando under Lieutenant E. G. D. Pounds and a U.S. special operations company that had been formed a few weeks earlier by Colonel Louis B. Ely, an intelligence specialist.

With faces blackened, the Royal Marines and GIs climbed down cargo nets hanging over the side of the frigate, dropped into rubber boats, and paddled ashore. Almost as soon as the raiders reached the beach, a confused firefight erupted. It raged for nearly an hour. As planned, the intruders withdrew and returned to the *Whitesand Bay*. Although the incursion cost the lives of three Americans, it may have reinforced the North Korean illusion that Kunsan was MacArthur's invasion target.

No means were overlooked to confuse North Korean intelligence or to lead it down the path to a faulty conclusion. Before sailing to Inchon, Lieutenant Colonel Raymond L. Murray's 5th Marine Regiment was pulled off the front line along the Pusan Perimeter and boarded a transport ship that was moored to the dock. The leathernecks were assembled on deck and heard officers lecture, over a loudspeaker, on In Min Gun defenses—at Kunsan. A few yards away, dockworkers, perhaps including spies or Communist sympathizers, got an earful from the phony briefing, as intended.

Forty-eight hours before D-day, Stratemeyer's aircraft winged over Ongjin, Chinnampo, Inchon, and Kunsan—each a west coast port—and dropped thousands of leaflets warning civilians to flee to the interior to escape looming violence. Deception planners could not ignore Inchon, because such an omission might pinpoint that port as the true target. The leaflet blitz was a con game of sorts, the idea being to keep the North Koreans from knowing which shell the pea would be under.

In another ploy to keep North Korean intelligence in a quandary over where the amphibious operation would hit, the battleship *Missouri* (on whose deck a Japanese delegation had formally surrendered five years earlier) barged into the harbor at Samchok, directly opposite Inchon on the east coast. Mighty Mo's big guns began belching, and a few hundred shells exploded in the town and along the docks.

As D-day grew closer, Commander Eugene Clark and his espionage team on Yonghung Island, south of Inchon, remained amidst the enemy and in danger of detection by the North Korean force on nearby Taebu-do. Seven days before Chromite was to hit, Clark's lookouts on the island's highest elevation called out that fifty North Korean soldiers were heading from Taebu-do to Yonghung in sail sampans and a motorized sampan with a 37-millimeter gun lashed to its bow. Clearly, the presence of the espionage team had been discovered.

Undaunted, Clark and many of his men got into their sampans, shoved off, and stood out to meet the oncoming hostile force in what would be an extremely strange "naval battle." Standing in the bow of his motorized sampan, Clark led the charge. While the North Koreans opened fire at a far distance with their 37-millimeter gun, which banged away futilely, Clark held his own fire and continued to close in. Then he loosed heavy bursts from his mounted .50-caliber gun. His initial rounds disabled the North Korean "gunboat," and succeeding bullets sent it gurgling to the bottom.[2]

Then Clark turned his automatic weapon against a sail sampan with eighteen soldiers aboard and sank it. With their gunboat on the bottom of the channel, the other sampans hightailed it back to Taebu-do.

Clark held no illusions that the brief but sharp shootout on the water would be the end of North Korean efforts to kill or capture him and his men. So on his return to Yonghung, he radioed for assistance, and in less than twenty-four hours, the U.S. destroyer *Hanson* hove to off Yonghung. Clark and one of his men paddled out to the ship and climbed aboard.

Clark talked with the *Hanson*'s skipper, Commander C. R. Welte, but refused to divulge his name or any other identifying information. All he would disclose was that he was on a highly important secret mission. At this point in time, Welte probably had no knowledge of the impending Inchon landing.[3]

Welte offered to take Clark and his group off the island, but the suggestion was declined. Instead, Clark asked that the *Hanson* pound Taebu-do with her five-inch guns and that carrier planes be brought in. Minutes later, the destroyer's guns began belching and poured 212 rounds onto the small island.

Within the hour, eight Corsair fighter-bombers from the U.S. escort carrier *Badoeng Strait* roared overhead. Circling like vultures, the Corsairs peeled off one at a time and dived toward Taebu-do, dropping bombs and firing rockets and cannon. By nightfall, the target was covered by a blanket of thick smoke and dust.

Feeling confident that the North Koreans on Taebu-do would cause no more trouble, Eugene Clark and his right-hand man, ROK Lieutenant Youn Joung, chugged up-channel in the motorized sampan that night to reconnoiter Palmi-do, a tiny island jutting out where Flying Fish and East Channels join. Slipping ashore, they paused to listen for sounds that might indicate the presence of North Korean soldiers. Satisfied that the island was free of the enemy, they scrambled up Palmi-do's 219-foot elevation and entered an old lighthouse, darkened since the war began.

Clark and Youn were delighted to discover that the North Koreans had not damaged the machinery but only disconnected the battery-powered rotor of the reflector and snuffed out the old oil lamp. Tinkering, Clark concluded that the reflector would rotate if reconnected, and there were still oil and a wick in the lamp.[4]

Back at his base, Clark asked by radio if the navy could use the lighthouse beam as a guide through treacherous Flying Fish Channel in the darkness of D-day morning. The navy was ecstatic. Yes, indeed, came the reply. It could well be the first time in the annals of warfare that a lighthouse in the midst of enemy positions would be used to guide in a hostile invasion armada.[5]

Now that Clark and his team had carried out their secret mission, there was nothing to do but wait. These were the hardest hours as he and his men had time to ponder their delicate situation. There they were on this tiny, sun-drenched island, framed by enemy soldiers who knew they were there. What if Chromite were called off at the last minute? What if the fleet were unable to navigate Flying Fish Channel and the invasion would fail? How would the espionage party get off the island alive? Each man knew the answer: In the larger scheme of things, they were expendable.

On September 10, ROK Navy Lieutenant Commander Lee Sung, in Patrol Craft 703, the same vessel that had landed Eugene Clark and his Trudy Jackson team on Yonghung, sailed into the bay at Haeju, a port near Inchon. Lee sighted a North Korean boat heading for the docks and ordered his three-inch gun to open fire. A shell struck the enemy vessel. Much to the astonishment of Lee and his crewmen, this seemingly inconsequential boat disintegrated in a gargantuan explosion that could be heard for miles.

Only much later would U.S. intelligence learn that the North Korean craft had been loaded with Soviet-built magnetic mines that were to be sown along Flying Fish Channel on the approaches to Inchon. Thus, a stroke of luck and the daring of Commander Lee may have prevented increased casualties, or even disaster, when the Chromite force arrived.[6]

Early on the morning of D-day minus 2, Douglas MacArthur lifted off in his personal plane, the *SCAP*, from Haneda airport outside Tokyo. No doubt the supreme commander was gripped by a maze of deep concerns, not the least of which was the weather. September was the monsoon season, and heavy winds and rains were sweeping across Japan and Korea. Because of the storm, pilot Tony Story had to land the plane at a small airport on Kyushu, the southernmost Japanese island, instead of at Fukouka as planned.

Climbing down the steps of the *SCAP*, MacArthur and his entourage, which included a few reporters sworn to secrecy, walked toward three parked automobiles. Outsiders seeing MacArthur for the first time found it hard to believe that he was seventy-two years of age. Tall and erect, he walked with a spring in his step. His eyes were clear and alert, and his face and hands showed no wrinkles. Although his hair had grown thin on top, it had still not turned gray.

As the three-car convoy headed for the U.S. Naval Base at Sasebo, it was evident to the knowing eye that American security officers had been at work; the metal pendant on MacArthur's automobile bore only four stars. There was only one five-star general in the Far East, as any lurking Communist spy would know. So the fifth star was missing to mask the true identity of the general riding in the vehicle.

Reaching Sasebo, MacArthur met more frustration. His flagship for the Inchon operation, the *Mount McKinley*, had not arrived because she had been caught in the storm. A few hours later, the *McKinley* sailed into Sasebo and was warped into the dock. MacArthur got aboard.

Close to midnight on September 13, the *McKinley* edged out of the harbor and set a course to link up with the invasion fleet at sea. There was no turning back: MacArthur had crossed his Rubicon.

During the first two weeks of September, brutal, no-holds-barred fighting had continued to rage along the Pusan Perimeter. North Korean atrocities intensified. Captured American soldiers were castrated before being shot in the head by Soviet-built submachine guns. GIs were tied up with barbed wire and their tongues were ripped out; then they were bayoneted and left to die.

On Hill 314, a key elevation overlooking Taegu, Lieutenant Colonel James Lynch's battalion of the U.S. 1st Cavalry Division drove a large enemy force down the reverse slope after a savage, hand-to-hand clash. Lynch's outfit suffered 229 casualties—one-third of its strength.

Sprawled on the bloody hill were more than two hundred dead North Korean soldiers wearing American uniforms, boots, and helmets. At their sides lay U.S. Garand rifles and carbines. Use of the GI clothing and weapons bore mute testimony to the effectiveness of UN airpower in cutting Communist supply lines.

Nearby were four GIs who had been bound with barbed wire, then hacked to death. An American lieutenant who had been tied hand and foot lay charred beside an empty five-gallon gasoline can. Before they had fled Hill 314, the North Koreans had burned him alive.[7]

Lynch's soldiers were enraged by what they saw and vowed revenge against the In Min Gun. Like most other GIs, they had arrived on the peninsula indifferent to the North Korean Communists. Now they hated their foe with a bloodthirsty passion.

On D-day minus 2 for Chromite, General Johnnie Walker received word that a ROK division had just mauled the North Korean 15th Division in a bitter fight on the perimeter. Walker was jubilant. The 15th Division was led by Major General Pak Sung-chol, who had been vice-premier in the North until losing a power struggle.

Grabbing his shotgun and climbing into his dusty jeep, the Eighth Army leader sped to the headquarters of General Chung Il-kwon, the ROK army chief of staff, and asked him to assemble all available officers. Some forty officers listened intently as Walker praised the tenacity of ROK fighting men. Caught up in his enthusiasm, he let slip the most closely guarded secret of the war: General MacArthur was sailing toward Inchon, where he would hit the In Min Gun far behind the battlefront.

Loud cheers rocked the room. In moments, Walker realized he had pulled a serious security blunder. So he told the group that no one was to even hint, much less talk about, the secret he had just divulged.

Like any capable war correspondent, Shin Hua-bong of the Associated Press (AP) was hovering outside the building. When the ROK officers, beaming and talking excitedly, strolled outside, Shin collared one of them, Major Kim Kun-bae, an old drinking buddy, guided him to a nearby bar, and fed the major whiskey shots.

"What's this I hear about General Walker making an absolutely fantastic statement to you officers?" the AP man asked when he figured the booze was starting to take effect.[8]

In journalistic jargon, Shin was "fishing," throwing his line into the water in the hope he would hook something of significance. Kim made no reply and continued to sip his drink. Then Shin sent out another seemingly casual comment: "I hear there is going to be a large amphibious landing at Kunsan."

"Not Kunsan!" the ROK major blurted. "It's Inchon!"[9]

Despite his tipsy condition, Kim quickly realized he had blundered. There could be hostile ears in the bar, so he vehemently denied his own disclosure, claiming that he had been joking.

Not to worry, Shin assured his buddy. Even if his statement had been true, the entire world would know about it in three or four days.

"Three or four days, hell!" the major snapped. "It's going to be the day after tomorrow!"

Shin, a conscientious journalist, was skewered on the horns of a dilemma. Through his own initiative, he had uncovered a blockbuster story and could scoop the scores of other correspondents on the peninsula. But should he sit on the story to protect the security of the Inchon landing? Or was it his obligation as a dedicated journalist to send the story to his Associated Press office in Tokyo? He sent it.

Within a few hours, Johnnie Walker received an urgent telephone call from one of MacArthur's security officers in Tokyo. Far East headquarters there had just received an inquiry from the AP wanting details on the looming landing at Inchon. Was anyone in Eighth Army responsible for this alarming leak?

Walker was angry and worried. As soon as his conversation with Tokyo concluded, he telephoned General Chung Il-kwon, in whose headquarters Walker had let slip the Inchon secret. Had any of the ROK officers let the cat out of the bag? Walker asked. Chung had no answer.

Deeply upset, Chung promptly rushed to call on President Rhee and turned in a letter of resignation. Rhee was not worried, and refused to accept it. In a rare flash of humor, the Old Patriot quipped: "Don't give it another thought, general. Kim Il Sung will think [any report of an Inchon landing] is just another Rhee dirty trick!"[10]

On September 14—D-day minus 1—Navy Commander Eugene Clark and his espionage team on Yonghung were preparing to strike camp and go to Palmi-do, where the lighthouse beam would be turned on at midnight to guide in the invasion fleet. As dusk fell, Clark's lookouts sighted a large number of sampans loaded with heavily armed In Min Gun soldiers fast approaching from the direction of Taebu-do. Unbeknownst to Clark, the North Korean commander at Inchon had shifted some two hundred of his men to Taebu-do with orders to wipe out the espionage team.

Cool and calculating as always, Clark called his men together and told them to make for Palmi-do, four miles away. Within minutes, the party shoved off in sampans, leaving behind the heavy equipment, including machine guns and the engine that drove the communications generator.

Soon after the last of Clark's men paddled away, the North Koreans stormed onto the beaches of Yonghung. Finding that their quarry had escaped, they murdered some fifty men, women, and children to demonstrate the fate of those who aid the Americans.[11]

Reaching Palmi-do, Clark and his men holed up until dark. Then, at midnight, they stole up to the lighthouse. Within minutes, the oil lamp was casting its beam down Flying Fish Channel. Clark scrawled on the lighthouse door: *"Kilroy was here!"*

11

Guiding In a Fleet

"IT'S AS BLACK AS A COW'S BELLY!"** reflected U.S. Navy Captain Norman W. Sears, who was in command of the spearhead flotilla of swift, maneuverable destroyers and light transports rendezvousing at the entrance to Flying Fish Channel. Crammed into three ships was Lieutenant Colonel Robert Taplett's marine battalion, the Wolmi-do assault unit. It was just past midnight on D-day, September 15, 1950.

For two hours, as the ships edged up Flying Fish Channel, the skippers and navigators peered intently at radar screens to detect obstacles to their passage. Lookouts in the bows could hardly tell the dark sky from the water. Suddenly, a welcome sight loomed ahead: a quick flash of light, then another, then a third. Captain Sears clicked a stopwatch: At the fortieth second, the light flashed on again, then twice more.

Sears was jubilant. The timing of the flashes was a predesignated code; Commander Eugene Clark had turned on the guiding oil lamp in the old lighthouse on Palmi-do.

Sears and other skippers could not see Clark in the blackness, but the Trudy Jackson leader had a balcony seat. Wrapped in a blanket against the nighttime chill, Clark was perched on top of the lighthouse as he watched the passing parade of ships.[1]

As the pink streaks of dawn broke the black sky, the eerie silence off Wolmi-do was split by the roar of six- and eight-inch guns on ten U.S. and British destroyers and cruisers. A crescendo of explosives saturated the North Korean stronghold. Then U.S. Navy Corsairs blasted the smoking mass with rockets, bombs, and cannon fire. Wolmi-do had been covered with lush pine, locust, and other greenery. Now it looked like Dante's inferno.

Just past 6:30 A.M., Taplett's marines hit the beach. Functioning like a well-oiled machine, they rapidly killed or captured four hundred shaken and demoralized North Koreans, seizing the island at a cost of seventeen casualties, all of them wounded.

Phase one of the bold invasion had gone off like clockwork, due in considerable part to the detailed intelligence radioed back by Eugene Clark and his Trudy Jackson team.[2]

According to plan, Captain Sears's flotilla pulled back to sea and Taplett's marines were marooned on Wolmi-do after the tide ebbed. Now oceans of oozing mud lay between them and Inchon.

Down-channel, the *Mount McKinley's* anchor rattled from the hawespipe at 5:08 A.M. Below deck, Douglas MacArthur, who had been up most of the night, awakened. After a shower and breakfast, he joined a bevy of admirals and generals who were watching Wolmi-do smoking in the distance. All around the *McKinley* lay the bulk of the invasion fleet—261 ships. On the transports were the remainder of Oliver Smith's 1st Marine Division and David Barr's 7th Infantry Division, along with support troops—71,318 men in all.

Wearing his trademark leather jacket and sunglasses, MacArthur asked Marine General Lem Shepherd, "Have we seen or heard anything of the Russians or Chinese?" All the brass were aware that if Soviet or Chinese soldiers or sailors were killed, wounded, or captured, international repercussions could give the war huge new dimensions.

"We have not," Shepherd replied.[3]

MacArthur turned to Admiral Doyle and remarked, "Say to the fleet, 'The navy and marines have never shone more brightly than this morning!'"[4]

Perhaps MacArthur already felt vindicated. He drafted a terse message to the Joint Chiefs, all of whom had fought against Chromite almost to the final moment: "First landing phase successful with losses light. All goes well and on schedule."[5]

There were no outbreaks of jubilation aboard the flagship. The trickiest part of the operation would come near dusk when the tide came in and the fleet started up Flying Fish Channel and the marines assaulted Inchon.

At mid-morning, Captain Carter Printup, skipper of the *McKinley*, was told by a lookout that a small, strange-looking craft was approaching. Peering through binoculars, Printup saw that it was a motorized sampan carrying what seemed to be a group of Koreans. As the craft drew closer, Printup could see a tall man standing up and waving a naval officer's cap. Leery that the strangers might have the sampan loaded with explosives and were preparing to crash into the *McKinley*, Printup signaled for the sampan to stand off, and he sent a landing craft with an ensign and a squad of heavily armed sailors to investigate. Drawing nearer, the ensign saw that the man in the naval officer's cap was not a Korean, but a deeply tanned Caucasian.

Leveling a tommy gun at the stranger, the ensign shouted, "Who in the hell are you?"

"Lieutenant Commander Eugene Clark of the United States Navy—and lower that popgun before you hurt somebody!"[6]

Minutes later, Clark was on the bridge of the *McKinley*. Operation Trudy Jackson was concluded.

After high tide returned in late afternoon, the big guns on six destroyers and four cruisers blasted Inchon with a deluge of shells. Then swarms of Corsairs pounded the city and the waterfront. Inchon became an inferno of fire and smoke. At 5:22 P.M., after the bombardment lifted, men of Colonel Lewis B. "Chesty" Puller's 1st Marines and Colonel Raymond Murray's 5th Marines hit the shore in amphibious tractors (amtracs) as isolated bursts of machine-gun fire hissed past and a few mortar rounds exploded. Thanks to the snooping of Eugene Clark and his sidekick, ROK lieutenant Youn Joung, the assault troops knew the height and contours of the seawall.

On Red Beach, Murray's marines hoisted scaling ladders and scampered over the concrete barrier. On Blue Beach, one group of Puller's marines, confused by the smoke, went astray and landed at the seawall to the left of the beach. In a few places, dynamite had to be used to blast holes in the barrier.

A barge carrying X Corps leader General Ned Almond and Vice Admiral Arthur D. "Dewey" Struble, commander of the Seventh Fleet, approached Blue Beach to observe the landings close-up. Just as their craft neared the seawall, a leather-lunged marine sergeant ashore bellowed: "Boat there! Get the hell out of here!"

Admiral Struble, recognizing a proper order when he heard one, promptly told the coxswain to turn the barge away—fast. Moments later, a huge explosion blasted a hole in the seawall at the point to which Struble and Almond had been heading.[7]

Rapidly, the marines fanned out into the battered and smoking city, and by midnight Puller's 1st Marines and Murray's 5th Marines were on their objectives. Some thirteen thousand men were ashore and the Inchon beachhead was secure. Twenty marines had been killed and 179 wounded.

It was a first-ever operation for the proud U.S. Marine Corps. Never before had leathernecks assaulted the heart of a city.

On the morning of D-day plus 1, Douglas MacArthur, eager to get ashore, arose at dawn on the *McKinley*. Along with an entourage that included an admiral, seven generals, and a bevy of media correspondents, the supreme commander went ashore at Inchon and drove inland in a caravan of jeeps. Rifle shots rang out periodically. Bullets never bothered MacArthur, so he kept going forward. Passing a dead North Korean soldier, he turned and remarked to a medical officer, "Doc, there's one patient you won't have to work on!"

Farther along, the touring VIPs came upon several T-34 tanks that were charred, twisted wreckage. "Considering they are Russian," MacArthur chuckled, "these tanks are in the condition I desire them to be."

As he forged ahead, a marine lieutenant charged up in a state of anxiety and blurted, "General, you can't come up here!"

"Why?"

"We've just knocked out six Commie tanks over the top of this hill!"

"That was the proper thing to do, Lieutenant."[8]

Ignoring the warning, MacArthur climbed from his jeep and strolled onto the crest of the hill for a look. The tanks were still burning and their half-cooked occupants were sprawled on top. Dead In Min Gun riflemen were around them.

Silhouetted against the sky, MacArthur stood for long minutes, hands on hips, glancing around. A firefight was raging just ahead, and Oliver Smith, leader of the 1st Marine Division, had grown anxious. While he certainly might have regretted MacArthur's being gunned down at any location, he particularly didn't want it to happen in a marine zone.[9]

Smith was enormously relieved when MacArthur decided he would return to the *McKinley*. There was ample cause for Smith's concerns. No sooner had the jeep caravan departed than Lieutenant George C. McNaughton and his marine platoon flushed seven fully armed North Korean soldiers out of the culvert atop which MacArthur had been standing while admiring the smashed enemy tanks.[10]

Communist newspapers and radio stations around the globe were stunned by what famed U.S. Admiral William F. "Bull" Halsey, a World War II hero in the Pacific, called "the most masterly and audacious strategic course in history." *Pravda*, Josef Stalin's propaganda mouthpiece in Moscow, declared that "General MacArthur landed the most arrant criminals at Inchon, gathered from the ends of the earth. . . . [These] American bandits were shooting every Inchon civilian taken prisoner."[11]

After plunging ahead, Oliver Smith's marines seized Kimpo airport; then they drove onward to Seoul, now heavily battered by bombing. Fighting was savage at times. *Pravda*'s correspondent in the city compared Seoul to Stalingrad, where the Soviet army withstood the siege of a powerful German force for months before eventually trapping and destroying the Nazi army.

"Seoul's streets are being barricaded with wagons, rice bags filled with dirt, and furniture," the correspondent wrote. "Every home is being defended as a fortress."[12]

Seoul was no Stalingrad. On September 28, thirteen days after the Inchon assault, Syngman Rhee's capital fell.

On September 16, General Johnnie Walker's Eighth Army, 180 miles southeast of Inchon, launched the second phase of MacArthur's one-two punch to kayo the In Min Gun. After a sluggish start, Walker's spearheads drove ahead rapidly. Each South Korean town overrun by the Eighth Army disclosed evidence of Communist "liberation" procedures. Only hours before GIs reached a community, North Korean commissars liquidated leaders with pistol shots to their heads. At Sachon, the retreating In Min Gun burned the jail and the 280 South Korean policemen, government officials, and landowners who had been penned up inside.

At Mokpu, Kongju, Chonju, and Hamyang, UN soldiers uncovered shallow mass graves stuffed with the corpses of hundreds of murdered civilians, including women and children. In and around Taejon, advancing GIs found the grisly remains of some five thousand executed civilians in huge communal graves. Buried with them were seventeen ROK and thirty-nine American soldiers, all of whom had their hands tied behind their backs. Two GIs and three civilians escaped the slaughter by feigning death and allowing themselves to be buried alive.

After the long drive to the northwest, Johnnie Walker's spearhead linked up with L Troop, 7th Cavalry, at a bridge forty miles southeast of Inchon at 8:36 A.M. on September 27. Half of the In Min Gun—some fifty thousand soldiers—were trapped in the South.[13]

In only twelve days, after three months of defeat, Douglas MacArthur and his fighting men had freed nearly all of South Korea of Communist domination and put Syngman Rhee back in Seoul's presidential palace. Final tabulations would show that since Inchon, MacArthur's forces had killed, captured, wounded, or driven northward between thirty thousand and forty thousand In Min Gun soldiers. But the Americans had paid a price: 536 dead, 2,550 wounded, and 65 missing in action.

When the two steel jaws of the MacArthur trap snapped shut, thousands of North Korean troops were cut off in the Kunsan region, one hundred miles south of Inchon. Isolated, hungry, demoralized, not certain what had taken place to the north, they wandered about aimlessly. One day, a T-6 training aircraft flown by U.S. Lieutenant George Nelson was winging over the countryside near Kunsan. These

T-6 trainers were forward-observer planes, and it was their pilots' task to locate enemy troops, tanks, artillery positions, convoys, or other targets; then they called in fighter-bombers.

Pilots of these light aircraft, which belonged to what was known as the Mosquito Squadron, often carried propaganda and surrender leaflets in their cockpits. When a North Korean troop unit was detected, the pilots would roll back their canopies and pitch out the leaflets over the enemy force.

On this occasion, Lieutenant Nelson spotted a group of some two hundred North Korean soldiers. He had used up his surrender leaflets earlier, but he had an idea. While circling the region, he took out a pad and wrote a terse message that told the North Koreans to drop their weapons and march to a nearby hill. There they would be picked up by U.S. troops and treated humanely. Nelson signed the note "MacArthur."

Swooping in low, Nelson dropped his note over the enemy soldiers. Then he circled for ten minutes. Much to his amazement, the North Koreans put their weapons on the ground and marched off to the designated hill. The pilot located an American patrol and radioed its leader directions to the unarmed enemy soldiers.[14]

As the spearhead of the Inchon-Kimpo-Seoul assault, Oliver Smith's marines suffered the heaviest casualties among MacArthur's forces. Their battle feats, however, did not impress Soviet Navy Captain G. Doidzhashvli, who launched a propaganda broadside for global consumption:

> When in the summer, the American imperialist marauders, the newly appeared pretenders to world domination, provoked the bloody holocaust in Korea, the Wall Street house-dog, General MacArthur, demanded that the American so-called "Marines" be immediately placed at his disposal. This professional murderer and inveterate war criminal intended to inflict a final blow [at Inchon] on the Korean people.
>
> The events in Korea have shown graphically that the Marine Corps stalwarts did not turn a deaf ear to the appeal of their rapacious leader [MacArthur]. They have abundantly covered Korean soil with the blood and tears of hundreds of thousands of Korean women, old people, and children.[15]

In Tokyo, forty-three-year-old U.S. Lieutenant General James M. Gavin, who represented the Weapons System Evaluation Group in the Pentagon, held a meeting with General Charles Willoughby, MacArthur's G-2. Almost on the heels of the 1st Marine Division, Gavin and a civilian associate, Edward Bowles, a Ph.D. from the Massachusetts Institute of Technology (MIT), had arrived at Kimpo airport while flames were still licking the buildings and scores of dead North Korean soldiers were sprawled around the premises. Now Gavin was expressing to Willoughby his deep concerns about telltale clues he had seen at Kimpo—stark evidence that China was about to leap into the war militarily.[16]

Known as "Slim Jim" to his troops while commanding the crack 82nd Airborne Division as a thirty-seven-year-old two-star general in Europe during World War II, Gavin had been greatly disturbed then by the fact that the U.S. bazooka rockets were impotent and bounced harmlessly off the heavy German tanks. Now he had come to Korea to evaluate the battlefield performance of the current antitank rockets.

While at Kimpo airport, Gavin was astonished to see an intricate arrangement of hardstands and revetments. These were the equal of any he had seen during the war in Europe, he told Willoughby. It seemed clear to Gavin that an enormous amount of sophisticated planning and construction had gone into the airport project, which was far too elaborate for the needs of the small and largely obsolete North Korean air force. Gavin explained to Willoughby that the Communists, since seizing Kimpo early in the war, had converted it into a modern military airport.

"Either Kim Il Sung has been wasting an enormous amount of money, time, and manpower in developing this airport or a first-class air power is about to jump into the conflict," Gavin warned Willoughby.[17]

Gavin thought he knew the identity of that "first-class air power"—Communist China.

Willoughby was unimpressed. Here was a newcomer to the Far East who had traipsed around a captured airport, then decided that China was about ready to intervene. If Mao Tse-tung was going to leap to the aid of his Communist neighbor, the G-2 chief responded, he would have done so as soon as the marines hit the seawall at Inchon.

Gavin replied that the Chinese probably had been taken by surprise by the audacious amphibious assault and had not had time to ride to the rescue of Kim Il Sung. "When Mao is ready, he'll come in!" Gavin declared. [18]

During his first week as a cadet at West Point, Douglas MacArthur had learned the tactical doctrine: When the enemy is on the run, keep him on the run. So he sought and obtained from President Truman permission to pursue the disorganized remnants of the In Min Gun across the 38th Parallel to bring an end to the war. MacArthur's directive, however, was drawn up by the National Security Council in

Washington, and it was a masterpiece of ambiguity and evasion. If there was "no indication or threat" of armed intervention by China or the Soviet Union, the directive stated, MacArthur was to make plans for the occupation of North Korea.[19]

In essence, Washington had assigned MacArthur the task of gazing into his crystal ball to fathom what was going on in the minds of Josef Stalin and his clique in the Kremlin in Moscow and Mao Tsetung and his coterie in the Great Hall of the People in Peking. If a UN offensive into the North went awry, the Washington power barons wanted to make certain the finger of blame would point elsewhere— that is, at MacArthur.

Bent on destroying the enemy, MacArthur issued orders to continue the advance. On October 1, elements of the ROK 3rd Division, advancing up the east coast, crossed the 38th Parallel. A few days later, patrols of the U.S. 1st Cavalry Division probed across the dividing line in the west.

Washington, meanwhile, received an alarming report from a CIA agent planted in the Indian embassy in Peking. Only hours after UN forces pushed past the 38th Parallel, the Chinese foreign minister, Chou En-Lai, had summoned K. M. Panikkar, the Indian ambassador, and told him pointblank: Should MacArthur cross the 38th Parallel, the Chinese army would be sent across the border from Manchuria to defend North Korea.[20]

India's neutrality in the Korean War had been regarded with deep suspicion by intelligence services in Washington, Tokyo, and Seoul. Studying the CIA-generated report in the White House, Harry Truman noted that Panikkar had in the past "played the game of the Chinese Communists fairly regularly." Dismissing the matter as a bluff, the president concluded that Chou's remarks to the Indian ambassador probably had been "a bare-faced attempt to blackmail the United Nations by threats of intervention in Korea." [21]

12

A Secret Trek to the Yalu

EARLY IN OCTOBER 1950, while UN forces were plunging into North Korea, Douglas MacArthur and his commanders remained in the dark about the true intentions of Mao Tse-tung and his Chinese generals. Most of the intelligence gathered by Charles Willoughby, the G-2 chief, were estimates and contrived analyses. Actually, there were no real means for discerning Peking's frame of mind with regard to Korea. The United States had no high-grade spies in the Chinese Communist capital, nor did it have the ability to accept and decipher Chinese radio communications.

Among the American officers frustrated about the intelligence blind spot in Peking was West Pointer James H. Polk, a member of Willoughby's staff. "One reason we were not reading Communist Chinese traffic at all was that they employed the Mandarin dialect," Polk would declare. "We had no Mandarin linguists. Chiang Kai-shek's people were reading [Peking's] traffic, but no one trusted what they produced because it was invariably biased or self-serving. I wanted to bring some of Chiang's people to Korea [to work under U.S. code breakers], but the Pentagon refused permission."[1]

No doubt Washington power brokers had felt that importing even a handful of Chiang Kai-shek's technicians to South Korea might trigger an armed intervention by the Communist Chinese.

Despite the lack of a direct wireless pipeline into Peking military headquarters, U.S. intelligence continued to collect alarming reports that Chinese forces, size and mission unknown, were assembling in the deep valleys just north of the Yalu River. In Washington, President Truman became deeply concerned when these reports reached his desk, and he ordered the CIA to conduct a comprehensive evaluation of Chinese intentions.

"The Chinese Communists, lacking requisite air and naval support, are capable of intervening effectively but not necessarily decisively," the CIA document declared. "Despite [bellicose] statements by [Foreign Minister] Chou En-lai, troop movements to Manchuria, and propaganda charges of [UN] atrocities and border violations, there are no convincing indications of an actual Chinese Communist intention to resort to full-scale intervention in Korea."[2]

In the Far East, MacArthur and his commanders could not rely on analytical intelligence from CIA headquarters in the old OSS compound at E and 25th Streets in Washington. So Lieutenant Commander Eugene Clark, who had led the Trudy Jackson espionage team at Inchon, was called in by U.S. intelligence officers and briefed on a new secret mission. After rapidly recruiting 150 ROK guerrillas and soldiers, Clark was to scrape up a flotilla of small boats and sail from Inchon up the west coast of Korea almost to the Yalu. His task was to learn the truth about the reports of Chinese troops massing on the other side of the river.

Along with probing Chinese activities (if any), Clark was to reconnoiter several small islands off North Korea and stake out flat pieces of terrain that would be large enough for U.S. pilots to crash-land damaged planes while on raids over North Korea.[3]

There was one more espionage task to be accomplished during the long and perilous trek. By whatever means, Clark was to "steal" a radar (or its key components) that reportedly was located in North Korea just south of the Yalu.

The radar-theft scheme seemed to Clark like a tall order. No doubt the facility would be heavily guarded. And the radar must weigh many hundreds of pounds. How was he supposed to disassemble components (he knew nothing about radar, nor would his ROKs have such knowledge), transport the parts onto tiny boats, and then run a gauntlet of North Korean gunboats seeking to sink the intruders' craft as they fled south?

If the awesome magnitude of the secret mission daunted Eugene Clark, he gave no sign of it. In short order, he rounded up his 150-man force (along with four women), armed them, and briefed them on the operation. They were issued suitable clothing, including Chinese-style padded garments that would be worn over their uniforms as both a hedge against the cold and a disguise. On October 15, Clark and his party, looking like a band of Chinese pirates, boarded four old power craft at Inchon and set a course northward.[4]

Five days later, North Korean Premier Kim Il Sung and Chinese General Peng Teh-huai, a confidant of Chairman Mao Tse-tung, were in a large structure along the Yalu River. Peng disclosed that Mao and his puppet Communist Central Committee had just made a crucial decision: A massive force of thirty-nine divisions of the Chinese People's Volunteers (as the army was called in Peking) was to congregate in secrecy along the north bank of the Yalu. General Peng had been appointed to command the army of some five hundred thousand men, most of them battle-hardened veterans of years of fighting on the Chinese mainland during World War II.

Peng, a man of few words, wasted none of them. Mao's goal, he told Kim Il Sung, was to wipe out the U.S. Army and secure a peaceful reunification of Korea under the Communist banner. No doubt Kim breathed a deep sigh of relief. He explained to Peng that the North Korean army had been virtually decimated by heavy American assaults and that he had only three divisions and two regiments more or less intact.

Advised by radio of the near collapse of the In Min Gun, Mao Tse-tung ordered General Peng to pick out a suitable date in the near future, then sneak his armies over the Yalu under cover of night and deliver a crushing blow against the oncoming Americans and ROKs.[5]

While these momentous events were taking place in the camps of the two Communist partners, Eugene Clark and his guerrillas were probing several unoccupied islands off the west coast of Korea and marking on maps a number of locations where U.S. pilots could "ditch" their damaged planes. Within a few more days, the espionage team reached a tiny island only ten miles south of the Yalu. A camp was set up and camouflaged. Even though the weather had turned quite cold, outdoor fires could not be set for fear the smoke would give away the presence of the intruders. To search out the radar, Clark sent patrols, clad in the padded clothing to blend with the native population, onto the mainland. The radar was never found, and Clark doubted whether it even existed.

However, the patrols returned with disturbing news. In talks with civilians, the intruders were told that Chinese in the region were boasting that they would soon cross the Yalu. Seeking to confirm these rumors, Clark dispatched a few other small teams to reconnoiter along the river. They came back with the report that Chinese soldiers were swarming around the region just north of the river barrier.

Clark radioed this alarming intelligence to his base: "Am confident of Chinese troop movement."[6]

Although the war seemed almost over in North Korea in mid-October, south of the 38th Parallel, deep behind UN lines, an estimated forty thousand Communist guerrillas were marauding around the countryside and inflicted heavy casualties on supposed rear-area U.S. and ROK personnel. Many of these guerrillas had been operating in the South since the war began, but their numbers had been greatly augmented by In Min Gun soldiers who had been cut off when Mac-Arthur's Inchon and Pusan forces had linked up a month earlier.

These Communist bands were heavily armed, and they ambushed vehicle convoys, raided villages for food and hostages, and sabotaged railroad lines. On October 15, one of these guerrilla units sneaked into Seoul at night, blew up a radio relay station, and shot several of its personnel. Five days later, the irregulars attacked about sixty ROK soldiers and policemen who were guarding the Hwachon Dam in the vicinity of the 38th Parallel. A few of the ROKs were killed in the shootout, and the others fled. In the carefully orchestrated raid, the guerrillas opened the dam's control gates, thereby causing the Puk-han River to rise so rapidly that a railroad bridge downstream was swept away. This maneuver effectively blocked a UN supply line until an alternate route could be found.

In the meantime, Hans Tofte, the daredevil Frank Wisner had sent to the Far East as operations chief for the Office of Policy Coordination, had assembled three C-46 cargo planes at his secret base near Atsugi airport in Japan. Bold letters on the sides of the fuselages identified the craft as belonging to the Civil Air Transport (CAT), a Chinese Nationalist commercial airline based in Taipei, Taiwan, Chiang Kai-shek's capital. Actually, these three twin-engine aircraft were part of the CIA's secret fleet that would be used for clandestine missions in Korea and throughout the Far East.

CAT's origins traced back to 1946 less than a year after World War II ended. Claire Chennault, a retired U.S. major general who had gained fame as leader of the free-wheeling Flying Tigers (American volunteer civilian pilots who fought the Japanese over China), and Whiting Willauer, a graduate of Harvard Law School, linked up to form a small civilian airline in China.[7]

CAT got off the ground, figuratively and literally, in October 1946 and soon was operating a fleet of thirty-nine C-46s, most of them U.S. war surplus. Along with carrying deep into the interior the mountains of supplies that had piled up at coastal ports while the civil was raging, the airline also took on passengers and brought out several thousand wounded Nationalist soldiers to hospitals in the major cities.

CAT's role in aiding Chiang Kai-shek was not lost on Mao Tse-tung. Communist radio broadcasts and propaganda leaflets warned that any CAT pilots or employees who were captured would be immediately shot.[8]

When Chiang Kai-shek and his army were driven from the mainland to Taiwan in late 1949, CAT followed and established its operational base in Taipei. The C-46s were largely intact, but there was no place to fly cargo and passengers. The airline was nearly broke.

In Washington, the CIA concluded that keeping CAT from folding its tent was in America's national interest. In March 1950, the faltering airline's owners inked an agreement with a Washington banker, Richard P. Dunn, acting as an agent for "undisclosed principals," a tactic designed to mask the CIA as the new owner of the airline. CAT would be used for authorized covert actions.

As a component of the "cover," banker Dunn took control of CAT's assets, and a holding company, Airdale Corporation, was formed under Delaware laws. All three of Airdale's directors belonged to the CIA. At the same time, these three directors, along with another CIA official, gave the agency a majority on the board of CAT Incorporated, the phony company established to operate the airline.[9]

Now, in October 1950, Hans Tofte, with three CAT C-46s at his disposal, put the finishing touches on an escape-and-evasion (E & E) plan. It focused on two small islands off the west and east coasts. Manned by CIA undercover agents, these islands would be the destination of U.S. combat pilots whose airplanes were badly damaged and had only a few minutes of flying time remaining. It could mean life or death to a pilot if he knew in which direction to fly and where to bail out.

Before lifting off on combat missions, pilots would be briefed in detail on the locations of bands of CIA-trained guerrillas across central North Korea. They would guide the airmen to the E & E islands. A pair of "fishing fleets," manned by Korean CIA agents, would sail up and down the east and west coasts to rescue pilots who had to bail out. Each pilot would carry four one-ounce gold bars to pay friendly Koreans for their help or to bribe hostiles who might otherwise turn them in to Communist police.[10]

It was over the use of the gold bars that Hans Tofte had his first real clash with the "Prussian Drillmaster," Charles Willoughby, MacArthur's G-2. Tofte planned to have the bars imprinted with the widely recognized chop of the old Bank of China. These bars could be obtained easily in Taiwan, but Willoughby objected, claiming that international currency regulations prohibited such imports to Japan and South Korea.

Never a man to take no for an answer, Tofte climbed into a CAT plane, flew to Taipei, purchased $700,000 worth of one-ounce gold bars, had them imprinted by the Bank of China, and returned to Japan—all within twenty-four hours.[11]

After Tofte's E & E plan was approved, he began searching for a secluded base where he could organize and train South Korean guerrillas for espionage and sabotage missions. Finally, he found an ideal locale—Yong-do, a tiny, hilly, wooded island in the Bay of Pusan.

With the help of the U.S. Counterintelligence Corps, Tofte and other CIA agents interrogated hundreds of refugees in camps around Pusan. Those displaying enthusiasm to help defeat the Communists were given cursory loyalty screenings, then accepted as guerrilla trainees. Tofte was especially delighted to find a sufficient number of men who had worked for the South Korean Telegraph Company and were skilled as radio operators.

In the wake of Mao Tse-tung's decision to intervene militarily in Korea, Chinese propaganda artists in Peking began whipping up a massive hate-America campaign. Most of the peasants had known the United States over the years as the benevolent nation that had rushed to their country's aid in time of famine, earthquakes, floods, and other natural disasters. America was the country that had sent thousands of its young men to help fight the Japanese in the 1940s. Now the goal of the Peking propaganda operatives was to erase these impressions and paint an ugly, brutal portrait of the "real America." Few of the Chinese people knew that they were being brainwashed for war.

An editorial in the widely read government-controlled newspaper, *Chinese People's Daily* kicked off the hate-America propaganda offensive:

> This mad dog [the U.S.] seizes Formosa [Taiwan] between its hindlegs while with its teeth it violently bites the Korean people. Its blood-swollen eyes cast around for something further to attack. This [the U.S.] is the paradise of gangsters, swindlers, rascals, special agents, fascist germs, speculators, debauchers, and all the dregs of mankind. This is the world's manufactory and source of such crimes as reaction, darkness, cruelty, decadence, corruption, debauchery, oppression, and cannibalism. . . . Conscientious persons can only wonder how the spiritual civilization of mankind can be depraved to such an enormous extent.[12]

In Washington, President Harry Truman remained disillusioned with the work of the CIA. Three years after its birth, it still was failing to provide analytical intelligence, Truman felt. Admiral Roscoe Hillenkoetter, who had had no background in the field prior to his appointment as CIA chief, continued to send the White House intelligence fragments collected from around the world with no effort at analysis.

Consequently, Truman telephoned General George Marshall, who had replaced Louis Johnson as secretary of defense, at his farm near Leesburg, Virginia. In essence, the president said the CIA was badly in need of new leadership, and he asked Marshall for a recommendation. Marshall suggested Walter Bedell Smith, a retired four-star general who had been Dwight Eisenhower's chief of staff during World War II and later was ambassador to the Soviet Union.

In mid-October 1950, the guillotine blade dropped and Roscoe Hillenkoetter's head fell into the basket. Almost within hours, Walter Smith, known throughout the U.S. Army as Beetle, took over the reins at America's clandestine agency.

A gaunt, ulcer-ridden, blunt-speaking man, the new director also was shrewd, dynamic, and widely experienced in global intrigue. He was an intimidating personality and a perfectionist. His tolerance for fools was zero. It was said around the CIA that Smith was the most even-tempered person in Washington—always angry.[13]

Smith landed at the CIA running, even though he was still recovering from a stomach operation that had dropped his weight from 185 pounds to 135. His first act was to read a highly critical report on the CIA, a document drawn up by Allen Dulles, Mathais Correa, and William H. Jackson, all New York City lawyers, at Harry Truman's request. Dulles had had extensive experience as OSS Station Chief in Switzerland during World War II. Handed to the president in 1949, the report faulted the fledgling CIA because most of the senior posts were held by military officers. Some of them were qualified; others were not.

Nothing had been done to implement recommendations in the report. Smith called Allen Dulles in New York and told him: "You wrote the report—now come to Washington and help me implement it!"

Then Smith contacted William Jackson, now associated with Jock Whitney in J. H. Whitney and Company, a Wall Street investment firm. Would Jackson come and help reorganize the CIA? He would.

Aware that President Truman had been displeased with the CIA during Hillenkoetter's watch for failure to provide analytical intelligence, Smith created a Board of National Estimates to take bits and pieces of information collected from around the world and produce reports that would eliminate this deficiency. To head this twelve-man panel, Smith tapped William Langer, a Harvard historian, and Sherman Kent, a Yale historian, as Langer's deputy. Both academics had served in the OSS Research and Analysis branch in World War II.

At the same time, Beetle Smith integrated the Office of Policy Coordination, headed by the human dynamo Frank Wisner, into the CIA and renamed it Clandestine Services.

Now that the cold war had turned into a hot war in Korea, Congress, deeply worried by Communist aggressions around the world, lavished funds on the revitalized CIA. There was virtually no congressional oversight to how the money was spent. With huge amounts of funds in the cash register, the agency began a heavy recruiting campaign and mushroomed in size. An aura of mystique that had clung to the agency since the OSS era and the promise of excitement served as magnets to draw talented men and women from universities, the armed forces, the scientific community, the banking fraternity, and prestigious law firms.

Cloak-and-dagger missions were laid on at almost anyone's behest. Many U.S. military leaders were enthusiastic about any covert operations that might ease the heavy Communist pressure against Douglas MacArthur and his UN army in Korea. Consequently, CIA tentacles began to extend into many locations around the world not directly related to Korea.

When Mao Tse-tung had taken over all of mainland China in late 1949, that sprawling nation became a vacuum for U.S. intelligence. Now several secret missions into China were launched, but they were largely ineffective. However, one CIA agent penetrated to Inner (southern) Mongolia, which merges with the northern provinces of China, and through an interpreter arranged with a tribal leader in the Ordon region to establish a CIA base for collecting intelligence. In return, the tribal chief would be supplied with tube wells to irrigate his farmlands. Mongol agents were recruited, trained, and provided with radios that they were instructed to use.

13

Three Communist Masterspies

WITH THE IN MIN GUN REMNANTS falling back in disarray and thousands of them surrendering, Douglas Mac-Arthur mapped out the tactical moves that, he was convinced, would swiftly lead to the UN force's occupation of all of North Korea and bring an end to the nasty, bloody conflict. His operational blueprint called for Ned Almond's X Corps to be packed into sea transports at Inchon and sail around the southern tip of the peninsula to assault Wonsan, more than halfway up the east coast, and then drive westward. At the same time, Johnnie Walker's Eighth Army would launch a sweeping maneuver eastward from the vicinity of Pyongyang. These two pincers would join and either trap the North Koreans or pin them against the Yalu River, where they would have to surrender or be destroyed.

On October 2, Oliver Smith's 1st Marine Division left Inchon with Admiral Dewey Struble's fleet of 250 ships. Things didn't go right. A minesweeping force under U.S. Navy Captain Richard Spofford arrived at Wonsan eight days later and discovered that the harbor was thick with sophisticated magnetic mines. These cunning devices were equipped with mechanisms that allowed ten or more ships to pass overhead before the explosion was triggered.

These mines and mine experts to sow them had been provided by the Soviet Union. Most of the underwater explosives had been moored or set adrift by Russian army personnel disguised as Korean fishermen in innocent-looking sampans. They knew their business: Two U.S., one ROK, and one Japanese minesweeper were blown to smithereens during the clearing operation, killing all crew members. Meanwhile, the 1st Marine Division transports marked time for two weeks, sailing up and down the Korean east coast, reversing their course every twelve hours.[1]

While floating helplessly at sea, General Smith learned that Wonsan had been captured by the ROK 3rd Division and the ROK Capital Division, and the two units were pushing ahead north of the port. On October 25, twelve days after Struble's fleet had arrived, the marines went ashore. Much to their chagrin, they learned that the popular entertainer Bob Hope had staged a USO show in Wonsan the night before they hit the beach.[2]

General Walker had grown suspicious that Kim Il Sung and his commanders were being tipped off in advance about Eighth Army tactical plans. Although most of his attacks since crossing the 38th Parallel had been successful, Walker thought that the North Koreans had developed an uncanny sixth sense enabling them to congregate forces at the right place at the right time to try to thwart the American advance.

Walker was convinced there was a Communist spy embedded in the Far East Command in Tokyo, or in major headquarters in Korea. He repeatedly told MacArthur of his qualms. The supreme commander ordered an intense investigation, but no potential source of leaks was uncovered in Japan or South Korea.[3]

Still, MacArthur remained concerned. "That there were serious leaks in intelligence was evident to everyone [in Tokyo and Seoul]," he would declare. His eye focused on Washington, where in the past two years a number of officials in the State Department had resigned abruptly during congressional hearings into suspected Communists in the federal government.

It was MacArthur's gut instinct, bulwarked by ample circumstantial evidence, that his top-secret operational plans were reaching Soviet intelligence in Moscow, from where the information was being shuttled to Peking, China, then on to Kim Il Sung in North Korea. Since the outbreak of hostilities, MacArthur had been sending detailed battle plans to the Pentagon, where copies were circulated to key figures in the White House, the State Department, and the Central Intelligence Agency. MacArthur strongly suspected that somewhere in that distribution list a Communist mole was operating.

In discussions with Johnnie Walker, MacArthur compared the tight security for the Inchon landing, in which the In Min Gun was taken by total surprise, with operations since that time, when the North Koreans seemed to have advance information. Comparing notes, the two generals recalled that the full operational plan for Inchon had not reached the Pentagon until only three hours before the marines stormed ashore. They estimated that it would have taken perhaps six more hours for copies to be distributed to the White House, the State Department, and the CIA. Any Communist spies in Washington would not have had time to get the top-secret plan to Pyongyang before Inchon was a *fait accompli.* Since then, MacArthur and Walker concluded, the traitor or traitors in Washington had had ample time before a UN tactical move to funnel top-secret information on Korea through the Moscow-Peking-Pyongyang conduit.

In a cable to the Pentagon, MacArthur requested that an intensive probe be launched to ferret out the traitors in the Washington bureaucracy who were responsible for feeding U.S. military secrets to Moscow, and thence on to Peking and Pyongyang. Much to the consternation of MacArthur and Johnnie Walker, the demand apparently fell on deaf ears.[4]

At this point, MacArthur had no way of knowing that the traitors in Washington were not Americans, but two top officials in the British embassy, Kim Philby, the first secretary, and Guy Burgess, the second secretary. They were aided and abetted by a third Communist spy, Donald Maclean, head of the American Department in the Foreign Office in London.

By any yardstick, Harold Adrian "Kim" Philby, was one of history's most successful and enduring masterspies. Born on New Year's Day 1912, he was the only son of Harry St. John Bridger Philby, a civil servant in the government of India. During World War I, the senior Philby was an aide to Winston Churchill, then a top official in the British Admiralty. In the 1920s, as an adviser to the king of Arabia, Harry Philby took to wearing flowing Arab costumes, became a Moslem, and assumed the name Haj Abdullah.

Harry Philby was known to British intelligence for his harsh diatribes against his government's policies in the Mideast. In 1940, after World War II had broken out in Europe, he was jailed for his outspoken disapproval of the British for going to war against Nazi Germany, which, at that time, had a friendship pact with Soviet dictator Josef Stalin. Perhaps from his father, young Kim inherited a bitterness toward the British establishment and a fondness for Communism.

Young Philby's disdain for anything British was accelerated after he entered elite Cambridge Trinity College in 1931. There he was exposed to the depth of feeling against the British hierarchy by British intellectuals of that era. At Cambridge antipatriotism was not just tolerated, it was fashionable. Marxism was not only respectable; membership in the Communist Party was considered a badge of honor. It is widely believed that Philby was recruited as a Soviet spy at age twenty-one while at Cambridge.

Despite his Communist-oriented background and his eccentric father's public harangues against the British establishment, Kim

Philby was appointed to a high-level post in MI-6, Great Britain's intelligence branch, when World War II broke out in 1939. Throughout the entire war, Philby's true allegiance was to Josef Stalin and the Soviet Union, and he fed nearly all of England's top secrets to his masters in Moscow.

Midway through that war, MI-5, British counterintelligence, became aware that there was a spy high up in His Majesty's government. Helping in the exhaustive search for the traitor was the traitor himself, Kim Philby.

In 1949, Philby was assigned to the British embassy in Washington as first secretary. This post put him in an especially advantageous position to spy on U.S. secrets. His duties included liaison with the CIA.

"There was an amazingly free exchange of information," a CIA officer would later declare. "Philby was privy to CIA planning. He told the CIA what British intelligence was doing, and, above all, he knew what the CIA knew about Soviet [intelligence] operations."[5]

Like most cloak-and-dagger agencies, the CIA is compartmentalized as security against penetration by spies—no one department knows the whole story. Because Philby had security clearance to speak with the CIA director (who reportedly briefed the Soviet spy on U.S. policy on occasion), Philby was cleared by every department. Since Philby himself had a long and ostensibly distinguished career in intelligence, CIA agents felt comfortable consorting with him. Consequently, through after-duty drinks with CIA men from various departments and discreet probing for information, Philby could have learned more about the secret agency than any person except for the director and a few of his closest assistants.

How much information was Philby able to extract from the CIA? "The sky was the limit," a veteran agency executive would say after retirement. "Philby could have learned as much as he wanted to find out."[6]

Later it would be charged that the high-grade intelligence supplied to Kim Il Sung by Philby (through the Moscow–Peking–Pyongyang conduit) on the glaring weakness of MacArthur's troops in Japan and the refusal of the Truman administration to furnish the ROKs with tanks, artillery, and warplanes, emboldened the North Koreans to invade their neighbor. Certainly all U.S. secret intelligence from the Far East went through the British embassy in Washington.[7]

In the event that Kim Philby would miss a piece of top-secret U.S. military information about Korea, it would be picked up by his consort, Guy Burgess, whose appointment as second secretary of the British embassy in August 1950 flabbergasted government officials in London. Burgess was a drunk and a homosexual, and he made no effort to conceal those facts.

Before Burgess had sailed for the United States, George Middleton, head of personnel in the Foreign Office in London, advised him to soft-pedal his staunch "socialist views" in Washington. Above all, Middleton stressed, the long-time diplomat should not get involved in any "homosexual incidents" that "might cause trouble."

Within a few days after Burgess reached Washington, many in the British embassy began to scrupulously avoid the newcomer, who loudly denounced General MacArthur and blamed the United States for the war in Korea. Burgess also lambasted America's long-time ally, Chiang Kai-shek, calling him the "Mad Satrap."

Royal Air Force Squadron Leader "Tommy" Thompson, the embassy security officer, reckoned that Burgess came to the office in a drunken stupor two or three days a week. Thompson thought Burgess was so highly unsuitable for the post that his being assigned to the embassy must be some sort of deep-laid plot by MI-5, the sophisticated British counterintelligence agency with a long history of conducting cloak-and-dagger machinations around the world.

Not only did Burgess leave British secret documents on his desk instead of locking them in a safe as required, he also infuriated the security officer by losing the pink slips that Burgess was supposed to fill in to explain and apologize for his carelessness. Thompson was frustrated and hampered by the Foreign Office's unspoken but hidebound concept that the only embassy people who might be disloyal were chauffeurs, typists, clerks, and other minor operatives recruited from the lower-middle class. It was expected that a security officer was to shadow these individuals, not waste his time on aristocrats like Burgess and Philby.

Although U.S. intelligence in Washington suspected Burgess as a flagrant security risk, no one, curiously, challenged the Communist spy when he asked agencies of the Truman administration for, and was given, information about the war in Korea—documents that had no true bearing on his job at the embassy.[8]

Backing up Burgess and Philby at the Foreign Office in London was the third member of the espionage clique, Donald Maclean, who had been posted at the British embassy in Washington two years before Philby reached the United States. Now thirty-seven years old, Maclean, like his crony Burgess, was an alcoholic and a homosexual. In his high position in the Foreign Office, he read all cable traffic from the Washington embassy, paying particular attention to copying documents relative to the U.S. war effort in Korea. These copies were slipped to his London undercover contact and soon were on the desks of Soviet intelligence officers in Moscow, from where they no doubt eventually reached Pyongyang by way of Peking.

Along with his heavy-drinking problem, Maclean had been undergoing intensive psychiatric treatments. Those factors no doubt contributed to his offbeat antics. While he was at the British embassy in Washington, the wife of a fellow diplomat told friends how Maclean often stopped at their house to visit. Instead of ringing the front-door bell, he clambered over a garden wall, barked like a dog, and pawed at the window to attract the occupants' attention.

Despite these idiosyncrasies and afflictions, Maclean, like Burgess, had an inner strength that permitted him to perform commendably as an agent for the Soviet Union. Incredibly, neither U.S. nor British security services suspected Maclean's undercover role.

In October 1950, three months after the North Korean invasion, Maclean, incredibly, was promoted to head of the American Department in the Foreign Office in London. As a department boss, he was on all the top-secret distribution lists, able to read documents prepared by the State Department in Washington along with the cable traffic about intelligence affairs and the war in Korea received from Kim Philby in Washington.

One night after a long dinner party in Chelsea, Maclean was thoroughly drunk and began a provocative conversation with a fellow Foreign Office official, Mark Culme-Seymour. "What would you say if I told you I was secretly working for Uncle Joe [Stalin]?" Maclean asked.

Embarrassed, Culme-Seymour made no reply.

"Well, I am!" the chief of the American Department snapped. "Go ahead and report me!" Then Maclean launched a lengthy diatribe against U.S. involvement in the Korean War and roundly damned General Douglas MacArthur.

At the Foreign Office the next day, Culme-Seymour was worried and confused about Maclean's remarks at the dinner party and confided in Cyril Connolly, a middle-level bureaucrat. They decided Maclean had merely been drunk and engaging in foolish chitchat. Besides, they concluded, if there was any question about Maclean's loyalty, MI-5 would doubtless have known about it. MI-5 didn't.

By the time October melted into November, the three British spies were in position to scan CIA and Defense Department reports, and also would have been able to advise the Communist leaders not only what MacArthur was going to do, but what he could *not* do. One CIA memorandum, approved by President Truman, recommended that MacArthur make no overt moves against Chinese units that had already been detected crossing the Yalu into North Korea to take up positions around the Sui-ho electric plant, which furnished power to southern Manchuria and to the tip of Soviet Siberia at

Vladivostok. No doubt this intelligence rapidly reached Mao Tse-tung in Peking.

How much crucial secret information about American battle plans and high-level government decisions with regard to the Korean War had the three traitors passed on to Moscow, thence on to Peking and Pyongyang? No one will ever know for certain. However, a top Washington intelligence officer would later declare: "I'd have given my arm to have had three comparable spies working for me!"[9]

14

A Colossal Intelligence Swoon

AT THE OLD OSS COMPOUND in Washington in mid-October 1950, the Central Intelligence Agency compiled an alarming report. It stated: "Large Chicom [Chinese Communist] purchases of drugs and medicines abroad during recent months . . . may indicate military stockpiling." The implication was that Mao Tse-tung was preparing to leap into the shooting war in Korea. As in most intelligence estimates, however, the CIA document hedged its bet by using such tentative wording as "may indicate."

The CIA, Charles Willoughby, and Eighth Army intelligence all seemed to agree that the Chinese had the *capability* to intervene. So the cardinal question was: What were the Chinese *intentions*?

Seeking a concrete answer to that crucial unknown, CIA agents in Japan found a former Chinese Nationalist officer who agreed to infiltrate Manchuria and evaluate the military situation there. It would be a perilous secret mission. If he were arrested, he would face excruciating torture and a slow, painful death.

This officer had fought with Chiang Kai-shek's forces in Manchuria, then had escaped to Japan when the Nationalists were defeated in the civil war. Many of his former colleagues had transferred their allegiance to the victors and now were leaders in Mao's People's Liberation Army. His mission would be to seek out his old comrades and try to subtly extract precise information on Chinese intentions. But could they be trusted out of friendship? Or would one of them turn him in to the Chinese secret police?

Clad in ordinary Chinese civilian clothes, the CIA spy slipped into Manchuria, circulated as much as possible without attracting suspicion, and spoke with a few old friends who were now officers in Mao's army. From his clandestine conversations with them and from his observations, he was able to establish with considerable precision the number of Chinese troops and their deployments along the northern regions of the Yalu—about three hundred thousand.

Along with the intelligence collected by Navy Lieutenant Commander Eugene Clark and his espionage party during their earlier trek to the Yalu, the information brought back by the former Chinese Nationalist officer reinforced the theory that Mao Tse-tung had the power to intervene, but the big question remained: *Would* he do so?

In North Korea on the morning of October 19, elements of Major General Hobart R. "Hap" Gay's 1st Cavalry Division were ready for a final attack to seize Pyongyang, Kim Il Sung's capital. Leaders of the cavalry outfit were in a hurry: Word had been received that the ROK 1st Division, advancing from the southeast, was about to break into the prized objective. It would be embarrassing if the ROKs entered Pyongyang first.

Much to the chagrin of Hap Gay, who had been General George Patton's chief of staff in World War II, and his leaders, the ROKs won the "race" and by nightfall reached the center of the city. Most of the bigshot Communists—Soviet and North Korean—had fled northward to the town of Sinuju, directly across the Yalu from Antung, Manchuria.

As had been his habit in three wars, Douglas MacArthur arrived in battered Pyongyang on the heels of the infantry. Glancing around in mock disbelief, he quipped: "Any celebrities here to greet me? Where is Kim Buck Too?"[1]

With the North Korean capital in Eighth Army hands, Johnnie Walker promptly launched a drive to the Chongchon River, forty miles north of Pyongyang. The Chongchon flows in the same southwesterly direction as the Yalu and is about sixty miles to the south of it. From the Chongchon, Walker would make his final lunge to the Yalu and victory in Korea.

Spearheading the attack would be an airdrop of four thousand paratroopers of the U.S. 187th Airborne Regimental Combat team led by Brigadier General Frank S. Bowen Jr., a forty-five-year-old West Pointer, who had been a staff officer in the Pacific in World War II and only recently had joined the airborne forces. The paratroopers would jump at two different points, both about twenty-five miles north of Pyongyang: Sunchon and Sukchon. MacArthur hoped that the airborne operation would cut off fleeing North Korean troops and government officials and rescue American POWs, who reportedly were moving northward in a train that moved only at night and hid in tunnels by day.

In the early afternoon of October 20, a sky armada of forty C-47s of World War II vintage and seventy-one C-119 Flying Boxcars reached the drop zones. General Bowen jumped first. It was a textbook-perfect operation. Airborne history was made: For the first time in warfare, heavy equipment, guns, and vehicles were landed by parachute. Only one paratrooper was killed in the descent; forty-five others were injured on crashing to earth.

Although the main body of the In Min Gun had slipped out of the airborne trap, the paratroopers at Sukchon dropped behind the last unit to leave Pyongyang, the 239th Regiment, whose mission was to stall the rapid Eighth Army advance. This regiment found itself assaulted from the north instead of the south. It put up a fierce fight, but Frank Bowen's paratroopers teamed up with the British Commonwealth 27th Brigade, trapped the North Korean unit in the hills, and virtually wiped it out.

About five miles northwest of Sunchon, the other airborne objective, GIs discovered a grisly scene around a railroad tunnel: the corpses of seventy-three murdered American soldiers. Twenty-three GIs, several of them wounded, who had escaped from their captors, told shocked U.S. officers of events.

Two trains, each loaded with about 160 American POWs, had pulled out of Pyongyang six days earlier, on October 17. These were the survivors of a group of nearly four hundred Americans the North Koreans had marched on foot northward from Seoul at the time of the Inchon landings. Moving in fits and jerks, the trains had to await repair of the tracks that had been cut by bombs. Along the way, six or seven GIs died of disease each day; their bodies were hurled from the boxcars by the captors.

Three days after leaving Pyongyang, while Bowen's paratroopers were bailing out, the second of the two trains halted inside the tunnel. Near dusk, the North Korean guards led the Americans from the tunnel to get their evening meal. As they waited for the food, the captors riddled them with Soviet-made machine guns. Those GIs who survived did so by feigning death. That night, the train continued northward.[2]

While Johnnie Walker's Eighth Army on the left and Ned Almond's X Corps on the right pushed steadily ahead, Radio Peking acknowledged what the Far East Command in Tokyo already knew: Chinese "volunteers" had crossed the Yalu into North Korea. Perhaps to lull the UN commanders into a false sense of complacency, the Peking broadcast insisted that the Chinese government was following such honorable precedents as that of Marquis de Lafayette and his French volunteers who came to the aid of the thirteen American colonies during the Revolutionary War.

Even after U.S. and ROK battle leaders reported sporadic clashes with Chinese Communist troops south of the Yalu, Charles Willoughby, MacArthur's G-2, downplayed the significance of the episodes. He reported to the Pentagon that the "most auspicious time" for the Chinese to intervene had "long since passed." It seemed illogical to Willoughby that the Chinese would plunge into the war so late and in the face of the victorious Eighth Army.[3]

The ominous threat of Chinese intervention intensified, however, when U.S. pilots sighted heavy southbound traffic on six bridges over the Yalu River. When Eighth Army reported that two Chinese POWs boasted that tens of thousands of their comrades were in North Korea, Willoughby held that their stories were "unconfirmed and thereby unaccepted."

In Tokyo on October 29, Willoughby received an urgent telephone call from Ned Almond, the X Corps leader: "I've got sixteen Chicom POWs here," Almond declared. In his thick Teutonic accent, the G-2 snapped, "I don't believe you!"

"Then why in the hell don't you come over and see for yourself?" Almond barked back.[4]

Willoughby flew to X Corps the next day and interviewed the sixteen captured soldiers. It was obvious that they were Chinese, but Willoughby discounted them as "stragglers."[5]

Despite what would seem to be compelling evidence that the Chinese were over the Yalu in large numbers, thirty-four-year-old Lieutenant Colonel James C. Tarkenton, Johnnie Walker's G-2, compiled reports that reflected Willoughby's viewpoint. Willoughby's opinions, in turn, mirrored those of the Big Boss—Douglas MacArthur.

Although relatively young and inexperienced in the subtleties of the intelligence business, Clint Tarkenton had done an outstanding job in the Pusan Perimeter in tracking the In Min Gun units. Now, however, Tarkenton missed the target. In an October 26 intelligence analysis, he declared that there was "no indication of open intervention on the part of Chinese Communist forces in Korea." Even after his own intelligence officers had interrogated ten Chicoms, Tarkenton continued to believe that there would be no large-scale intervention by Mao Tse-tung's army.[6]

Ten days before Colonel Tarkenton arrived at that intelligence estimate, elements of the Chinese Fourth Field Army had begun crossing the Yalu on foot at night into North Korea. Hiding in tunnels and huts in the day, they assembled on the western side of the high mountain spine of Korea opposite the oncoming Eighth Army. Led by General Lin Piao, who alternately had been fighting the Japanese and Chiang

Kai-shek's Nationalists since 1934, the Fourth Field Army was the most battle-hardened military formation in the Far East.

At the same time, 150 miles to the east, components of the Chinese Third Field Army, under General Chen Yi, also were sneaking across the Yalu at night and assembling in front of Ned Almond's advancing X Corps. In overall command of the Chicom forces was General Peng Teh-huai, whose headquarters was in Mukden, the Manchuria city from where Captain Jack Singlaub, the CIA agent, recruited a few-score spies to infiltrate the North Korean government and military from 1946 through 1949.

When the massive secret influx of the Chinese People's Volunteers was completed, there were 180,000 troops in the west opposite Eighth Army and 120,000 soldiers in the east in front of X Corps. Augmenting this powerful force were an unknown number of soldiers of the shattered North Korean army.

On a collision course with these 300,000 Chicoms were seven U.S. divisions, six ROK divisions, two British Commonwealth brigades, a Turkish brigade, a British commando company, and battalions from Canada, the Netherlands, Thailand, and the Philippines—totaling some 247,000 men.

By Western standards, the Chinese Communist armies were primitive. They had few tanks or other tracked vehicles and only a handful of modern antiaircraft guns. Their small arms (rifles, pistols, and machine guns) had been collected from numerous sources (Soviet, U.S., Japan), so they used a wide variety of ammunition, complicating supply problems. They were weak in heavy artillery. Radio communications were rudimentary.

Although deficient in these areas, the soldiers of the Third and Fourth Field Armies were highly motivated, having been told by political commissars that they would be fighting to protect their homeland from "the running dog of Wall Street's greedy capitalists, General MacArthur." They were tough and well disciplined, accustomed to marching long distances at night while hand-carrying mortars, shells, machine guns, and other heavy equipment. Having honed their skills in the China wars, the veterans were experts in guerrilla-type warfare: surprise ambushes followed by quick withdrawals.

In Washington, President Truman and the Joint Chiefs had grown edgy as reports of the capture of Chinese Communist soldiers in North Korea continued to arrive. They were haunted by the possibility of an all-out war against China and/or the Soviet Union, a potentially horrendous conflict for which the U.S. armed forces were ill prepared to fight. So, at Truman's direction, the Joint Chiefs pro-

posed that MacArthur halt his advance short of the border with Manchuria and Siberia to avoid creating a spark that might trigger a huge
conflagration. MacArthur seemed to agree, replying that it was his
intention to consolidate positions south of the Yalu and then replace
the GIs with ROKs.[7]

In Tokyo, MacArthur had been flooded with so many often conflicting
reports about Chinese troops in North Korea that he decided to have
a look for himself. On November 25, he flew to Eighth Army headquarters on the Chongchon River and, bundled up against the icy
blasts of wind and bone-chilling cold, he chatted with GIs heading
toward the mountains in front of the Yalu.

Before climbing into the *SCAP* for the flight back to Tokyo, Mac-
Arthur told his aides he wanted to fly the length of the Yalu to reconnoiter with his own eyes. His staff officers were worried. The
lumbering aircraft was unarmed, and there were Chinese antiaircraft
guns just across the river and within range.

MacArthur's aides grew even more alarmed—ostensibly for the
supreme commander's safety—after he remarked casually that he especially wanted to see Sinuju, the North Korean town located where
the Yalu empties into the Yellow Sea. It was in Sinuju that Kim Il
Sung had reestablished his government. It was near Sinuju that as
many as seventy-five modern Chinese MIG aircraft had been sighted
by U.S. pilots. MacArthur waved his aides aboard, and *SCAP* lifted off
for the Yalu.

Shortly after takeoff, one officer stole up to Lieutenant Colonel
Tony Story, MacArthur's personal pilot since World War II days, and
pleaded with him to fly along some other river. The boss wouldn't
know the difference, the aide insisted. Story refused. Then General
Courtney Whitney, also a MacArthur confidant going back to the last
war, expressed the opinion that all of those on board should at least
wear parachutes. MacArthur chuckled and said, "You gentlemen can
wear them if you want to, but I'll go down with the plane!"[8]

Reaching the Yalu, MacArthur instructed Story to turn east and
follow the river at a height of five thousand feet. All that unfolded
before the supreme commander's eyes was a bleak expanse of barren,
frozen countryside, jagged hills, and yawning crevices. However,
carefully concealed in this forbidding terrain were a few hundred
thousand men of the Chinese army, who had moved up at night and
hid during the day. A phantom force, coiled and ready to spring.

In Mukden, Manchuria, General Peng Teh-huai and his combat commanders had put the final touches on an operations plan designed to
annihilate the unsuspecting UN forces advancing toward the Yalu.

Peng and his generals had a tactical advantage of the kind that battle leaders only dream about: They knew in advance MacArthur's plan for his end-the-war offensive. Apparently, this priceless intelligence had reached the Chinese high command by way of the Philby-Burgess-Maclean conspiracy. The three Communist spies were still reading top-secret documents sent to the Pentagon by MacArthur and relayed to the British embassy in Washington.

Armed with this high-grade intelligence, General Peng, a crafty veteran of nineteen years of fighting against the Japanese and Chiang Kai-shek's Nationalists in China, planned to launch his surprise assault in two phases. In the first phase, Lin Piao's Fourth Field Army would jump off on the night of November 26. His heaviest blow would hit the ROK II Corps, which was in the mountains on the extreme right of Johnnie Walker's army, and wipe it out. Then Lin's forces would wheel to the west, cut in behind Eighth Army, and charge to the Yellow Sea below Sinanju, thereby trapping Walker's troops.

Peng's second phase would begin about 150 miles to the east on November 27. General Chen Yi's Third Field Army would surround and destroy Oliver Smith's 1st Marine Division and David Barr's 7th Infantry Division spearheads in the vicinity of the Chosin Reservoir, whose hydroelectric plants, among the world's largest, supplied power for much of northern Korea. Then Chen's troops would overwhelm the bulk of Smith's and Barr's outfits, which were stretched out along a single narrow road all the way to the port of Hungnam, seventy-five miles to the south.

Knowing MacArthur's tactical plans, including troop dispositions, in advance, had other enormous benefits to the Chicom generals. They would feel secure in the knowledge that there would be no surprise amphibious landing to their rear, such as the masterpiece MacArthur had pulled off at Inchon that temporarily changed the course of the war.

On the night of November 26, it was bitterly cold and eerily quiet along Walker's Eighth Army front. A bright moon was beaming down on the killing grounds. Suddenly, the GIs and ROKs were awakened in their sleeping bags and huts by a frightening cacophony of blaring bugles, beating drums, clanging cymbals, shrill whistles, rattles, and flares shot into the wintry sky. Then Chinese assault troops, chanting slogans and screaming "kill GI," charged forward, hurling grenades and firing bursts from submachine guns.

Taken completely by surprise, much as the Americans had been when hit by the German offensive in the Battle of the Bulge six years earlier, Walker's men were shocked, even paralyzed. All along the Eighth Army sector, the conflict turned into a mosaic of company, platoon, and squad death struggles. Ambushed from the flanks and rear, cut off from contact with higher headquarters, tiny bands of near-frozen and confused GIs, often outnumbered ten to one, fought back. It was reminiscent of Indian warfare in the days of America's Old West.

Grand strategy had flown out the window. Seventy-two hours after the first Chinese blows had struck, Johnnie Walker's objective was no longer the Yalu River, but rather, to save his command from annihilation. He ordered Eighth Army to pull back all the way to Pyongyang, sixty miles to the south.

On November 27, a day after the Chinese "volunteers" had smashed into Eighth Army, Colonel Raymond Murray's 5th Marines and Colonel Homer Litzenberg's 7th Marines were trudging westward through a blizzard. On the eastern side of the Chosin Reservoir, a 7th Infantry Division task force of twenty-five hundred men, led by Colonel Alan D. "Mac" Maclean, a former star tackle on the West Point football team, was pushing northward. Weather conditions were severe. Temperatures seldom rose above zero in the daytime and plunged to as low as minus thirty-five at night. In this brutal arctic climate, weapons froze, food froze, blood plasma froze, and vehicle engines froze.

Shortly after nightfall, General Chen's Third Field Army, which had been waiting for the U.S. spearheads to go deeper into his trap, struck. Simultaneously, the Chicoms hit Murray's 5th Marines, Litzenberg's 7th Marines, and Maclean's task force. Within twenty-four hours, these units were cut off when Chinese units got behind them and blocked the single, narrow road that led south to Hungnam.

Nowhere was the situation more desperate than in Mac Maclean's sector, where the GIs and attached ROKs were battling for their lives. At one o'clock that afternoon, General Ned Almond, the X Corps leader, arrived by helicopter at Maclean's command post. Unfolding a map on the icy hood of a jeep, Almond exuded optimism. "The enemy delaying you for the moment is nothing more than remnants of Chinese units fleeing north," the general assured Maclean. "We're still attacking, and we're going all the way to the Yalu. Don't let a bunch of Chinese laundrymen stop you!"[9]

Almond was unaware that Maclean's task force was being chopped to pieces. Moreover, his viewpoint had been clouded by Charles Willoughby's intelligence estimates, in which the presence of huge numbers of Chicoms had been discounted. Almond's own G-2, Colonel William W. Quinn, had agreed with Willoughby's assessment.

15

CIA Target:
Douglas MacArthur

FOR THE FIRST TIME since the U.S. government had abandoned his beleaguered forces in the Philippines in the early black months of World War II, Douglas MacArthur was shaken by events with which he was involved. In the Dai Ichi building in Tokyo, he remarked to a confidant: "The evacuation of all or part of the Americans in Japan"—forty thousand of them, mostly civilians—"might become necessary!"[1]

The implication shocked the confidant. If the UN forces were annihilated, the Chinese, perhaps in tandem with the Soviets, might invade Japan, which had no armed forces. Josef Stalin's covetous eye had long been on that nation's enormous industrial capacity. He had once been quoted as saying, "Give me Japan, and I'll have the whole world!"

In Washington on November 30, four days after the Chinese army struck, Harry Truman met with the press at the White House. After he said that "we will take whatever steps are necessary to meet the military situation [in Korea] just as we always have," Jack Dougherty of the *New York Daily News* asked, "Will that include the atom bomb?"

"That includes every weapon we have," Truman replied.

"Does that mean, Mr. President, use against military objectives or civilian?" Robert Dixon of the International News Service inquired.

"It is a matter that the military people will have to decide," Truman responded. "I am not a military authority that passes on these things."[2]

Within minutes, the Associated Press, International News Service, and United Press flashed Truman's incendiary remarks around the world. Shock waves were triggered. Clement Attlee, the British

113

prime minister, whose Labour government was under heavy attack by the Conservatives for the nation's escalating involvement in the Korean War, was "shocked and astounded." He and his cabinet had taken Truman's pronouncement to mean that Douglas MacArthur was being handed the authority to use A-bombs against China, North Korea, or the Soviet Union as he saw fit.

Aware that global hornets' nests had been stirred up, White House damage-control parties swung into action. Charles Ross, Truman's press secretary, issued a "clarifying statement" to the press. "The use of any weapon is always implicit in the possessor of that weapon," the press release said. "Only the president can authorize the use of atomic bombs."[3]

America's traditional allies were reassured—partially. However, clues would emerge that Harry Truman had deliberately dropped the A-bomb remark, a subtle reminder to Josef Stalin and Mao Tse-tung that massive involvement in Korea could trigger swift and massive retaliation from the United States.[4]

In Korea, Johnnie Walker's Eighth Army, although under almost constant attack from all sides, continued a generally orderly retreat to Pyongyang. On the fourth day of the pullback, however, the general, realizing that one of his U.S. divisions had been badly mauled and three ROK divisions had virtually disintegrated, knew that he did not have the strength to defend Pyongyang. Huge clouds of black smoke spiraled into the slate-gray sky over the city as countless tons of supplies and equipment were burned. Walker's new defense line would be along the frozen Imjin River, twenty-five miles north of Seoul.

One hundred fifty miles to the east, Oliver Smith's marines and David Barr's 7th Infantry Division GIs were surrounded, cut off from their base at Hungnam. The scholarly, soft-spoken Smith set the tone when he told his battle leaders: "We're going to attack in another direction!"[5]

The GIs and marines formed into a long column and headed southward along the narrow, ice-covered, corkscrew road. They had to hack their bloody way through masses of Chicoms, who were swarming over the snowy razorback ridges and steep, icy gorges to ambush the retreating Americans.

At 11:30 P.M. on December 11, the final elements marched and rolled into the Hungnam region. On hand to greet and congratulate the warriors on their epic feat was Douglas MacArthur. Although about a thousand men had been killed, wounded, or were missing during the "breakout to the coast," the marines and GIs brought with them most of their vehicles, tanks, artillery, and wounded—along with the frozen corpses of their comrades.

In the United States, twelve thousand miles from frozen North Korea, the media editorial writers fell all over one another in trumpeting howls of calamity. *Time* magazine: "It was a defeat—the worst defeat the United States ever suffered. . . . Days passed before its enormity finally became plain." *Newsweek* magazine: "America's worst military licking. . . . It might become the worst military disaster in American history."

Indeed, the U.S. forces had suffered a humiliating defeat on the battlefield, but they had not been "ingloriously crushed," as one American newspaper phrased it. Nor had MacArthur's men suffered "staggering casualties," in the words of a national magazine. Rather, the Korean retreat generally had been orderly. Only the U.S. 2nd "Indianhead" Infantry Division had been seriously mauled, and its 25 percent casualties were light in comparison to the 60 to 80 percent losses of some U.S. units when Adolf Hitler had launched his surprise assault in the Battle of the Bulge.

With a distraught and ill-informed American media steadily stoking the fires of doom and gloom, an epidemic of "bug-out fever" broke out in Washington. Beetle Smith, the CIA director, made a stunning recommendation to President Truman and the Joint Chiefs: "We should get out of Korea now. Otherwise the Russians will bleed us to death in Asia!"

In light of entry into the war by China, with its almost limitless manpower, thinking in the Truman administration began to shift gears. No longer would the reunification of the two Koreas be the U.S. goal; rather, saving MacArthur's forces was now the principal objective.

Consequently, General Joe Collins, the army chief of staff, was rushed to Tokyo to confer with MacArthur about an Eighth Army evacuation to Japan. However, Collins found that the Far East commander had regained an upbeat mood. Pyongyang had fallen and Seoul would be lost temporarily, MacArthur told Collins. Although UN forces had been hit hard, they had not suffered the "staggering casualties" portrayed by the U.S. radio and print media.

After Collins returned to Washington and briefed the president and his leaders, Secretary of State Dean Acheson wrote in his diary: "The hysteria about evacuation has subsided."[6] Still, Washington power barons needed a scapegoat for the humiliating reversal in Korea. The finger seemed to be pointing at Douglas MacArthur.

As Washington criticism of the Far East commander grew more strident, MacArthur learned from contacts in the capital that Beetle Smith, who had been director of the CIA for only two months, had launched a secret effort to get the general sacked. Unrecognized (or ignored) at the time of his appointment, Smith had one serious obsession: He had long detested MacArthur. That antipathy, undoubtedly, had been born and nurtured during Smith's four years as alter ego to General Eisenhower during World War II. Going back to the 1930s, when Eisenhower had been a major and a not-too-adoring aide to four-star General MacArthur in the Philippines, a subtle feud had simmered between America's two most widely known officers. That animosity had flamed even more intensely after Eisenhower became Allied supreme commander in Europe in World War II and received the lion's share of troops, aircraft, weapons, supplies—and the public spotlight.

Now, in mid-December 1950, while MacArthur was establishing a new defensive line in Korea, Smith contacted Pedro A. Del Valle, a retired Marine Corps lieutenant general, in Buenos Aires, where he was South American president of International Telephone and Telegraph. Del Valle had served with great distinction as a division commander in the Pacific in World War II and was highly regarded in Washington. Smith invited the former marine to come to Washington at his earliest convenience to discuss an important matter.

A month earlier, Del Valle had submitted to the Joint Chiefs his plan to "combat Communism on a global basis," so he presumed that the comprehensive document had been shuttled on to the CIA and Smith wanted to discuss its recommendations.

Two days later, Del Valle flew to the capital and met with Smith at the CIA compound. Prepared to elaborate on his anti-Communist agenda, Del Valle was astonished when Smith failed to even mention his plan and, instead, asked the retired marine general to join the CIA station in Tokyo. His mission there would be to "pull the rug out from under MacArthur," Smith said.

The CIA chief apparently believed that Del Valle was the ideal man for the machination. "I know you have crossed swords with MacArthur out in the Pacific [during World War II]," Smith stated.[7]

Like many U.S. Army officers in Europe in the fight against Nazi Germany, Smith had gained the popular impression that all marines in the Pacific disliked Douglas MacArthur. That notion was only partly true. Many marine leaders, including Del Valle, greatly admired the army supreme commander. Smith could not have picked a less likely candidate to perform the undercover hatchet job.

Straining to conceal his anger, the Old Marine replied, "Far from being an enemy of General MacArthur, I consider him the greatest soldier-statesman this country has had!"[8]

There were tense moments of silence. Then Del Valle got to his feet to leave. "I'm sorry this discussion turned out badly, but I simply cannot accept this offer," Del Valle declared firmly. "I certainly will do nothing to upset General MacArthur's position in [the Far East]."

On his way out, the Old Marine bumped into Allen Dulles, the number-two official at the CIA. Dulles, a pipe-smoking man whose tweedy clothes and rimless glasses exactly fit Hollywood's image of a kindly old college professor, had gained a sterling reputation in the spook community for his espionage deeds as Office of Strategic Services station chief in Switzerland during World War II.

Now Dulles greeted Del Valle with a wreath of smiles. It was as though the two men were secretly involved in a devious plot against Mao Tse-tung or Kim Il Sung. Presumably under the false impression that the Old Marine had eagerly gobbled up Beetle Smith's offer, Dulles declared that he was extremely happy that Del Valle was "joining us."[9]

It was obvious to Del Valle that Smith's scheme to "pull the rug out" from under MacArthur had been no spur-of-the-moment decision. Wise old owl Dulles had his hand in the scheme as well. Without a change of expression, Del Valle assured the surprised Dulles that he had no intention of "joining us" and that he would have no part in a scheme against MacArthur by his own countrymen in Washington.

Still angry about Beetle Smith's proposal, the retired marine general returned to Buenos Aires and wrote a letter to MacArthur. Because he did not mention his encounter with the CIA leaders in Washington, Del Valle's missive may have puzzled the Far East commander. The Old Marine merely assured MacArthur of "my staunch support, admiration, and approval." It was doubtful whether the five-star general ever knew about Beetle Smith's plot to use Del Valle against him.[10]

Back in Korea, after Johnnie Walker's Eighth Army had taken up its new defensive line along the Imjin River, the pursuing Chinese "volunteers" had outrun their supply lines and halted. This unexpected development enabled Walker to bring Eighth Army up to full strength with replacement soldiers brought from Pusan. Weapons and vehicles were replaced, ammunition was replenished, and the GIs received heavier winter clothing.

On the morning of December 23, Walker climbed into his jeep beside his driver, Master Sergeant George Belton, and headed over the icy roads toward the front lines. The general felt that Belton was going too slowly and ordered him to speed up. Just as the jeep approached a convoy of ROK vehicles coming toward it, a ROK weapons carrier traveling behind Walker's jeep pulled out to pass and smashed into the left rear of the general's vehicle. Under the impact, the jeep swung around on the ice-covered road; then it rolled over several times. Belton and Walker's aide, Lieutenant Layton "Joe" Tyner, who had been in the back seat, were thrown clear and escaped with only painful injuries. Walker was killed instantly.

On learning of Walker's death, President Syngman Rhee was so distraught that he ordered the immediate execution of the ROK driver of the weapons carrier involved in the accident. However, American officers intervened and saved the life of the unfortunate Korean, who, instead, was sentenced to three years in prison.

Christmas Day had a very special meaning to General Ned Almond: He landed near Pusan with the last of his X Corps evacuees from Chinese-besieged Hungnam. In a seaborne operation that reminded Almond of the British army's evacuation from Dunkirk, France, across the English Channel to England in the early days of World War II, a fleet of 193 vessels, in a two-week operation, had carried out 105,000 U.S. and ROK troops, 17,500 vehicles, and 350,000 tons of cargo. Along with the fighting men, the seaborne armada brought out 100,000 North Korean civilians who feared they would be murdered by the In Min Gun for helping the Americans.

Early on the morning of December 26, Lieutenant General Matthew B. Ridgway, whom the Joint Chiefs had plucked from behind a desk in the Pentagon to replace Johnnie Walker, was escorted into Douglas MacArthur's office in the Dai Ichi building in Tokyo. Known as a rugged, no-nonsense man of great personal courage, Ridgway had led the crack 82nd Airborne Division in Sicily, Italy, and Normandy. Later, he had commanded the XVIII Airborne Corps in Holland, the Battle of the Bulge, and during the final Allied offensive deep into Germany.

Now the paratroop general was greeted warmly by MacArthur, who briefed him on the situation in Korea, told him that Almond's X Corps would be a component of Eighth Army, and warned him not to underestimate the skill and courage of the Chinese army.

Ridgway asked one question: "General, when I get over there and find the situation warrants it, do I have your permission to attack?"

That upbeat approach was music to MacArthur's ears. "Matt," he replied, "do what you think is best. The Eighth Army is yours!"[11]

On New Year's Eve, five days after Matt Ridgway reached South Korea, the cold and desolate landscape along the frozen Imjin River suddenly echoed with the eerie sounds of bugles, drumbeats, whistles, and exploding rockets. All along the Eighth Army front, the Chinese struck. Furious firefights erupted. Ridgway's line bent, then buckled. Realizing it would be impossible to hold Seoul, the Eighth Army commander issued orders for the evacuation of the South Korean capital.

While packing to leave Seoul, Matt Ridgway found a pair of pajamas with a huge hole in the seat of the trousers. Impishly, he tacked the trousers up on his office wall. Above them in large block letters, he wrote:

TO THE COMMANDING GENERAL
CHINESE COMMUNIST FORCES—
WITH THE COMPLIMENTS OF
THE COMMANDING GENERAL
U.S. EIGHTH ARMY[12]

Then Ridgway took his leave, and Seoul fell to the Communists for the second time in six months on January 4, 1951.

Knowing that a weakened Eighth Army could not hold against the rain of Chicom trip-hammer blows, Ridgway ordered a fighting withdrawal to a new defensive line behind the Kum River, thirty miles below Seoul. Despite the retreat, the general was cautiously optimistic. Now he had a relatively solid front for 135 miles across the narrow waist of the peninsula. His line was anchored at each end by the Yellow Sea and the Sea of Japan. Ridgway also was encouraged by the fact that the Chicoms had outrun their supplies and had to halt.

Eighth Army, by now, had taken on a truly United Nations character. Fifteen countries had troops in Korea: the United States, Australia, Great Britain, Canada, Turkey, Belgium, Sweden, Thailand, the Philippines, the Netherlands, Greece, France, South Africa, India, and New Zealand. Altogether, Ridgway's force numbered about 365,000 men. Opposing Eighth Army were an estimated 485,000 Communist troops, mainly Chinese.

With a lull on the battlefield, Ridgway gained the time to rebuild and revitalize his largely demoralized Eighth Army and to infuse it with his own fighting spirit. Like a whirling dervish, the general, by jeep and by helicopter, visited the command posts of each major unit. In all ranks, from generals to teenage machine gunners, he sensed anxiety, a grim foreboding of disasters yet to come.

Before his departure from Washington, Ridgway had told the Joint Chiefs that he intended to be "ruthless with our general officers" who were not measuring up. After his tour of Eighth Army, Ridgway rolled out the guillotine. In rapid order, heads fell into the basket: Major General Robert B. McClure, who had commanded the 2nd Infantry Division for only a month; David Barr of the 7th Infantry Division, Hobart Gay of the 1st Cavalry Division, John Church of the 24th Infantry Division, and William B. Kean of the 25th Infantry Division. These generals were replaced largely by younger men who had the Ridgway seal of approval as aggressive battlefield leaders.

Ridgway's action triggered nervous tics in the Pentagon. Concerned about a congressional investigation into the rash of firings, the Joint Chiefs orchestrated a finely tuned public relations campaign. Rather than having Eighth Army announce the sackings, the Pentagon issued a carefully worded press release to make it appear that the command changes were routine. Most of the media bought the Pentagon line. Stories appeared that the five generals were being brought back to posts of major significance.[13]

16

Top Secret: The Li Mi Project

I N WASHINGTON, there was deep apprehension in the wake of General Peng Teh-huai's full-blooded New Year's Eve offensive. Although the assault had run out of steam, it was clear that Peng would regroup and strike another massive blow at Eighth Army, an attack that could plunge all the way to the southern port of Pusan.

These Washington jitters intensified after W. Stuart Symington, the suave, cerebral chairman of the National Security Resources Board, dropped a bombshell on January 11, 1951. Symington, who had been the first secretary of the Air Force in 1947, was known for his calm and dispassionate approach to major problems—a reputation that now went by the boards.

In a report to President Truman, Symington declared that the survival of the United States "is imminently threatened by Communist aggression." Within eighteen months, the Soviet Union would have the nuclear strength to "blast the heart out of the United States."[1]

Then Symington outlined recommendations in which he out-hawked General MacArthur. First, the United States should rapidly pull out of Korea, which, as General Omar Bradley, the chairman of the Joint Chiefs, had stated, was the wrong war at the wrong place at the wrong time. Then, the U.S. Navy should blockade Mao Tse-tung's Chinese mainland, strengthen Chiang Kai-shek's forces on Taiwan, heavily bomb Communist supply and communications lines in Korea and China, pulverize industries in Manchuria with B-29 Flying Fortress raids, and promote extensive guerrilla warfare behind Communist lines in Korea.

121

"The hour is late," Symington warned. "The odds may be stacked against the free nations, but it is still possible to take the offensive in this fight for survival."[2]

Harry Truman had great confidence in the opinions of Stu Symington. In this case, however, the president chose to ignore the advice of his National Security Resources Board Chairman. Truman's policy would remain: Contain the conflict on the Korean peninsula.

In frozen Korea, General Matt Ridgway continued to stabilize his lines, bring in reinforcements through Pusan, and brace for the next Communist blow. Among his vexing problems was the crucial matter of Eighth Army security in the rear areas, now flooded with tens of thousands of refugees, largely North Koreans.

When the Chinese armies had launched their surprise offensive in late November, as many as two hundred thousand North Koreans had left their homes in the dead of the peninsula's coldest winter in two decades to seek safety in the South, away from Communist oppression. Huge masses of civilians, many of them ill and starving, trudged along the clogged roads ahead of the retreating Eighth Army. Elderly men and women, frail and with faces blue from the piercing cold, were carried on "A" frames on the backs of younger men. Other refugees were packed in or on top of or clung to the sides of antiquated, wheezing trains heading away from the North.

There was no way for the refugees to escape the below-zero temperatures and the sleet and icy blasts. At night, they lay exhausted in the deep snow alongside the roads. Many froze to death. Their families shed a few tears, then moved on. More than sixty thousand North Korean civilians would die during the mass exodus to the South.

Blending in with the swarms of refugees were untold numbers of Kim Il Sung's spies, guerrillas, and saboteurs who were infiltrating into the South to carry out specific undercover missions. In an effort to stymie or slow down this mass infusion of enemy agents, the Eighth Army Counterintelligence Corps launched its own covert war within a war.

The historic mission of the CIC was to protect an army's security through the detection of espionage, treason, and subversive activity. Now, in Korea, it had been handed an almost impossible mission: to screen all the refugees—a task akin to reversing the flow of the Mississippi River. The CIC had limited manpower, so the best it could do was to have small detachments fan out behind and along UN lines and conduct spot screenings in the hope of snaring an occasional subversive.

Most of the male refugees wore the traditional Korean long, flowing garments of white cloth. Many men were captured while carrying weapons under these loose clothes and, under heavy interrogation, admitted they had been sent by In Min Gun intelligence officers to organize guerrilla bands in the South behind UN lines.[3]

Instead of the handful of subversives they had hoped to collar, the CIC sleuths were amazed at the large number that were swooped up in their loose dragnet. Four suspects were caught red-handed while signaling with mirrors, presumably as a means of communicating with the advancing Communist troops. Among those apprehended in the refugee ranks were twelve Koreans who confessed they belonged to an espionage ring that was to operate in the Pusan region, the UN's major supply port. All carried broken spoons as a means of identification with one another and with North Korean spies already in the South.

Other spot screenings resulted in the arrest of seven Communist couriers ranging in age sixteen to seventy-five. Each carried an identical Japanese coin as a means of identification. Each had been assigned a short-range mission: to seek specific intelligence about UN military positions and return immediately to the North.

A few days later, the dogged CIC gumshoes collared a ring of thirty-one Communist spies, including five women. Grilling disclosed that their mission was to find out if General MacArthur was employing Japanese as combat troops. If the Japanese, who had occupied Korea for several decades and were hated in both the North and the South, were engaged in the fighting, that discovery could provide the Chinese and the In Min Gun with ammunition for a massive propaganda barrage aimed at turning Korean public opinion against the Americans.[4]

The CIC agents discovered that North Korean intelligence had devised a simple system that would permit some spies among the hordes of genuine refugees to recognize one another. Male agents wore a white bandage spotted with blue ink dots on the little finger of the left hand. Female spies wore black blouses and black jackets, and they carried a small piece of white cloth in one hand and an apple in the other.[5]

Matt Ridgway was furious when he learned of the large number of Communist subversives snared in the CIC dragnet. At a staff conference, he stressed that he intended to deal harshly with the spies and saboteurs who "hid behind innocent civilians." One general had a solution: "We cannot execute them, but we can shoot them *before* they are taken prisoner." Another general suggested: "Turn them over to the ROKs—they'll take care of them."[6]

By "take care of them," he had not meant that the ROKs would provide the subversives with food and shelter.

While the CIC's spy hunt was taking place in South Korea, Frank Wisner, the dynamic chief of the CIA's Clandestine Services in Washington, came up with a scheme to take some of the Communist pressure off MacArthur's forces by causing Mao Tse-tung and his high command in Peking to divert attention and troops from Korea. Wisner labeled it the Li Mi project.[7]

The centerpiece of Wisner's plan was Chinese Nationalist General Li Mi, who, after Mao's Communist army had overrun all of China, led fifteen hundred of his men into adjoining Burma, where they had been marooned since late 1949. Despite frequent clashes with elements of the Burmese army, General Li had established a camp in an isolated, mountainous locale and sent word for other scattered Nationalists to join him in throwing Mao Tse-tung's army out of China—a preposterous goal inasmuch as Mao had over two million battle-tested men under arms.

Bands of Nationalists rallied to Li's banner, however, and by early 1951, he had some five thousand veteran fighting men in his camp, all of them poorly armed and equipped.[8]

Frank Wisner proposed rearming and energizing Li's anti-Communist troops and having them invade the neighboring Chinese province of Yunan. Hopefully, this incursion would draw Mao's focus away from Korea, at least long enough for MacArthur's forces to be strengthened and reorganized.

In light of the worried mood in Washington at this time, President Truman stamped his approval on the top-secret Li Mi project.

On February 6, 1951, the covert operation was launched when CIA agents, flying Civil Air Transport planes (the CIA's secret airline), picked up weapons and ammunition on Okinawa and flew the lethal cargo to Bangkok, Thailand. Numerous flights would follow. Taking charge of the weapons, ammunition, and supplies when they reached Bangkok was Sherman B. Joost, ostensibly the president of the commercial Sea Supply Company, but actually a CIA operative.

A graduate of Princeton University, Joost was an old hand at cloak-and-dagger activities. During World War II, he had been a key OSS figure in Burma. Now it would be his mission to coordinate and expedite the flow of war accoutrements to General Li in Burma.[9]

Sneaking the weapons and ammunition into Li's secret camp required a complicated series of transactions—and no doubt a few bribes. Joost had the cargo loaded into heavy wooden boxes stamped with such labels as Kitchen Appliances and put aboard the CAT planes at the Bangkok airport. With CIA agents at the controls, the plodding transports took the goods to two towns in northern Thailand, which borders Burma on the east.

Under the supervision of other CIA agents, the heavy cargo was transported to the nearby Thai border. There it was turned over to certain elements of the Thai police, who were, perhaps, more motivated by thick rolls of Uncle Sam's dollars than by political differences with Communist China. These Thai contacts kept their part of the secret arrangement, and a heavy influx of weapons, ammunition, and supplies reached General Li Mi, who called his ragtag force the National Salvation Army.

In early April, General Li led his reequipped but largely untrained contingent on an arduous march of more than 170 miles across rugged terrain. All the way, CAT planes dropped supplies by parachute. Reaching the Yunan border, the National Salvation Army plunged ahead without significant resistance for another sixty miles.

Suddenly, local Communist units struck in force and a fierce battle erupted. Two weeks later, General Li's National Salvation Army, which had launched its operation with high hopes, was back in Burma after being chopped to pieces.

Not all CIA covert missions are resounding successes. The Li Mi project was largely a flop, although it well may have diverted Mao Tse-tung's gaze from Korea for brief periods.

In Rangoon, the capital of neutral Burma, U.S. Ambassador David M. Key, who had known nothing about the Li Mi project in advance, was furious after belatedly learning of the operation. He fired off a harshly worded cable to Washington:

> This adventure has cost us heavily in terms of Burmese goodwill and trust. Participation by Americans well known to GOB [government of Burma] . . . Denial of official U.S. connection with these operations meaningless to GOB in face of reports they constantly received that [General Li Mi's] troops were accompanied by Americans and received steady supply of American equipment, some dropped by American planes.[10]

In the wake of the unmasking of the CIA's hand in the operation, the State Department in Washington promptly unfolded the Li Mi project cover story. Assistant Secretary Dean Rusk sent a cable to Ambassador Key explaining that an "exhaustive investigation" had been conducted and that Key was authorized to "categorically deny to GOB that there was or could be in future any official or unofficial U.S. government connection with secret operations in Burma."[11]

When the British government became incensed after the Li Mi project leaked, CIA Director Beetle Smith, an old hand at dealing with

London bureaucrats from his World War II days as Ike Eisenhower's right-hand man, clung to the cover story. Swearing that the government of the United States had no involvement in the incursion by the National Salvation Army, Smith told the British that he suspected some freelance American gun-smugglers may have been trying to line their pockets by arming General Li Mi.

While the Li Mi project was unfolding, General Matt Ridgway launched his revitalized Eighth Army in an all-out offensive. Kicking off on January 25, 1951, the GIs, marines, and ROKs ran into fierce opposition, but by February 9, Chinese resistance had collapsed at many points. Inchon and Kimpo airport were captured without a shot being fired.

By mid-February, the Chicoms and their North Korean allies were in full retreat. Eager to pursue the enemy, Ridgway triggered Operation Killer, whose goal was to annihilate as many enemy soldiers as possible—the ultimate objective of any war.

In Washington, the code name "Operation Killer" offended State Department bureaucrats and Harry Truman's chief civilian advisers, who supported the president's limited-war concept. These political appointees and bureaucrats thought the war should be prosecuted on the sly without all the bloodshed.

Despite the squeamish outcries from some in Washington, Operation Killer went forward against more obstacles than just the customary tenacity of the Chinese. An early spring had thawed the frozen hills, and the GIs, marines, and ROKs had to fight in torrential rains, stumbling knee-deep in the stinking muck of melting rice paddies, and fording swollen rivers whose currents tried to drag them downstream to their deaths.

By the end of February, the last Communist footholds south of the Han River collapsed. As Eighth Army warriors advanced, there were startling signs of how U.S. firepower, the brutal winter, and disease had wreaked havoc on General Peng's armies. Shallow mass graves were uncovered in many places. Chinese cadavers by the thousands dotted the hills. Veterans of World War II said they had never seen such slaughter.

Eighth Army's psychological warfare branch leaped to take advantage of the Chinese massacre. Retreating Chicoms were showered from the air with hundreds of thousands of leaflets that simply said: *General Peng, count your men!*

On the night of March 14, patrols of the ROK 1st Division probed the outskirts of Seoul and found the city empty of Communist forces. For the fourth time in eight months, the South Korean capital changed hands. Few buildings remained standing, and there was no power, light, or water. Food was scarce. Of the peacetime population of 1,500,000, only about 200,000 ragged, hungry, and bewildered civilians remained to "greet" the UN soldiers who poured into Seoul.

Early in 1951, the Communist high command in Peking received a report from an inspecting officer in Korea that told in stark detail how the brutal, subzero winter and existing without shelter on a few bites of raw potato a day had taken their toll on tens of thousands of Chinese soldiers, now immobilized by pneumonia, intestinal diseases, frozen limbs, and bronchial ailments.

In February, the CIA in Washington learned from an agency spy in the Indian government of Prime Minister Jawaharlal Nehru that the Chinese Communists had chartered a Norwegian ship and sent it to Bombay, India, to take aboard tons of medical supplies and the equivalent of three field hospitals complete with surgeons, doctors, and nurses, along with their gear.

Nehru, who had been preaching the need for peace, brotherhood, and understanding, professed to be neutral in the struggle in Korea. But his government, no doubt with his knowledge, had been providing propaganda and diplomatic aid to the Communists—and now Nehru was going to play an active covert role.

Washington was alarmed by the disclosure from the CIA spy. If the medical personnel and cargo reached the Chinese in North Korea, thousands of their soldiers could recover and join in the next Communist offensive against General Ridgway's force, killing large numbers of UN troops. But how was the ship to be halted? Norway, although a member of the United Nations and professing to be neutral, had permitted its shipping firms to continue to trade with the Communist enemy.

In Washington, the CIA flashed an urgent message to Hans Tofte, the agency's station chief in Japan, and to other stations in the Far East: Stop the ship. That assignment was fraught with diplomatic perils. Involved would be two "neutral" nations, Norway and India. Although the cable from CIA headquarters did not mention it, the clandestine job was to be done in such a manner that the finger of suspicion could not point at the United States.

Tofte knew he had been handed a tall order. He talked with the U.S. Navy, which did not want to get involved even with unmarked vessels. Likewise, the U.S. Air Force rejected bombing a ship flying a neutral flag on the high seas, for the source of the attack would be evident to the entire world and provide an enormous propaganda bonanza for the Communists.

However, the two services did agree to peripheral roles in the operation, code-named Stole. Keeping out of sight over the horizon, a destroyer would monitor the route of the cargo ship and radio its findings to Tofte in Japan. If the freighter docked in a North Korean port—which was unlikely—the U.S. Air Force agreed to bomb the vessel.

At one point along the Norwegian freighter's trek, Alfred T. Cox, the CIA chief for the British crown colony of Hong Kong, was notified that the ship might make a stopover at that busy port. Cox, a man of action, began hatching a plan to scuttle the ship if it arrived.

Cox was an impressive combination of brains and brawn. While a student at Lehigh University in the late 1930s, he had been captain and quarterback of the football team, co-captain of the baseball team, and a star guard on the basketball varsity. Along with his athletic skills, he earned a coveted Phi Beta Kappa key for outstanding academic achievement.

As an army reserve officer when the U.S. was bombed into World War II, Cox went on active duty in early 1942, earned his parachute jump wings, and volunteered for Wild Bill Donovan's OSS. In August 1944, he jumped far behind German lines at the head of an elite force of two officers and thirteen enlisted men when the Allies invaded southern France. There Cox and his men marauded around the countryside, blowing up bridges, tunnels, and railroad tracks and ambushing German troops.

Returning to the United States as a major, Cox was sent to China by Donovan. There Cox organized a commando school for Chinese troops, and in July 1945 he launched Operation Apple—the first combat jump by Chinese soldiers—behind Japanese lines.[12]

After World War II ended, Cox, who had been promoted to lieutenant colonel, spent two restless and boring years as a manager in a corporation in the United States. Then he was recruited by Frank Wisner, chief of what was then the OPC, and sent to the Far East in early 1950, before the outbreak of the Korean War.

Now, less than a year later, Cox had his sights set on the imminent arrival in Hong Kong of the Norwegian "mercy ship." He collected a large supply of explosives and prepared to blow up the freighter, even in a port of a friendly nation, Great Britain. No doubt Cox was disappointed to learn that the ship was continuing northward.

This development left the halting of the ship in the hands of Hans Tofte, who hatched his own plot. In a CAT aircraft, he flew to Formosa, gained an audience with Chiang Kai-shek, and briefed the Nationalist leader on his plan. Chiang agreed to help.

Within hours, a small fleet of dilapidated Nationalist vessels, with Al Cox and other CIA agents aboard, set sail. Guided by radio messages from the shadowing destroyer, the gunboats intercepted the freighter north of Formosa. Cox and the other Americans remained discreetly out of sight below, while Chiang's boarding parties scrambled onto the cargo ship, kept the Norwegian crew at gunpoint, and transferred the medical goods and equipment onto one of the unmarked Chinese ships. Then the freighter was permitted to continue its journey, knowing only that it had been raided by a cutthroat band of Oriental pirates.[13]

Meantime, at the Dai Ichi building in Tokyo, Douglas MacArthur cabled the Pentagon for approval of an unique operational plan he had conceived to end the war. First, he would "clear the enemy rear all across the top of North Korea by massive air attacks." Then he would "sever Korea from Manchuria by laying a field of radioactive wastes— the by-products of atomic manufacture—across all of the major lines of enemy supply." Finally, he would "make simultaneous amphibious and airborne landings at the upper end of both coasts of North Korea—and close a gigantic trap."

MacArthur concluded that this operation, which he described as "something like Inchon only on a much larger scale," would cause the Chinese army in Korea either to starve or to surrender.[14]

Twenty-four hours later came a brusque reply from the Joint Chiefs: "No!"[15]

Douglas MacArthur, who, since his early West Point days, had held that "in war there is no substitute for victory," had convinced himself that there was a conspiracy in Washington to deny him the means to finish the mission he had been assigned: driving the Communists from North Korea and reuniting the South and North under a democratic government. He was scornful of the Joint Chiefs for what he regarded as their loss of will to see the Korean mission through.

The telecon circuits between Tokyo and the Pentagon chattered around the clock. When MacArthur asked for permission to bomb an important North Korean supply depot near the Soviet border, the Joint Chiefs rejected the urgent request. MacArthur asked for clarification, and the Pentagon brass replied only that no wider war was desired. Failing to use U.S. power against Chinese military bases made no sense, an angry MacArthur fired back, because Mao Tsetung already was building a one-million-man strike force to hurl MacArthur's troops out of Korea.

Unbeknownst to MacArthur, the UN resolution calling for the reunification of the two Koreas by force had, by mutual consent of its members, been quietly abandoned. If Ridgway's army could just hold on, the UN and the Truman administration were ready to settle for a status quo—two Koreas, each distrustful of the other.

Douglas MacArthur was not the only top general in Korea having squabbles with the hierarchy. Frustrated by the failure of his all-out offensive to reach Pusan, General Lin Paio, leader of the Fourth Field Army, who had launched his drive with such high hopes, complained loudly that he had not been provided with the tanks and warplanes he had been promised. These complaints did not sit well with his superior, General Peng Teh-huai, at supreme headquarters in Mukden. Consequently, Lin was sacked, and Peng took charge of the prosecution of the war in Korea.

17

A Raid to "Kidnap" a Corpse

I N THE FAR EAST COMMAND HEADQUARTERS in Tokyo in early
March 1951, Brigadier General Crawford F. Sams, Mac-
Arthur's chief health officer, ripped open an envelope marked Top
Secret. Inside was a deciphered report from a secret agent operating
deep behind Chinese lines near Wonsan, Korea's east coast seaport.
Sams intently scanned the terse message and felt a surge of alarm.
Swarms of Communist soldiers were dying from a mysterious disease
whose symptoms were severe backaches and headaches, soaring tem-
peratures, and ugly, oozing body sores.

Sams feared that this epidemic might have been carried from
Manchuria by Chinese soldiers. It was in Manchuria that the Black
Death, as the horrible ailment was called, reputedly had its origin. If
the epidemic was indeed the Black Death, the plague could sweep
through MacArthur's forces in the South, inflicting unthinkable numbers of casualties. Mortality from the Black Death was nearly 100
percent.

A week later, a mimeographed sheet that another spy had pilfered
from a Chinese army hospital in North Korea reached Crawford
Sams's desk. Issued by a Chicom medical unit, it provided corrobo-
rating proof that a widespread epidemic was raging within Chinese
ranks. Under the heading "Disease," the medical report stated:

1. The number of patients in an NKA [North Korean Army] hospital
   in our vicinity has increased to over four hundred. Several patients have died lately. The hospital announced that this disease
   has reached epidemic proportions, and that two-thirds of the hospital staff has been infected.

2. Many native families [have been] infected with this disease and
   three children died from it.

131

3. Quite a few of [the patients] have soreness of waist and legs and also scabies.

4. Close cooperation between military and political cadre and medical organizations is needed to fight this disease and secure the health of our troops.[1]

The report urged troop commanders to take several preventive measures that, to General Sams's skilled eye, would be almost useless in halting the epidemic. "Kill the lice" movements should be initiated, the Chicom physicians declared. People when perspiring should remove their damp clothes and hats, and straw used for foxhole bedding should be left in the sun for a long period of time. And soldiers who had been scampering up and down mountains almost continually were urged to "get plenty of exercise."[2]

Based on the compelling intelligence that a serious plague had hit the Chinese troops and North Korean civilian population, Crawford Sams decided to go ashore near Wonsan for a firsthand inspection to evaluate the accuracy of the Black Death reports. Years earlier, he had witnessed a similar epidemic in Egypt and would recognize symptoms of the dreaded disease.

It was a decision that might well cost Sams his life, either from catching the Black Death or from being shot as a spy. Moreover, for an American general to slip ashore far behind enemy lines into territory occupied by Chinese troops was hardly like taking a Fourth of July river excursion back home.

Sams had another deep concern. If he and his companions were to be captured while ashore, the Communists would reap an enormous propaganda bonanza for global consumption. Sams could envision the headlines: "American army doctor sent to North Korea to spread germs among the innocent civilians."

To avoid touching off panic in Tokyo, Sams kept the true nature of the secret mission from his own staff. To explain his absence, he had orders cut for him to make a routine visit to Eighth Army headquarters in South Korea.

Navy Lieutenant Commander Eugene Clark, who had led the Trudy Jackson espionage mission at Inchon prior to MacArthur's landing, was tapped to go ashore with General Sams. Clark, understandably, was worried about being infected by the plague, but Sams administered inoculations to all of those going on the mission—and prayed to God that the medicine would ward off the deadly disease.[3]

Early on the morning of March 8, Sams, Clark, and ROK Navy Lieutenant Youn Joung (who had been with the Trudy Jackson team), along with a tiny group of volunteers, sailed northward from Pusan in a small vessel carrying equipment to diagnose blood smears. Three days later, Sams and Clark decided the ship was too slow and cumbersome, so the group transferred to an American destroyer, the *Wallace L. Lind,* and continued the trek.

When the *Lind* reached the vicinity of Wonsan, churning seas delayed the landing for two days. When the waters calmed, Sams, Clark, and Youn climbed into the *Lind's* whaleboat and headed for shore near the town of Chilbo-ri. Darkness concealed them from hostile eyes. Several hundred yards from the beach, the three intruders slipped into a rubber raft and paddled as silently as possible.[4]

When the three paddlers were about a hundred yards from shore, they were gripped by concern. Just ahead of them, on a road that ran along the waterline, a long convoy of Chicom trucks, their headlights splitting the blackness, was rolling southward in the direction of the battlefront. Moments later, there was the roar of powerful engines overhead, and the sky burst into iridescence. U.S. planes, their pilots unaware of the Black Death mission, had dropped flares over the convoy—and the three intruders.

Then a rash of bombs exploded along the road. Fighter planes raced up and down the line of vehicles with machine guns blazing. Several trucks burst into flame; the men in the rubber raft could see the Chinese soldiers scampering inland to get away from the death-dealing warplanes.

When the aircraft had flown away, Clark and Sams held a whispered debate: Should they go on to shore or cancel the mission? The violent air attack had scattered the Chicoms in the convoy, and the intruders could stumble onto a band of them and be taken prisoners or killed. However, when the truck cavalcade resumed its journey, Sams and Clark decided that survivors had climbed back aboard, so the landing party paddled on to shore.

Like giant cats, the three men began stealing through the night. They wore standard combat garb, but no insignia. Because they were armed with pistols, it seemed likely that they would be executed as spies if captured. So Sams carried hypodermic needles containing a liquid with which each man could commit suicide by injection if capture were imminent.

About an hour after leaving the beach, the intruders linked up with their predesignated contact, a Korean CIA agent named Koh, who had parachuted into the region a week earlier. Koh, a cheerful man who spoke perfect English, led the party inland for a mile to a cave that served as his hideout.[5]

After daylight, Clark and Youn set off to reconnoiter a nearby town, whose hospital reportedly had many Black Death patients. They would try to "kidnap" a corpse and haul it back to the cave to be examined by Crawford Sams. In the meantime, Sams remained in the cave to interrogate two other Korean CIA agents who had para-chuted with Koh. These men had had close-up looks at plague victims.

Thirty minutes after leaving their hideout, Clark and Youn reached the town, which had been battered earlier by air strikes and seemed to be virtually deserted. Outside the hospital, which had been partially destroyed, the intruders saw three Chinese guards armed with rifles. Inside this structure, Clark and Youn believed, could be found one or more corpses.

Now a major problem was at hand: How could the three Chinese sentries be dispatched without raising a ruckus that could bring other Chicoms in the town rushing to the hospital? Whispering, the intruders hatched a scheme. Using nearby buildings for concealment, Youn crawled to the side of the hospital and created a heavy rustling of the underbrush where he had concealed himself. Two of the guards at the front door came to investigate. Then, Eugene Clark slipped up to the remaining sentry at the front entrance and silenced him with a swift thrust of a trench knife.

This brief encounter caused a noise, and one of the two guards who had gone to investigate the rustling created by Youn dashed back to the front door of the hospital. Clark jumped on the man as he rounded the corner of the building and slit his throat with a razor-sharp knife. Meanwhile, Youn plunged a handheld bayonet into the third sentry's chest. Gurgling, the Chicom crumpled to the ground and died almost instantly.

Acting swiftly, Clark and Youn dragged the three Chinese bodies into nearby vegetation and then sneaked into the hospital in search of a corpse to "kidnap." But all the patients were alive. What to do now? Kill an ill victim and haul him back to the cave? The two intruders decided to go back and discuss a plan of action with General Sams.

MacArthur's health chief had good news. It would not be neces-sary to kill a patient and cart the carcass to the coast and a rendez-vous with the ship that was to pick up the party. After lengthy questioning of the two CIA agents, who already had seen stricken victims close up, Sams was convinced that there was indeed an epi-demic raging in the region, but it was smallpox, not the Black Death.

Greatly relieved by the diagnosis, Sams, Clark, and Youn walked back to the coast, recovered their inflatable rubber raft, and paddled out to a rendezvous with the destroyer *Lind*.

Seventy-two hours later Sams was back in Tokyo and reported to Douglas MacArthur that the threat of a Black Death plague infecting UN troops in Korea was unfounded.[6]

Although the "germ raid" had produced negative intelligence, Crawford Sams's fertile mind began spinning with visions of a propa-ganda coup that could be exploited throughout the Far East. During his mission, Sams had seen that the North Korean civilians were in a state of near panic because many of them were dying from the small-pox epidemic and the Chinese and North Korean authorities were doing nothing to halt the spread of the infectious disease. Lack of preventive measures by the Communists was not entirely due to in-difference, Sams knew. Rather, they were incapable of responding to the deadly situation.

"We have missed the boat in not throwing this fact back at the Communists," Sams declared in a written report. He strongly recom-mended launching a massive propaganda blitz throughout Asia, tell-ing about the Communists' medical failure in North Korea. This could be accomplished, Sams added, through the Voice of America radio network [broadcasting from Seoul], by millions of leaflets, and through the global media.[7]

"If I had anything to say about it," Sams continued, "I would constantly be hammering at the fact that diseases were sweeping North Korea, not only among civilians, but also military forces, be-cause the Communist military and civil people were incompetent and unable to control the [outbreaks]. I would hammer then to the other people of Asia that if the Communists invaded their country, they can expect widespread and deadly epidemics, because the [invaders] don't know how to control them. On the other hand, the United Nations forces are able to control these diseases on their side of the lines."[8]

General Sams's novel propaganda proposal was forwarded through channels to the Pentagon. There, for whatever reason, it was pigeonholed or fell through a bureaucratic crack.[9]

In Tokyo, Douglas MacArthur and his confidants had become deeply suspicious that certain delegates to the United Nations in Lake Suc-cess, New York, were secretly sympathetic to the Communist cause in the Far East and conspiring against U.S. interests. Although the war against the Communist aggressors was being fought under the auspices of the UN, several of its member nations were providing the Chinese army and the In Min Gun with the means to fight. Along with his generals, MacArthur was angry about the refusal of the Washing-ton power brokers to face up to the astonishing fact that these UN nations were trafficking with the Chinese and North Koreans, either for financial profit or for ideological reasons.[10]

Intelligence obtained from secret sources by General Willoughby provided stark evidence that war matériel was reaching Mao Tse-tung through back channels that ran from Ceylon and Indonesia to Macao to Hong Kong, the British crown colony on the south coast of China. These clandestine dealings between China and some nations belong-ing to the UN flourished even though they were handled virtually under the shadow of the large British naval base on the northeastern coast of Hong Kong.

Most of the secret transfer of war matériel to China took place at Kowloon, a town a mile across the bay from Victoria, the capital of Hong Kong. Docks for the ships that came to the colony were in Kowloon, and the town had rail connections that could whisk the surreptitious cargoes inland to Chinese military bases.

In the spring of 1951, Willoughby's staff compiled an alarming intelligence report that disclosed the steadily increasing trafficking:

> Hong Kong has become important as a supplier of strategic matériel to the Chinese Communists. Total trade in Hong Kong for 1950 amounted to over seven billion Hong Kong dollars ($500,000,000), an increase of almost fifty percent over 1949. Chinese Communist imports [at Hong Kong] during the last quarter of 1950 included vehicles, transport equipment, rubber, chemicals, drugs, iron, steel, and machinery.[11]

Meanwhile in mid-March 1951, rumors about Soviet plans to leap into the shooting war in Korea were floating around Tokyo, London, Seoul, and Washington. These conjectures intensified after Josef Stalin, in an interview in *Pravda,* declared in a bellicose tone that "the war in Korea can only end in a defeat of the [UN forces]."

In Washington, J. Edgar Hoover, the director of the FBI, intensified the nervous tics among leaders in the Truman administration when he disclosed privately that his agency had obtained intelligence indicating the Soviets would plunge into the war in Korea in April with massive army, navy, and air assaults. This same source said that Josef Stalin, who had the largest peacetime army that history had known, might also invade Japan and Alaska at the same time.

Some Chicom POWs corroborated these reports: Soviet ground troops and aircraft would soon overtly intervene. On Taiwan, Chiang Kai-shek's intelligence officers chipped in with another chilling report: Two Soviet armored divisions had already sneaked across the Yalu River and were concealed in North Korea, and large numbers of Soviet ground formations were holed up along the Tumen River just north of the Siberia-Korea border.

In Moscow, the British military attaché cabled London that a "reliable source" (presumably a spy planted in the Soviet high command) had informed him that a call had gone out for "volunteers" to fight in Korea.

As a consequence of these storm warnings from numerous sources around the globe, the Pentagon sent a cable to Douglas Mac-Arthur in Tokyo: "It must be emphasized that [Soviet] military forces in the Far East are considered to be currently organized, equipped, and disposed in such a manner to permit initiation of action without warning."[12]

Adding fuel to the alarming possibility of Soviet intervention were intelligence reports from a variety of sources that Josef Stalin had been heavily beefing up the weak Chinese air force in recent weeks. By early March 1951, MacArthur's intelligence estimated that the Chicom air force had expanded to 650 first-rate aircraft, including large numbers of Soviet-built MiG-15 jet fighters.

Haunting intelligence officers in Tokyo, Washington, and Seoul was an unanswered question: Were these sleek, swift, modern aircraft that had been spotted repeatedly in the skies over North Korea being flown by Chinese or Soviet pilots? If Russians were at the controls, it could be a telltale sign that the Soviets were preparing to intervene under the guise of "volunteers."

If the Soviets were to strike, Matt Ridgway had no intention of seeing Eighth Army caught off-guard as it had been four months earlier when the Chinese "volunteers" launched a full-blown offensive. So he had his staff develop a tactical plan whereby all UN forces would pull back immediately to the old Pusan perimeter and there conduct a rear-guard action prior to their evacuation from Korea. A single code word was secretly distributed to all top battle commanders. If the word were flashed, the withdrawal was to begin "without the slightest delay."

No doubt Matt Ridgway harbored another deep concern: If Josef Stalin overtly leaped into the conflict, the Soviets might drop A-bombs on crucial targets, one of which could be the chief Eighth Army supply base in Pusan. One Soviet A-bomb could take out four-fifths of his ammunition stockpiles in Pusan, Ridgway estimated. Such a frightening eventuality would leave Eighth Army helpless, unable to evacuate and thereby facing annihilation.[13]

If the Soviet clique in the Kremlin were to envision a major advantage in employing A-bombs to wipe out Ridgway's forces, it would most certainly lead to World War III. Already B-29 Superfortresses based on Okinawa had been allotted a total of twenty A-bombs. All that was needed would be the flashing of a code word to implement Operation Shakedown—the dropping of the A-bombs on Soviet military targets at Vladivostok, Port Arthur, the Sakhalin Islands, Darien, and elsewhere in the Far East.[14]

18

Father Sam and the Soviet Agent

SEVERAL HUNDRED MILES TO THE EAST of the Korean killing grounds, a bright sun cut through the frigid morning sky as a C-119 Flying Boxcar touched down on the runway of a Tokyo airport and rolled to a halt. Out hopped a large number of combat GIs and marines, who had been afforded the extreme luxury of shaves, showers, and clean uniforms before taking off from Taegu for six days of R & R (rest and relaxation) in Japan. It was March 3, 1951.

The R & R program had been established by General Ridgway earlier in the year when it became clear that the incessant burdens of battle were taking a heavy toll on morale in his ranks. He wanted his men to have something to look forward to other than danger, loneliness, and exhaustion—or to the prospect of being hauled off in a body bag. The hope for R & R buoyed the spirits of many war-weary men. All ranks, from private to high officer, were eligible for participation in the program.

After the brief respite in Japan, where their only danger would be the possibility of falling off a bar stool or being struck by one of Tokyo's wild-eyed taxi drivers, the warriors would be refreshed in mind and body, ready on returning to Korea to take up where they had left off.

In Tokyo, the "vacationing" soldiers and marines were put up in style at comfortable hotels that had been taken over by the U.S. Army. Most of the younger Americans on R & R spent their time in the many commercial nightclubs that offered excellent Japanese beer, talented Japanese combos and female vocalists, and flocks of often attractive young Tokyo women waiting to be picked up.

Among the combat veterans debarking from the Flying Boxcar that morning was thirty-seven-year-old Major Francis L. Sampson, the Catholic chaplain of the 187th Airborne Regimental Combat Team, with which he had jumped behind retreating North Korean forces near Pyongyang a few months earlier. Known to a legion of admiring paratroopers as Father Sam, the chaplain had survived numerous brushes with death while serving with the 101st "Screaming Eagles" Airborne Division during World War II. In the darkness of D-day morning, he had parachuted into Normandy, landed in water over his head, and nearly drowned while tangled in his harness.

A few days later, the padre was captured by German paratroopers while ministering to a large number of seriously wounded GIs. The captors put him against a wall to shoot him, but he was snatched from the jaws of death at the final moment when a German officer rushed up to halt the execution. A short time later, he escaped.[1]

In September 1944, Sampson bailed out with the Screaming Eagles over Holland, survived that operation unscathed, then was captured three months later at Bastogne in the Battle of the Bulge while far ahead of American lines searching for wounded comrades. During captivity in a bleak stalag (German prison camp) for six months, the scrappy padre was a royal pain in the neck to the German commandant, constantly demanding adequate food, better living conditions, and access to religious materials for the POWs. Even when the stalag guards threatened to shoot him if he didn't shut up, Father Sam continued to badger his captors until they caved in to his demands.

Now, five and a half years after his liberation from the stalag, Major Sampson was in Tokyo and eagerly looking forward to sleeping in a comfortable hotel bed, eating sumptuous meals, engaging in heavy-duty relaxation, and playing a few sets of tennis with a borrowed racket. A gifted athlete, he had won numerous army tennis championships.

His hopes were dashed on the second day of R & R when he was rushed to a Tokyo hospital to undergo immediate surgery to remove his appendix. While recovering, Father Sam learned that he would not be going back into combat. No doubt some high-ranking officer had concluded that the chaplain had endured enough of war's brutality for one lifetime. His new assignment was with a logistical unit in Tokyo, thereby setting the stage for one of the strangest undercover scenarios of the Korean War.[2]

In his new job, Father Sam was able to indulge himself in his favorite sport, tennis. Two evenings a week, he played a few sets at the Tokyo Tennis Club, to which high-ranking officials in the various national embassies belonged. On one of these visits, Sampson was approached by a big, strapping, athletic-looking young man who asked if he would care to play a set or two with him. The newcomer spoke good English, but with a pronounced accent. When he introduced himself, Sampson failed to catch his name but thought it was of Polish or Hungarian origin.

After the tennis competition, Sampson's new friend invited him to dinner at a Japanese restaurant, and the chaplain accepted. During the meal, the American learned that his companion was not Polish or Hungarian, but a diplomat assigned to the Soviet embassy. The chaplain was mildly surprised because the Soviets in Tokyo kept to themselves and seldom mixed with Americans. Before parting, however, the two men arranged to play tennis on the following weekend.

On returning to his quarters, Sampson began having qualms about his social relationship with the Russian, although the other man avoided political remarks and engaged only in friendly chitchat. The chaplain decided it would be prudent to at least report his encounter to the proper authorities, so the next morning he called at the CIC headquarters in Tokyo. There he received a heavy jolt. His new friend was Yuri Rostovorov, the chief of the Soviet secret police in Japan.[3]

Rostovorov, the CIC officers told Sampson, had been involved in transferring intelligence from Moscow before the North Korean invasion of the South the previous year. He was also the coordinator and supervisor of the Communist espionage apparatus in Japan, and part of his job was to obtain intelligence that could be useful to the North Korean armed forces.

Sampson was amazed. Did the CIC officers believe that he, a dedicated and decorated major in the U.S. Army, was somehow involved in Communist espionage in Japan? Was he being suspected of disloyalty? Much to his relief, he quickly learned that he was not a suspect. Rather, the army sleuths wanted him to become what amounted to an undercover counterintelligence agent. He was asked to continue his casual social relationship with Yuri Rostovorov and to report everything that was said.

"Look," Father Sam replied, "I'm a priest, an army chaplain, a paratroop officer, and I have a ton of work to occupy my time. I'm not interested in getting hooked up in this cloak-and-dagger stuff. Besides, all of this is way out of my field, and I'd surely ball it up for you."[4]

The CIC officers refused to take no for an answer. All Sampson would have to do, they insisted, was to continue to play tennis with the Soviet official and to dine with him on occasion. "We will take care of the rest," one officer declared.

Sampson pondered briefly over what was meant by "the rest" that the CIC was going to "take care of." However, he decided that as an officer in the U.S. Army, it was his duty to aid his country when called upon, just as he had done many times on the battlefield. So he finally agreed to cooperate with the CIC.

During the following month, the two unlikely friends, Father Sam, the advocate of democracy, and Yuri Rostovorov, who symbolized Communism, dueled on the tennis court twelve times and dined together on six or seven occasions. Politics or their divergent philosophical viewpoints were never broached.

At this time, unbeknownst to Major Sampson, his old outfit, the 187th Airborne Regimental Combat Team, was preparing to bail out near Munsan, twenty miles northwest of Seoul. Going along with them would be Captain Joseph Dunne, a wiry, enthusiastic, and energetic man who had sought the Catholic chaplain's post when he heard that Father Sam was not coming back.

Shortly after the paratroopers' jump on Munsan, Father Dunne was seriously wounded when the ambulance in which he was riding was blown up by a land mine. His feet and legs were torn and twisted badly, and he was evacuated to a hospital in Tokyo for complicated surgery in an effort to save his life. While at the tennis club, Major Sampson learned about Dunne, and he told Yuri Rostovorov that he was going to Tokyo Army Hospital to see a seriously wounded friend.

Much to Sampson's surprise, the Russian asked if he could go along. What angle did the chief of the Soviet secret police in Japan have in traipsing off to a medical center to visit a wounded American paratroop chaplain? Sampson saw nothing harmful in the request, however, so the two men left for the hospital.

When they entered Father Dunne's hospital room, he had regained consciousness from surgery only a few hours earlier. A nurse whispered to Sampson that he had nearly died from shock on the operating table. Although ashen-faced and gripped by enormous pain, Dunne greeted his fellow chaplain and asked for his prayers. Rostovorov was introduced as "a member of the Soviet embassy in Tokyo," and Dunne, smiling through his physical anguish, shook hands and greeted the stranger warmly.[5]

In the following weeks, Major Sampson continued his tennis playing and dining with Rostovorov and reporting to the CIC about what had been discussed. Perhaps to the frustration of the army sleuths, there never had been anything of consequence to report.

Eventually, Father Sam was ordered to return to the United States for a new assignment. A few months later, the chaplain was contacted by a CIC officer and asked to report to a certain building at a specific time. Sampson probed his memory for some act he might have taken inadvertently during his association with the CIC in Japan that might have gotten him into hot water.

On reaching the designated building, Sampson was escorted down a long hallway and motioned into a room. There, to his amazement, stood a familiar figure—Yuri Rostovorov, grinning broadly. The chaplain could hardly believe his eyes. Then he was told that the Soviet official had recently defected to the United States.

In a long and animated private conversation, Rostovorov told Father Sam that he had become disillusioned with Communism and had been anguishing for months over whether to defect. His mind had been made up to take the crucial step, he said, because of the deep impression Father Dunne had made by his friendly demeanor toward an "enemy" while lying in excruciating pain on a hospital bed.[6]

Back in Korea in the spring of 1951, Matt Ridgway's Eighth Army and the combined Chinese and North Korean forces had been engaged in a bloody death struggle along the 38th Parallel. UN airpower and massed artillery had been inflicting massive casualties. Ridgway's intelligence disclosed that enemy soldiers were usually hungry and had virtually no medical care when sick or wounded, and that many of them had not the foggiest notion what they were fighting about. This situation was an ideal one to be exploited by Eighth Army's PsyWar branch.

Conditions were so bad for the Communist soldier that he was willing to risk being shot by his own officers if he tried to surrender. So PsyWar printed hundreds of thousands of cleverly worded "safe-conduct passes" with a facsimile of Matt Ridgway's authentic signature. One side was printed like genuine money to ensure that it would be picked up. The passes stressed that the surrendering soldier would be given plenty of food, adequate shelter, and medical care, and would have the chance to see his family again one day.

The text was in Chinese, Korean, and English and stated:

Attention all soldiers of the United Nations forces. This safe-conduct pass guarantees humane treatment to any Chinese or North Korean desiring to cease fighting. Take the man with this pass to your nearest commissioned officer at once.[7]

Political commissars attached to each Communist unit tried to frighten soldiers from even picking up the passes. They were told that the Americans had saturated the paper with disease organisms that would cause a man to die a lingering and hideous death. If a man did try to use a pass, the commissars stressed, UN soldiers, especially the Americans, would brutally torture and then kill a man as soon as he surrendered. There also were hints that the family of any soldier using the pass would be maltreated or murdered.

Once the blizzard of safe-conduct passes fell along the Communist positions, many soldiers, either fearful of the consequences or else dedicated to their cause, ignored them. Thousands of others, however, surrendered at the first opportunity.

Around the world, meanwhile, the finely tuned Communist propaganda machine cranked out a new charge against the United States. A report by the phony Moscow-sponsored Catholic Committee for World Peace and Against Communist Aggression swore it had irrefutable evidence that the United States had shipped huge amounts of mustard gas to Japan and was dropping the deadly material on towns and villages in North Korea. Radio Peking and Radio Moscow backed up the accusation, blaming "the war criminal MacArthur" and his "military madmen."

Then the Communist-controlled Hungarian Red Cross demanded that the UN General Assembly take action against the "American imperialists to prevent the atrocity of using poison gas in their war of aggression in Korea." *Pravda* published a series of inflammatory articles castigating the United States for dumping poison on North Korean civilians. Photos of groups of dead civilians were splashed across the front pages of the world Communist press under such headlines as "Innocent North Koreans Murdered by U.S. Poison Gas."

Non-Communist newspapers, including many in the United States, printed the poison-gas charges. Most of the media inserted disclaimers in which the Pentagon branded the accusation an "outlandish lie." But the damage had been done: Large numbers of readers started to believe there was merit to the Communist accusations.

Douglas MacArthur in Tokyo and the power barons in Washington were on a collision course. MacArthur, already turned down on his tactical plan to isolate the Chicoms by scattering atomic wastes along their supply lines, now asked for permission to bomb the North Korean port of Rashin, some thirty-five miles below Soviet territory in Siberia. Huge amounts of war supplies came through Rashin by way of Vladivostok, Siberia, MacArthur explained. In one day alone, air reconnaissance had spotted 350 railroad freight cars waiting to be loaded.[8]

MacArthur's request was rejected. Rashin was so close to Siberia that the Soviets might launch a reprisal air assault against UN installations, it was explained. Two weeks later, MacArthur cabled Washington for approval to bomb the North Korean hydroelectric plants along the Yalu River. No, responded the Joint Chiefs.[9]

MacArthur was bitter at Harry Truman, telling aides that the president's "nerves are at the breaking point."[10]

On the heels of the latest rejections from Washington, MacArthur received a copy of a document drawn up jointly by the State and Defense Departments and circulated to all UN allies for approval. It read, in part:

"[Every effort] should be made to prevent the spread of hostilities and to avoid the prolongation of the misery and loss of life [in Korea]. Since aggression against South Korea has been repelled, the UN is prepared to enter into arrangements [with the Communists] which would conclude the fighting."

In response, MacArthur issued to the press a "military appraisal," which was widely interpreted as an ultimatum for the Chinese army to surrender. Mao Tse-tung's forces had "shown a complete inability to accomplish by force of arms the conquest of Korea," MacArthur declared. "I stand ready at any time to confer in the field with the commander-in-chief of the [Chicom] forces in an early effort to find any military means whereby realization of the political objectives of the United Nations in Korea . . . might be accomplished without further bloodshed."[11]

In the wake of MacArthur's public pronouncement, Radio Peking exploded: "The war criminal general has made a fanatical but shameless statement with the intention of engineering the Anglo-American aggressors to extend the war of aggression into China. MacArthur's shameless trick will meet with failure."[12]

Pravda blasted MacArthur as "a maniac, the principal culprit, the evil genius" of the war in Korea.[13]

CIA leaders in front of Civil Air Transport (CAT) airplane. From the left, Hans Tofte, CIA chief in Japan; a South Korean guerrilla officer; and marine Lieutenant Colonel "Dutch" Kraemer. (Joseph C. Goulden collection)

Captain Robert I. Channon (third from the right holding coat) gets an unexpected honor guard of fellow Airborne Rangers on leaving for the U.S. after a tour behind Communist lines. (Courtesy Col. Robert I. Channon)

Underwater demolition team member Milt Von Mann (nearest camera) shortly before he went on a raid to blow up a Communist general's train. (Courtesy Dr. Milt Von Mann)

U.S. Major John K. Singlaub (right), in Mukden, Manchuria, where he was head of the CIA station. There he recruited and trained spies that were sneaked into North Korea prior to the outbreak of the war. A Chinese Nationalist general is at the left. (Courtesy Maj. Gen. John K. Singlaub)

Mud flats at low tide after U.S. marines landed on Wolmi Island during the Inchon operation. Commander Eugene Clark's espionage team reconnoitered Wolmi before the attack. (U.S. Marine Corps)

When Seoul was recaptured by U.S. forces in September 1950, GIs found the city saturated with large posters of Soviet dictator Josef Stalin. (U.S. Marine Corps)

An emotional President Syngman Rhee clasps the hand of General Douglas MacArthur at a ceremony in Seoul when the city was recaptured, September 29, 1950. (National Archives)

President Harry S. Truman (third from the left) and his key advisers on the Korean War. From left: Special Assistant Averell Harriman, Secretary of Defense George C. Marshall, Secretary of State Dean Acheson, Treasury Secretary John Snyder, Army Secretary Frank Pace, and General Omar Bradley. (Harry S. Truman Library)

After MacArthur's spectacular landing at Inchon, the ROKs wanted the world to know that they were the first UN unit to drive into North Korea. (United Nations)

CIA operative Marve Curry, boss of all the Korean guerrillas, at his command post atop a mountain at a secret training base on Yong Island in the Bay of Pusan. (Joseph C. Goulden Collection)

A Korean guerrilla recruit stands in a mock-up of a C-47 airplane door as he takes parachute training under the direction of two CIA men. (Joseph C. Goulden Collection)

The U.S. Navy provided transportation and landed Korean guerrilla bands north of the 38th Parallel. (Joseph C. Goulden Collection)

Major Francis L. Sampson
(Father Sam), assigned to keep
tabs on the Soviet secret police
chief in Tokyo. (Courtesy of
Maj. Gen. Francis L. Sampson)

CIA Director Walter "Beetle" Smith planned to
"pull the rug out from under" General MacArthur.
(U.S. Army)

Communists in the POW camp on Koje Island. The sign at the right in Korean and English states that articles and packages were not to be passed through the fence, an order totally ignored. (U.S. Army)

Masses of Korean refugees head southward away from the battlefront. Many Communist spies infiltrated behind UN lines with these genuine refugees. (U.S. Army)

Korean guerrillas undergoing final inspection on Yong Island before departing on a mission behind Communist lines. Smiling faces reflect high morale. (Joseph C. Goulden Collection)

Soviet masterspy Kim Philby beams after being "cleared" of espionage accusations. (Imperial War Museum)

Donald Maclean (right), key Soviet spy, with two top officials in the British embassy in Washington prior to the outbreak of the Korean War. (Imperial War Museum)

Communist leaders in the Korean conflict. Premier Kim Il Sung of North Korea (upper left), General Pen Teh-huai, commander of the Chinese armies (above), and Mao Tse-tung, strongman of Communist China (left). (U.S. Air Force)

Two GIs of the 2nd Infantry Division hold a Communist propaganda poster showing Americans being driven into the sea. (U.S. Army)

Main Eighth Army supply port of Pusan. General Matthew Ridgway was concerned that his force would be marooned if Communists dropped the A-bomb on the city and harbor. (U.S. Army)

A Chinese POW at Koje assaults an International Red Cross official. Following orders, GIs stood by and did nothing. (National Archives)

Communist POWs on Koje had compounds festooned with huge posters of Josef Stalin and defiant slogans. (National Archives)

North Korean General Nam Il (center) was the ostensible head of the Communist peace-talks delegation. Actually calling the shots was Chinese General Hsieh Fang (far left). (National Archives)

The U.S. Air Force's "secret weapon" was a two-and-a-half-inch barb called a tetrahedron that punctured the tires of Communist trucks and left them vulnerable to air attack. (U.S. Air Force)

Alan Winnington (center, holding magazine) of the Communist *London Daily Worker* wrote the germ-warfare "confessions" of American POW pilots. (National Archives)

19

An Espionage Conspiracy Unmasked

GENERAL EARLE "PAT" PARTRIDGE, leader of the U.S. Fifth Air Force in Korea, was a frustrated man. Although his pilots and air crews had been inflicting heavy damage on Communist rear-area installations, he told his staff: "I believe [our] paramount deficiency today . . . is our inability to seek out and destroy the enemy supply convoys at night."[1]

Pat Partridge, a tall, thin man with a shock of gray hair, had gained heavy combat experience in World War II, both in North Africa and in England, where he had been chief of staff of XII Bomber Command and leader of the 3rd Air Division of the Eighth Air Force. Korea, he soon discovered, was an entirely different kind of war, for which new tactics, some of them bizarre in concept, had to be created.

As the In Min Gun had done earlier in the war, the Chicoms sought to escape devastating air attacks by moving truck convoys at night and hiding them by day. Colonel Virgil L. Zoller, commander of the 3rd Bombardment Wing, said that his night intruder aircraft were having a difficult time even locating, much less bombing and rocketing, the enemy convoys. "We're usually groping in the darkness," Zoller explained.[2]

Some unheralded individual within Zoller's organization hatched a scheme whereby lumbering, night-flying C-47s would scatter hundreds of thousands of tacks on selected North Korean roads known to be heavily used by the Chicoms to supply their troops. The tacks, it was hoped, would puncture the tires of enemy trucks, and soon after dawn, Zoller's fighter planes would seek out and destroy the stalled vehicles.[3]

"It's a hell of a crazy idea," remarked one officer, "but then, so was that of Columbus crossing the Atlantic!"

Within a few days, U.S. airpower joined the covert war. Operation Tack was launched. Groups of C-47s, winging through the darkness at heights of only ten to twenty feet, sprinkled eight tons of roofing nails along four highways south of Pyongyang, the North Korean capital. While zipping along one of these routes, Major Robert V. Spencer piloted his plane so low that it almost collided with three Chinese tanks. Only by swiftly pulling up at the last moment did Spencer avoid a fatal crash.

Shortly after daybreak, swarms of Fifth Air Force fighters roared over the targeted highways and destroyed twenty-eight trucks that had been stalled by tire punctures. After studying strike results, however, Pat Partridge concluded that Operation Tack had been only moderately successful. Many trucks had rolled on undamaged because the roofing nails often landed on their sides instead of with the points facing skyward.

What was needed, Partridge and his staff decided, was some sort of "gizmo" that would more effectively blow out tires. So the Far East Material Command hatched a "secret weapon"—only two and a half inches long and manufactured at a cost of less than two cents. Called a tetrahedron, it had several barbs, so no matter which way the item landed, at least one sharp point would be on top.

A few nights later, eighteen C-47s sprayed the Chicom supply roads at six points with ten tons of the "secret weapons," which were virtually invisible in the darkness from the driver's seat in a truck. Dawn brought Partridge's fighter planes, and many stalled vehicles were shot up. Adverse weather conditions, however, kept the pilots from assessing how much damage they had been able to inflict.[4]

One unexpected bonus resulted from the periodic spreading of tetrahedrons: Chicom truck convoys were slowed because one man often would be assigned to walk in front of a vehicle along road sections thought to be vulnerable to tetrahedron "attack." Only when the truck column commander felt the road topography was not suitable for scattering the multibarbed items did he order a resumption of normal speed.

On April 5, 1951, two Douglas MacArthur bombshells exploded in the media. Their shock waves reverberated in the White House, the Pentagon, and the State Department, creating a man-made tempest in the temples of power.

For an article in the *Freeman*, having been asked why South Koreans had been denied heavy weapons and equipment before the outbreak of the war, MacArthur replied that it had been a "basic political decision beyond my authority"—a jab at Harry Truman and Dean Acheson.

At the same time, the London *Daily Telegraph* published a story in which MacArthur was quoted as having told a reporter that "United Nations forces were circumscribed by a web of artificial conditions in a war without a definite objective. . . . The situation would be ludicrous if men's lives were not involved."[5]

An even heavier blockbuster struck Washington that afternoon. Republican Joe Martin, the Speaker of the House, took to the floor to read a letter he had received from MacArthur: "It seems strangely difficult for some to realize that here in Asia is where the Communist conspirators have elected to make their play for global conquest," the general stated, "and that we have joined the issue thus raised on the battlefield, that here we fight Europe's war with arms while the diplomats still fight it with words."[6]

After several somber consultations, the Joint Chiefs voted unanimously to sack MacArthur because "the military must be controlled by civilian authority in this country." Chairman of the Joint Chiefs Omar Bradley presented the verdict to Harry Truman, who replied that he already had decided to take such an action.

Truman's firing of national hero Douglas MacArthur triggered an outcry that echoed across the United States. A Gallup poll disclosed that 66 percent of Americans did not approve of Truman's action; only 25 percent stood behind the president. A White House official admitted that in the first 27,363 letters and telegrams, those critical of Truman ran twenty to one against those in the president's corner.[7]

In Tokyo soon after daybreak on April 12, General of the Army Douglas MacArthur left the U.S. embassy for Atsugi airport. Some 250,000 Japanese people lined the streets and stood silently in their ultimate gesture of deep admiration. Shaking hands with him as he prepared to climb the steps of the *Bataan* was his successor, Matt Ridgway. For the first time in fourteen years, MacArthur was going home—not as a disgraced Old Soldier, but as a departing hero.

On April 14, Lieutenant General James A. Van Fleet flew in from Washington to take command of Eighth Army. Ironically, he was secretly even more bitter than MacArthur about the stalemate and what many generals felt was the "no-win" policy of the Truman administration.

Known as Big Jim to colleagues, Van Fleet had been a star fullback on the undefeated West Point football team of 1915. His graduating class included Dwight Eisenhower and Omar Bradley. As a captain in charge of a machine-gun unit, he had been wounded in the Meuse-Argonne battle a few days before the World War I armistice.

In June 1944, Van Fleet was only a colonel while his West Point classmates were wearing three and four stars. He led the 8th Infantry Regiment of the 4th "Ivy" Infantry Division in the assault on Utah Beach in Normandy. In the weeks ahead, his combat skills earned him rapid promotions to an assistant division commander, a division commander, and leader of III Corps.[8]

Now at Taegu, Eighth Army intelligence greeted Van Fleet with news that General Peng Teh-huai, the Chicom commander, had brought in massive reinforcements from China, and seventy of his divisions were arrayed along the battlefront. Radio Pyongyang made no secret of Peng's goal: the destruction of the UN forces.

Van Fleet was ready to meet the challenge. "We must expend steel and fire, not men," he told his staff. "I want so many artillery-shell holes that a man can step from one to the other!"[9]

In bright moonlight on the night of April 22, an estimated 337,000 Communist troops joined in the assault, one of the largest since World War II. So closely massed were Peng's soldiers that they were slaughtered in droves by Eighth Army artillery and warplanes. Four days after the Big Red Attack jumped off to wipe out Van Fleet's forces, it sputtered to a halt short of Seoul, Peng's initial major objective.

While the savage fighting had been raging, U.S. Counterintelligence Corps sleuths uncovered evidence that the Communists might have had a spy planted in Eighth Army. While spot-checking letters mailed by members of the armed forces, the CIC sleuths came across an envelope addressed to: Josef Stalin/Premier/Moscow, Russia. Steaming open the envelope, the security agents read a message urging Stalin to exert his influence to bring the Korean hostilities to a close and cease antagonizing the United Nations so the war could end and "we can all go home."

A return address identified the writer, a teenage infantry private, who was interrogated by suspicious CIC men. No ulterior motive was uncovered. The frustrated youngster had merely been expressing the view held by most of the other GIs in Korea: End this seemingly endless war so "we can all go home."[10]

Meanwhile, dramatic behind-the-scenes events were unfolding in Washington and London. Although President Truman, the Joint Chiefs, the State Department, and the CIA were unaware of it at the time, these startling developments would have an enormous impact on the war in Korea.

Kim Philby, the Soviet masterspy and first secretary of the British embassy in Washington, learned that the Foreign Office in London and MI-5 (British counterintelligence) were closing in on an unidentified espionage agent who was thought to hold a key post in the British government and was passing U.S. top-secret information on the Korean War to the Communists. Philby was still privy to reports sent by General Ridgway in Tokyo to the Pentagon. He maintained his contacts with CIA officials, including an alleged briefing on intelligence activities by the agency's director, Beetle Smith.

At first, Philby thought that he himself was the target of the British search for the traitor, but careful examination of the dispatches from London disclosed that the prime suspect was Donald Maclean, Philby's long-time conspirator and chief of the American Department at the Foreign Office in London.

As first secretary, Philby was asked to join in the investigation to root out the Soviet spy. Although the CIA, MI-5, and J. Edgar Hoover's Federal Bureau of Investigation all knew that Maclean was the suspect, his name was never mentioned in discussions or on paper. Early in the probe, a CIA official asked Philby if he knew "him." Astute, self-assured, and as collected as always, the first secretary puffed on his pipe for a few moments and replied vaguely, "Yes, I seem to recall that I once met him at Cambridge [University] at one time or the other."[11]

In London, Maclean must have sensed the dragnet was closing in on him. His associates in the Foreign Office noticed that he had grown steadily more irritable and was given to long periods of brooding silence punctuated by outbursts of cursing both the U.S. and the British governments.

In Washington, Guy Burgess, the second secretary of the British embassy, was speeding through the Virginia countryside one day when he was halted and given a ticket by a highway patrol trooper. Burgess pleaded diplomatic immunity, and the ticket was voided. However, a routine report was filed with the FBI, and that agency's investigation disclosed that the man with Burgess in the automobile had a long record of homosexual activities.

A copy of the FBI finding was routinely sent to Burgess's superior, Ambassador Oliver Franks, who promptly decided it was time to sack the second secretary. His decision was reached on a security basis because of Burgess's open relationship with a homosexual. Franks still had no inkling that his problem subordinate had long been slipping top-secret U.S. Korean War military secrets to Moscow, from where they were passed along to Peking and Pyongyang.

Burgess, no doubt relieved that he had not been unmasked as a Communist spy, sailed on the luxury liner *Queen Mary*, and disembarked at Southampton on May 7. Eleven days later, he agreed to lunch with Donald Maclean at the RAC Club, an out-of-the-way place where they were not likely to bump into diplomatic colleagues—or

MI-5 sleuths. During lunch, Maclean, impeccably dressed in a gray suit and black bow tie, suddenly burst out: "Guy, I'm in terrible trouble. I'm being followed by the dicks."

Both men expressed deep concern over the "appalling situation" in Korea, fearing that the United States "might expand the conflict and provoke World War III." It was characteristic of their mind-set to see the United States as the aggressor and North Korea and Communist China as simply defending themselves.[12]

Finally, Maclean remarked dolefully that the two conspirators should clear out of London and flee to the Soviet Union. Burgess, having been kicked out of the Foreign Office and sensing that he, too, was, or soon would be, under surveillance by the relentless MI-5, replied that he might as well go along.[13]

As Maclean had suspected, the trap was about to snap shut. On the morning of May 25, a tense secret meeting was held in the Foreign Office. Among those present were key officials in MI-5, who laid down damaging evidence of espionage against Maclean, information that had been collected over many weeks. Foreign Secretary Herbert Morrison gave the green light for Maclean to be heavily interrogated by crack MI-5 investigators.

It was nearly noon on a Friday, however, so the grilling was put off until Monday. It was thought that a delay of two days was unimportant because the weekend in British life was a sacrosanct period during which normal affairs were suspended. This erroneous assumption saved Maclean and Burgess.

At about 9:30 A.M. that same Friday, while the meeting was being held at the Foreign Office, Burgess was awakened by a jangling telephone. Since he was unemployed, there had been no reason for him to rise early. Later that day, he planned to sail for France and a brief vacation with a young homosexual he had met coming over on the *Queen Mary.*

Picking up the receiver, Burgess got a jolt. The call was from someone in the know—whose identity would never be known for certain—tipping him off about the forthcoming Foreign Office investigation of Maclean. Deeply alarmed, Burgess quickly packed some clothes in a suitcase, put three hundred pounds (about $1,200) in a briefcase, hired an automobile, and picked up Maclean. The two men drove to the dock at Southampton. Abandoning the automobile, the two spies leaped aboard a cross-Channel steamer.[14]

After reaching France, Burgess and Maclean vanished. Intensive efforts by MI-5 gumshoes to track them down were fruitless. It seemed logical to assume that the Soviet secret service had arranged the escape from England or possibly had taken the two Britons under its wing once they arrived in France. Whatever may have been the case, the two British traitors would surface in Moscow months later.

When word of the flight of Burgess and Maclean reached the British embassy in Washington, Kim Philby expressed shock that two trusted civil servants could be Communist spies. He kept his poise and grew more confident in the days ahead when the top-secret cables from London gave no hint that the Foreign Office suspected that Burgess and Maclean had a confederate in Washington.

An enormous flap erupted in London after it was disclosed that Burgess and Maclean had been Soviet spies whose treachery had inflicted incalculable harm to the security of Great Britain's and UN forces in Korea.

Despite the charmed life Kim Philby had been leading, it appeared that he may have been suspected of complicity. In late June he was called back to London, then posted to the embassy in Beirut, Lebanon. There he would no longer have access to top-secret information about Korea.

Only Josef Stalin, Kim Il Sung, Mao Tse-tung, and their key leaders would be aware that the Communist pipeline into the Pentagon and the highest councils of the U.S. government had been shut off. No longer would Chinese and North Korean generals be privy to UN battle plans and White House decisions in advance.

20

A POW Camp Propaganda Machine

SOON AFTER MATT RIDGWAY took command from Douglas MacArthur, he decided to move the 139,000 Communist POWs at various camps in South Korea to a secure location offshore where the chances of escaping or rioting would be lessened. The prisoners were not only a security hazard, but they posed enormous logistical and administrative problems for Eighth Army.

A few weeks earlier, MacArthur had asked the Joint Chiefs for permission to move the POWs off the peninsula, possibly to the United States or Okinawa. For undisclosed reasons, the request was rejected. Now, without consulting the Pentagon, Ridgway began shifting the POWs to Koje, a small island in the Korea Strait a few miles south of the Eighth Army's bustling supply port of Pusan.[1]

Once a land of lush green hills where the deer roamed freely and the crystal-clear streams ran with trout, Koje's pristine beauty began to fade in early 1951 when some 150,000 civilian refugees poured onto the island to join the 50,000 natives already living there.

Before the POWs were moved, U.S. Army engineers rushed to Koje and built four large barbed-wire enclosures, each split into eight compounds. Inside these stockades the engineers threw up hundreds of jerry-built huts. When the masses of POWs arrived, the compounds were jammed with many times their capacity. Koje became an ideal breeding ground for conspiracy and revolt.

As U.S. intelligence would eventually discover, the North Koreans had established a secret special unit outside Pyongyang. This unit's undercover operatives were to permit themselves to be captured to get inside POW camps and organize the inmates, send back intelligence, and foment violence. Before departing for the battlefront to surrender, these agents were given two months of instruction in Communist dogma. Once inside the POW compounds, they were to spread word among the inmates that the Communists were winning the war and that the UN forces would soon be driven into the sea or pull out of Korea. If they held firm, the POWs were to be told, they would be hailed as heroes when they returned to the North.

No sooner had the POWs been put behind the barbed wire at Koje than Colonel Lee Hak Ku, the youthful former chief of staff of the North Korean 13th Division that had spearheaded the invasion of the South in June 1950, took control of the camp inmates. A few months earlier, Lee had awakened two sleeping soldiers of the U.S. 8th Cavalry Regiment and told them he wanted to give up.

At the time of Lee's surrender, the In Min Gun still had hopes of smashing the UN army in Korea. But U.S. intelligence officers apparently had not found it curious that this high-ranking associate of Kim Il Sung had merely come forward and let himself be taken prisoner. It would appear that Lee's action had been premeditated to allow him to get inside a POW camp and take command. To the Communists, a POW camp was an extension of the battlefield.

A young, friendly man who spoke fluent English, Colonel Lee played his conspiracy role to the hilt. He hit it off well with the U.S. camp administration, was cooperative, and cheerfully did everything asked of him.[2]

Because there was still much construction to be done at the camp—a hospital, mess halls, workshops—Lee was put in charge of POW building crews. Soon metal shears, hammers, pliers, and other tools vanished and were hidden inside the compounds. Strips of barbed wire were cut away and concealed. With these accoutrements, Lee supervised the clandestine fashioning of a variety of crude but deadly weapons.

Oil drums, which served as garbage cans, were converted into forges for making spears, knives, hatchets, and swords. The barbed-wire strips were fitted with wooden handles to be used as flails. Black powder was created from wood ashes, and nitrates were extracted from urine. The powder was put in C-ration cans to become hand grenades. Stolen gasoline was poured into bottles for Molotov cocktails. Prisoners cut gates in the barbed wire, then camouflaged the openings.

Not long after the Koje camp opened for business, a military police detachment arrived from Camp Gordon, Georgia, to take over security. Back in the States, the MPs had been given lectures on how to handle POWs. The instructors, however, had not known any more about the topic than had the MPs.

The MP commander promptly called in his officers. "Men, our job is to teach these prisoners democracy," he said. "We're going to treat these people as human beings. If a POW is abused or an American strikes one of them, the American will be court-martialed. If we are going to teach these people democracy, we can't do it by being a bunch of bullies!"[3]

The naive pronouncement had simply reflected the instructions handed down by the State Department in Washington. Bureaucrats there had theorized that lenient treatment of POWs would result in favorable recognition for the United States around the world.

It was stressed to the MP officers and men that no matter how unruly, obstinate, arrogant, or violent the Communists became, they were to be handled with kid gloves. There would be no bed checks, no roll calls, no inspections of the huts and workshops.

On his arrival at Koje, each POW received a clean mattress cover and new clothing. U.S. Army fatigues were in short supply, so many prisoners were issued spiffy new American officers' dress uniforms. In the mess halls, POW cooks worked with shining new utensils, pots, and pans. Prisoners were given ample helpings of rice, fish, and vegetables—far more food than 90 percent of them had ever eaten at one sitting. Communist doctors who staffed the hospital were provided with ample drugs and medicines. Large amounts of athletic equipment were brought in for the prisoners.

Representatives of the International Red Cross and the United Nations Commission on Korea paid frequent visits to Koje. They met with Koje's POW leaders to advise them of their rights. Were the prisoners being provided with the things they needed? No, was the reply. They asked for mimeograph machines, and the paper and ink to go with them. These items were quickly furnished by the U.S. camp administrators, who dared not ask why POWs needed them.

As the days slipped past, it appeared to the Americans that the POWs were docile, contented, and keeping busy in their workshops. GI guards did not enter the workshops for fear of bringing harsh criticism from the State Department and the United Nations Commission on Korea. Therefore, the Americans were unaware that the POWs were not only building an arsenal of crude weapons but were also cranking out thousands of inflammatory propaganda pieces on the mimeograph machines.

In keeping with the wishes of the State Department, U.S. officers had been giving a series of lectures on democracy. Although attendance was voluntary, large numbers of POWs attended the sessions. Many went out of curiosity, others were die-hard Communists who took strident issue with any favorable view of democracy. As a result of these lectures, the POWs' initial propaganda leaflets were aimed at the prisoners themselves. These pieces were intended to wipe away any doubts about the glories of Communism that the lectures may have encouraged.

Although the Americans knew about the propaganda blitz inside the camp, they did not seize the mimeograph machines. To the contrary, when the POW leaders demanded more mimeograph machines and much larger supplies of paper and ink, the requests were granted.

Emboldened to find that the camp administrators were not lifting a finger to halt their propaganda operation, the POW leaders decided to expand their coverage to Koje's civilian residents and refugees. Arrangements were made for Communist agents outside the barbed wire to pick up bundles of leaflets and distribute them throughout the island.

One evening, Major William E. Gregory, a tall, red-haired reserve officer and chief engineer on Koje, returned to his quarters and found a POW leaflet on a table in his living room. He asked his young Korean servant to tell him what the piece said. Beaming, the native replied, "Oh, the Communists are telling our people what fools you Americans are!"[4]

Now the barbed-wire propagandists concocted a scheme to spread their leaflets around the Pusan region on the peninsula. This goal would require organizing an elaborate distribution system, a logistics problem that proved easy to solve. Leaflet bundles, wrapped in plain brown paper, were passed through the fence to agents among the horde of civilian peddlers, prostitutes, and black-market operators arrayed there each day. Bored GI guards paid no attention to the clandestine transactions because notes and packages were regularly exchanged along the fence line.

Once the bundles were out of the camp, they were turned over to couriers recruited from among the hundreds of Pusan civilians who served the Americans on Koje as cooks, maids, laundrymen, gardeners, barmaids, and barbers. These workers made the round-trip from Pusan each day. Poor, largely ignorant of the philosophical clash between democracy and Communism, these Koreans were delighted to pocket small fees for merely carrying bundles from Koje to Pusan. Few, if any, of the couriers realized that they were cogs in an elaborate Communist propaganda machine.

After crossing the Korea Strait in one of the old diesel-powered boats that chugged back and forth, the couriers were met at the Pusan dock by Communist agents who took charge of the propaganda packages. Then other agents distributed the leaflets throughout the city.

These printed sheets were designed to create confusion, doubt, fear, and unrest. Kim Il Sung and Mao Tse-tung, the leaflets stated, had sent their "heroic volunteers" to rescue the people of South Korea from the clutches of the American warmongers, who wanted to enslave all the brown people in Asia. The bloodshed, grief, and destruction in Korea were caused by the Wall Street capitalists and their "running dog, the arch-criminal Syngman Rhee," and anyone collaborating with Rhee would be executed. These were potent propaganda broadsides when flung against the already bewildered, frightened, and largely illiterate civilians.

Inland from Pusan, most of the Koje-produced leaflets were distributed around the villages and towns in the valleys and on the mountains by Communist guerrillas. When the In Min Gun collapsed at the time Johnnie Walker's Eighth Army broke out of the Pusan perimeter in September, perhaps twenty thousand soldiers had been cut off and faded into the countryside. There they linked up with Communist guerrillas to form a formidable armed force deep behind UN lines.

When ROK units were sent into the mountains to track down the guerrillas, they often found the Koje propaganda leaflets. The villagers knew which men among them had helped distribute the papers. Through fear, or through sympathy to the Communist cause, they refused efforts by the ROK soldiers to coerce them into identifying those involved.

These Communist guerrilla bands often melted into the civilian population by day, then launched hit-and-run raids at night. Truck convoys headed northward from Pusan to the battlefront were ambushed. UN installations were attacked. A favorite trick of the guerrillas was to set up a machine gun alongside the railroad tracks at a desolate location. Under cover of darkness, they would wait until a brightly lighted hospital train, painted extensively with red crosses and carrying hundreds of wounded men from the front, was abreast. Then they would rake the coaches with a fusillade of machine-gun fire. Patients and medical personnel were killed and wounded.

All the while, Colonel Lee Hak Ku, leader of the POWs at Koje, was busily organizing a communications network. In the 64th Field Hospital inside the barbed wire, he set up a system that permitted men in the different compounds to communicate with one another. Prisoners who had messages to pass along would feign illness to be admitted to the hospital. There they circulated the reports from ward to ward, either by word of mouth or by wrapping a note around some object and pitching it into a ward. After the message had been read, patients in that ward would throw the note-and-object into another ward.

Lee also created a direct pipeline between the Koje camp and intelligence officers at Pyongyang, three hundred miles to the north. When he had an important message to send, he would give it to one of the prisoners assigned to a work detail outside the compound. The POW would conceal the note in a predesignated spot. After dark, a civilian agent would pick up the message and take it to Pusan the next day. There the note would be given to a "runner" who would head northward, infiltrate the battle lines, and reach Pyongyang.

When intelligence officers in Pyongyang wanted to send orders or other information to Lee, they used radio transmissions that were picked up near Pusan by technicians equipped with Soviet-built receiving sets. These agents wrote down the messages, then shuttled them by couriers to Lee's operatives in the Koje civilian population. Then the notes were slipped to POWs on the work details outside the compound. They, in turn, took the messages to Colonel Lee.

In May of 1951, the power barons in Washington were, in the words of Dean Acheson, "casting about like a pack of hounds searching for a scent" in hopes of sniffing out a crack in the Communist diplomatic armor that could result in peace negotiations. Long gone were the lofty pronouncements of reuniting the two Koreas under the banner of democracy. A major obstacle to covertly seeking peace talks was that the Truman administration did not formally recognize either Kim Il Sung's North Korean government or Mao Tse-tung's Chinese regime.

Assistant Secretary of State Dean Rusk, who, as an army colonel in the Pentagon in 1945, had been instrumental in establishing the 38th Parallel as a dividing line, dramatized Washington's dilemma. "We do not recognize the authorities in Peking for what they pretend to be," he said. "It is not the government of China. It does not pass the first test. It is not Chinese."[5]

Kim Il Sung's North Koreans had launched the conflict by invading the South, the Chinese were carrying much of the fighting burden, and the Soviets had been and were providing most of the accoutrements of war to the two Communist armies. "The perplexing question is, with whom can a peace treaty be negotiated?" Secretary of State Dean Acheson asked in a cabinet meeting.[6]

Ernest Gross, the number-two man at the United Nations General Assembly, reported that he had detected a hint from Soviet diplomats that Josef Stalin was interested in a negotiated settlement in Korea. Charles "Chip" Bohlen, who had spent the World War II years at the U.S. embassy in Moscow and spoke Russian fluently, was dispatched to Paris by the State Department. There he tried to enter into discussions about peace negotiations with a diplomat at the Soviet embassy. His efforts were in vain.[7]

Then, in mid-May, a mysterious figure identified only as a "Western European diplomat with credentials of reliability" passed word to the State Department that Mao Tse-tung would be willing to discuss peace in Korea.

Following this tip, Acheson hatched a secret scheme. No written instructions were given. Only a handful of top people in the White House, State, and Defense were informed. Centerpiece of the clandestine mission would be Charles Burton Marshall, a top official on the Policy Planning Staff of the State Department.

Marshall was to travel incognito to the British crown colony of Hong Kong, on the China coast, and locate a few possible "go-betweens" recommended by the CIA. Marshall would carry with him a letter intended to convince Mao Tse-tung that Washington and Peking should reconcile their differences in Korea. Moreover, the message would point out, the Soviet Union was the real enemy of both Communist China and the United States.

If he could make contact with top-level Chinese officials in Hong Kong, Marshall was to practice a subtle form of psychological warfare. He was to remind them that the United States had not been *directly* involved in the savage civil war between Mao's forces and those of Chiang Kai-shek on the Chinese mainland, and that the United States had tried to keep its embassy in Peking open until its diplomats had been expelled in early 1950.

Marshall left Washington in the dead of night. Soon after his arrival in Hong Kong, he discovered that the would-be contacts suggested by the CIA were unreliable at best. Frustrated, Marshall left his confidential message with a person who claimed to be a distant relative of Mao Tse-tung's wife. This conduit to Peking was an extreme long shot, but it was the best the diplomat could do. So he departed for Washington, never knowing whether his letter actually reached the Chinese Communist dictator.[8]

21

The Donkeys of Yellow Sea Province

W ITH THE ARRIVAL OF 1951, U.S. Colonel John H. McGee, commander of a secret unconventional warfare unit based at Taegu, was ready to launch a clandestine campaign behind Communist lines in North Korea. His "assets," as undercover operatives were called, would penetrate hostile territory by parachute, by boat, and on the ground to organize and train guerrilla bands, collect intelligence, and conduct raids and sabotage operations.

McGee's organization had the designation EUSAK Miscellaneous, a deliberately vague title to mask its true nature. EUSAK was an acronym for Eighth United States Army in Korea, and Miscellaneous reflected the array of nationalities and military specialties that McGee had recruited.[1]

Although the United States had gained much experience in conducting unconventional warfare and in supporting and guiding guerrilla bands during the Second World War, this expertise had largely evaporated when the armed forces went on a peacetime footing and downsized. After the conflict erupted in Korea, McGee, then a lieutenant colonel on Douglas MacArthur's staff in Tokyo, proposed the formation of an unconventional warfare organization whose activities would be a mixture of those performed by America's OSS and Britain's Commandos in World War II. MacArthur, eager to strike back at the rampaging North Korean army, gave McGee's plan a green light.

McGee, a husky, friendly man, had an ideal background for his job. During the early days of a woefully weak America's involvement in World War II, he had been captured by the Japanese in the Philippines. While being shipped by boat to Japan to labor in the coal mines, McGee jumped overboard, swam ashore, and escaped into the mountainous, forested interior of the Philippines. For the remainder of the war, he led native guerrilla bands in forays against the Japanese.

Now McGee was in another war and was confronted with a major problem: Where would he obtain men with the skills and resourcefulness necessary to conduct clandestine operations? Some of his people came from the old Korean Military Advisory Group. They were conversant with Korean geography, customs, and habits. A few others, who had had experience with the OSS, were recruited, but they basically were planning and administrative officers.

What McGee needed were free-spirited, highly motivated men for field operations, the type Wild Bill Donovan, the OSS founder and leader, had admiringly called "cowboys." They had been described by Donovan as "hell-raisers who are calculatingly reckless, of disciplined daring, and trained for aggressive action."

Within the U.S. Army in the Far East there was no one group with a monopoly on cowboy types. But McGee knew that the several companies of U.S. Airborne Rangers in Korea had an extremely high ratio of warriors who were capable of functioning for long periods in relative isolation behind enemy lines, were accustomed to being deprived of the amenities that most soldiers took for granted, and were bold enough to inspire confidence among the guerrilla forces they would be organizing, training, equipping, and often leading. McGee recruited many of his cowboys from these elite outfits.[2]

At Fort Benning, Georgia, the Airborne Rangers had undergone rigorous training in dropping behind or infiltrating through enemy lines to destroy headquarters, ammunition and supply dumps, communications facilities, bridges, tunnels, and other key targets. They were also tough fighting men. The *Ledger-Inquirer*, in nearby Columbus, Georgia, had said of the Rangers: "Each is a one-man gang who can sneak up to an enemy sentry, chop off his head, and catch it before it makes noise by hitting the ground."[3]

Now that he was ready for action, Colonel McGee focused on North Korea's Yellow Sea Province (Hwanghae Province), which lies northwest of Seoul and south of Pyongyang. When Johnnie Walker's Eighth Army had passed through this region on the way to the Yalu River in the fall of 1950, U.S. intelligence officers were astonished to discover that this province was a hotbed of anti-Communism and long had had an armed guerrilla movement aimed at Kim Il Sung's regime in Pyongyang.

This North Korean militant opposition to Communism had origins tracing back to the decades of Japanese occupation. During that period most of the people in the province envisioned an eventual free and united Korea, and their ties were to Seoul, the historic capital of the ancient country. This dream was shattered in 1948, when the Soviets installed Kim Il Sung as the puppet ruler of North Korea.

Kim and his Communist commissars began to drastically revise the province's political, social, and economic structures along lines set down by Moscow. Soon large numbers of the province's young men took refuge in the mountains and thick forests and formed into guerrilla bands.

Arming themselves with a motley collection of weapons, the guerrillas began waging undercover warfare against tax collectors, agriculture agents (who were seizing private property), and other symbols of the Pyongyang regime. When Kim Il Sung, in preparation for the invasion of the South, had a draft act passed, students and others described as patriotic youths fled to the mountains and greatly expanded the guerrilla ranks.

As the UN forces had swept northward through the region, the anti-Communist guerrillas and their sympathizers came out into the open and were hailed as heroes by most of the Yellow Sea Province population. Then came the Chinese Communist military tide flowing southward, and the guerrillas had to flee for their lives. Since the roads leading southward from Yellow Sea Province were controlled by the Chinese army, most of the guerrillas joined large numbers of refugees in a trek to the west coast. There U.S. and British naval units evacuated them to four offshore islands: Paengnyong, Taechong, Sok, and Cho.

During the mass evacuation, the navy task force commander signaled Tokyo about the presence of the North Korean guerrillas. Tokyo, in turn, notified Colonel McGee at Taegu. Wanting to capitalize on this unexpected development, McGee dispatched U.S. Major William A. Burke to the island of Paengnyong in February 1951 to assess the situation. In a week, Burke reported that with the U.S. and British navies controlling the seas along the west coast, these guerrillas were capable of conducting forays onto the North Korean mainland.[4]

Under the guidance of Major Burke, the four islands off North Korea were rapidly converted into guerrilla bases. McGee sent detachments of two U.S. officers and nine enlisted men to conduct guerrilla training on each of the islands. ROK marines provided security against the quite real threat of Chinese assaults from the North Korean mainland. EUSAK Miscellaneous poured in arms, ammunition, and equipment.

By the spring of 1951, there were several thousand anti-Communist North Korean guerrillas on the four islands. Although the U.S. advisers made suggestions and guided operations, the guerrillas largely ran their own show. They called each unit a donkey, a puzzling term that the Americans eventually concluded had probably been derived from the Korean word *dong-il* (liberty).[5]

Their command structure was civilian oriented. A donkey commander, known as a gun leader, was elected by a simple majority of the unit. Once elected, he had the power of life and death over his men, but he could be removed from command by a two-thirds vote. In some donkeys, the gun leaders appointed subordinate officers; in others, the posts were filled by elections.

In most cases, each donkey consisted of men from the same districts in the Yellow Sea Province, resulting in tight unit cohesion and loyalty. On most occasions, a donkey conducted forays in its own home district, whose geography, landmarks, roads, and buildings they knew. If a guerrilla were detained by Chinese security officers and interrogated, he could plausibly explain that he was a local fisherman, farmer, laborer, or low-ranking Communist official—and the natives in his district would back his story.

These forays were fraught with peril. Despite their cover stories, captured guerrillas often were tortured to force them to spill secrets of their organization. If a guerrilla was wounded seriously while on a raid, there was no way to evacuate him. To spare him certain torture and to protect the security of the donkeys and their offshore bases, he was shot in the head by his own comrades.

In South Korea in early May, Captain Robert I. Channon, whose 3rd Airborne Ranger Company had been fighting as straight infantry, was ordered to report to Colonel McGee at Taegu for a special assignment. A few weeks earlier, at a bleak height aptly called Bloody Nose Ridge, Channon had been wounded in both legs while leading a wild, uphill bayonet charge that helped rout a dug-in Chinese force. He had refused medical evacuation from the ridge until he had put his men into position to repel an expected counterattack.

Although Channon's legs had not healed fully, he was eager to begin the wide-ranging mission to which he had been assigned by Colonel McGee. The Ranger captain was to fly to the offshore island where Major Bill Burke was in command, to inspect its defenses and to conduct a reconnaissance by boat sixty miles to the north in search of other islands as potential sites for guerrilla bases. Once those functions had been completed, Channon was to travel to the Han River estuary, one hundred miles east of Burke's island, and dismiss a maverick donkey leader who was refusing to take orders from the Korean major in command of several islands in the estuary.

Channon's first stop, the island of Paengnyong, was too small and hilly for a landing strip. So the C-47 in which he was a passenger had to make a bumpy landing on the beach. As soon as Channon climbed out, the plane took off to avoid being shelled by Chinese artillery on the North Korean coast only six miles away.

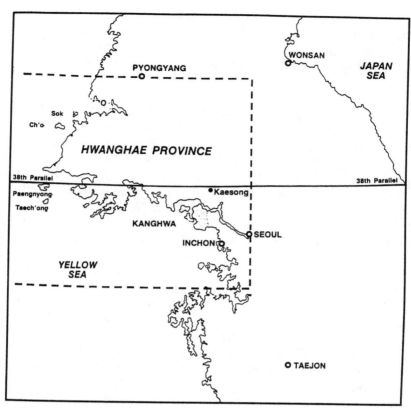

Yellow Sea (Hwanghae) Province area of guerrilla activities

Channon promptly contacted Major Burke, who put him in charge of demolitions training for the guerrillas until sea transportation became available and he could go on his reconnaissance mission. Three days later, Channon, Burke, and a few other officers were seated around a table in a mess tent eating lunch. Suddenly, a guerrilla trainee, cupping a grenade in both hands, barged through the tent flap and put the explosive device on the table in front of Burke. "No good!" the Korean shouted and dashed back outside.

The Americans stared bug-eyed at the grenade. Its firing release handle was off and the activated grenade should have exploded in four and a half seconds, blowing the Americans to smithereens. The guerrilla was right—it was "no good." However, it still could explode at any moment.

Lifting the grenade gingerly, Burke passed it to Channon and said, "You are in charge of demolitions. Get rid of the damned thing!"

Cushioning the grenade in both hands, Channon carried it a considerable distance from the tent and detonated it with a small TNT charge.[6]

Eventually, Channon's transportation—a seventy-foot-long, swift, maneuverable craft called a crash boat—arrived at Paengnyong, and he and two CIA agents climbed aboard. The crash boat belonged to the CIA, but it was manned by six U.S. Air Force crewmen. The skipper, a young sergeant, set a course for a flyspeck island called Hacwira, sixty miles north of Paengnyong. At a fishing village there, the CIA agents recruited ten civilians into the pilot escape-and-evasion network that was being established in North Korea and on the offshore islands along the west coast. The native recruits were taught how to give signals to a downed UN pilot to indicate they were friendly; how to get word to UN lines that they had a pilot in their care; and how to conceal him until an evacuation team arrived by sea or by air.

Channon reconnoitered a few more islands to determine their suitability for guerrilla base camps, then told the skipper to head southward for the 120-mile trek to the broad estuary of the Han River. There several small islands were occupied by donkeys, and on one of the patches of land was the maverick guerrilla leader who refused to take orders from the Korean major in charge of clandestine operations in the estuary.

After barreling across the water at high speeds, the crash boat slowed almost to a crawl, then halted as it reached the first of the islands in the mouth of the Han. Off in the distance loomed the first destination, the island of Taesuap-to, where a donkey leader Channon had brought with him was to be put ashore to take charge of operations there.

After shutting off the engines, the crash-boat skipper told the Ranger, "I can go no farther. We're in a tidal region and the boat might get hung up on mud flats when the tide drops for thirty feet or so." A dispute erupted. Channon insisted that the boat continue to Taesuap-to regardless of risk. "If we get hung up on the mud flats," the skipper responded, "the Chink artillery will blast us." Besides, the airman said, putting the donkey leader ashore was the Ranger's mission, not the skipper's. He was only the chauffeur.

Time was short. So Channon, the donkey leader, and a Korean interpreter scrambled into a bright yellow inflated raft and began paddling toward Taesuap-to, five miles away.[7]

The current was swift and the tide was tricky. Channon felt as though he were trying to paddle up Niagara Falls. Suddenly, after going for about a mile, the interpreter called out "Look!" and pointed ahead at a two-masted sailing junk. All hands hunkered down in the raft to reduce their profiles. As the men watched anxiously, the junk abruptly altered its course and sailed directly toward the raft. If this was a Chinese Communist craft, Channon reflected, he and his companions were doomed.[8]

The three men were aware that the first burst of fire from the junk would sink the raft, but they drew their pistols, determined to get off their shots before going under. The junk drew closer. And closer. When two hundred yards away, it turned and lined up broadside to the raft as though preparing to fire a deck gun. "This is it!" Channon thought.

Moments later, a Korean voice wafted across the water. The interpreter in the raft replied. Channon and his companions issued sighs of relief: There were friendlies in the junk.

When the junk drew up to the raft, Channon arranged for its skipper to take the donkey leader to Taesuap-to. Then he and the interpreter paddled the raft back to the crash boat.

The next stop was the nearby island of Gyodong, where the Korean major whose orders the dissident donkey leader had ignored was headquartered. There the Ranger, the major, and the interpreter boarded a sailing junk and headed for the adjacent island of Kanghwa and a showdown with the maverick.

Late in the afternoon, Channon and the others went ashore on Kanghwa and made contact with a British secret agent who had been working with the balky donkey leader. The leader called himself Lieutenant Un, a *nom de guerre* (war name) to protect his family in the Yellow Sea Province from savage retribution at the hands of the Communist authorities there. The Englishman, who had been an undercover agent in Yugoslavia during World War II, praised the achievements of Lieutenant Un and the eight hundred North Korean guerrillas in his donkey. He reported that they had carried out many raids as far north as thirty miles, ambushing Communist troops, burning supply warehouses, blowing up ammunition caches, and shooting up barracks. Many members of their families had been tortured and murdered by the Chinese and North Korean troops. So Lieutenant Un and his guerrillas showed no mercy on clandestine missions into Yellow Sea Province.

The Briton agreed to arrange a meeting with the donkey leader. The next morning he drove Channon, the Korean major, and the interpreter to a large manor house, where they dismounted inside the walled courtyard. Minutes later, there was the sound of screeching tires, and a battered old jeep burst through the open gate. Seven men were crammed into the vehicle: Lieutenant Un and his driver were in front, five bodyguards were in or hanging on in the rear. All the new-comers were armed to the teeth, and extra bandoleers of ammunition were draped from their shoulders and across their chests. The scenario reminded Channon of the Hollywood movies of Mexican bandits barging into a town in the era of the Old West.[9]

The jeep jerked to a sudden halt. The bodyguards leaped to the ground and surrounded the Ranger and his companions while their leader dismounted. The Englishman introduced Channon to Lieutenant Un, who glared icily at the American. Then the two groups went into the manor house, and a heated discussion between the Korean major and the maverick raged for thirty minutes. Both were jabbering at the same time. Finally, Channon broke up the gathering, and arrangements were made to have a party that night.

From his talk with the British agent and his own observations, Channon had drawn the conclusion that it would be a serious mistake to sack the donkey leader. Channon was convinced that Lieutenant Un's seasoned and highly motivated guerrillas would be valuable assets to the UN war effort with Un as their commander.

That night, about an hour into the party, Channon told Lieutenant Un (through an interpreter) that he had been sent to relieve him of his guerrilla command. Un's anger was apparent. He reached down to the pistol on his hip. Channon clamped a hand onto the holster top and said, "Now, listen to what else I have to say!"

Un relaxed slightly. "I do not think you should be relieved," the American said. "Tomorrow I will slip back through the lines on the mainland and recommend to our leader [Colonel John McGee] that you be retained in command." Un's face brightened. The party lasted into the wee hours.

Soon after dawn, Channon and the British agent jeeped to the river bank, where the vehicle and its occupants were loaded onto a wooden raft and ferried to the Kimpo peninsula, a no-man's-land on the mainland that separated Chinese and British forces. Warily driving southward, the two men crossed British lines and continued to Yongdungpo, about halfway between Inchon and Seoul. There the Ranger intended to telephone Colonel McGee at Taegu but, by happenstance, the EUSAK Miscellaneous commander was in Yongdungpo.

Channon located the colonel in an officers' mess. "Glad to see you, captain," McGee said. "We thought you and the others on the crash boat had been lost at sea!"[10]

Channon spent an hour briefing McGee on the guerrilla situation in the Yellow Sea Province offshore islands and on the nonconformist Lieutenant Un and his donkey on Kanghwa. McGee pondered the Ranger's strong recommendation that Un be retained as commander of his donkey and be supplied with weapons, ammunition, medicine, and equipment by EUSAK Miscellaneous. McGee gave his approval provided that Un agreed to take orders from the Korean major in charge of clandestine operations in the Han estuary islands.

Now Channon was confronted by the daunting task of retracing his route through no-man's-land and on across the water to Kanghwa, where he would advise the dissident Un of Colonel McGee's demands.

Meanwhile, the British agent had returned to his brigade and taken his vehicle. So Channon scrounged a jeep from an American engineer unit near Inchon, and arranged for a driver and a lieutenant to ride shotgun. Neither of the engineers displayed enthusiasm about the prospect of trekking through no-man's-land, which was often probed by Chinese patrols.

At dusk, the party in the jeep reached the hamlet where Channon and the Englishman had come ashore from Kanghwa the previous day. Few natives remained in the village. But Channon located a fisherman on the waterfront, and through hand motions and pidgin English made it known that he wanted the man to ferry him to Kanghwa. To punctuate his request, the Ranger loosened the flap on his pistol holster.

Channon and the fisherman climbed into a sampan and cast off. By now it was pitch-black. Soon, the American became concerned: the swift current seemed to be carrying the sampan far off course. But the native knew his business. Much to Channon's amazement, the craft made landfall at the village on Kanghwa from which he and the Briton had departed twenty-four hours earlier.

Using an ancient crank-operated telephone in the shabby, dimly lit police station, Channon telephoned Un's command post. An hour later, a wheezing old truck arrived and carried the Ranger inland to Un's headquarters.

Fifteen minutes later, the donkey leader entered the room where Channon was waiting. Anger and doubt were etched on Un's face. He seemed to be convinced that the Ranger had come back to tell him he was being sacked, and that his donkey would be turned over to a more reliable leader. No interpreter was present, so the two men could not communicate. Tension was thick.

Through hand gestures, Un managed to convey to Channon that he should spend the night there and a discussion could be held after daylight when an interpreter would be present. Two of Un's men escorted Channon to a small sleeping room. Deep concern gripped Channon. In essence, he was a prisoner of the maverick leader, and his throat might be slit while he slept. Channon laid his pistol near his bed.[11]

Early the next morning, with the interpreter present, the Ranger captain explained to Un that he had obtained permission to bring his donkey under the auspices of EUSAK Miscellaneous, which would provide him with more weapons, ammunition, equipment, and a means to care for his wounded men, and that Un would remain in command. Un immediately accepted the arrangement.

Un balked, however, at the suggested command setup, refusing to serve under his arch-rival, the Korean major in charge of guerrilla activities in the Han estuary. Notified of that obstacle, Major Bill Burke came up with a solution satisfactory to Un: A U.S. Army captain would replace the major as commander in the estuary.

His mission successfully completed, Captain Channon left for Taegu and a new assignment.

22

Widening the Unconventional Warfare

BY THE LATE SPRING OF 1951, it had become clear to official Washington that the war in Korea would be a prolonged and bitter conflict. So President Truman performed a flip-flop. He lifted his earlier ban on providing Chiang Kai-shek with material aid and authorized the widening of the undercover warfare to harass the Communist Chinese mainland to tie down tens of thousands of troops, thereby preventing them from being shifted to Korea. This large-scale assistance program would be veiled in a cloak of deep secrecy.

During the 1940s, the United States had funneled billions of dollars in military and economic aid to Chiang Kai-shek's Chinese Nationalists and had little to show for it. After Chiang was driven from the mainland by Mao Tse-tung's Communist forces in late 1949, the Truman administration decided to separate itself from Chiang. At a National Security Council meeting on December 29, 1949, Truman ordered a cutoff of all material assistance to the Chinese Nationalists. The president declared that if Mao Tse-tung were to invade Taiwan, Chiang's capital, the United States would take a neutral position. Translation: Chiang and his Nationalist army had been written off as expendable.

After the Korean War erupted, Truman revised his policy and ordered the U.S. Seventh Fleet to patrol the waters between Taiwan and the Chinese mainland to protect Chiang from invasion by Mao's forces and prevent Chiang from invading the mainland.

General MacArthur had been incensed by the deployment of the Seventh Fleet. Its presence gave a "tremendous advantage" to Mao,

MacArthur felt, because his Communist army would no longer be tied down on the mainland to repel an invasion by the Chinese Nationalists. In MacArthur's view, Washington should have remained silent to keep Mao guessing and off balance.[1]

Soon after Truman had made his secret decision to expand the covert war in the Far East, James Smith, who had fought with the 1st Marine Raider Battalion in the Pacific during World War II, learned from a friend in Washington that a secret agency there was recruiting combat veterans with experience in raids and infiltration tactics. Smith had tried to reenlist in the marines when the Korean War began, but was turned down. Too old, he was told. At the time, he was twenty-nine years of age.

Now Smith sensed an opportunity for action, so he called at the designated building and was surprised to see no men in uniform there. An interviewer in civilian clothes offered Smith a job as employee of an import-export firm that was operating in the Far East. By now, realizing that the import-export company was a CIA front, the former marine signed on.[2]

A short time later, Smith and a group of other new "employees"— former marines or OSS veterans—were flown across the Pacific to Chin-men, one of four widely spaced islands off mainland China and a few hundred miles southwest of Korea that would serve as bases for training guerrillas and launching hit-and-run raids. Not long after his arrival, Smith was introduced to his boss, who was operating under the cover of branch manager of the phony import-export firm. Actually, he was a CIA agent in charge of U.S. activities on Chin-men. Smith would never learn his true name, but from his military bearing and haircut, and the phraseology he used when giving orders, he concluded that the branch manager was a colonel or brigadier general in the army or marines.

Soon Smith and a few score of other "employees" of the import-export firm were busily engaged in military instruction of the eight hundred guerrillas on Chin-men, with an emphasis on demolition, silent killing, seaborne infiltration, and hit-and-run raids. A small fleet of Chinese junks, powered by diesel engines, was surreptitiously collected. Disguised with sails to look like fishermen's craft, the junks would be used to carry guerrilla bands.[3]

When clandestine operations were launched against Mao's mainland, the junks carrying the guerrillas had no problem filtering through the Seventh Fleet blockade. While much of the world envisioned hundreds of U.S. warships steaming up and down the Chinese coast to prevent Chiang and Mao from assaulting each other, in reality the Seventh Fleet was a shadow force of no more than twelve to fifteen vessels—and most of them were in port at any given time. With the change in policy by the Truman administration to provide secret assistance to Chiang, it was doubtful that the fleet commander made an effort to detect and turn back the guerrillas' junks.

To avoid an accidental confrontation between the junks and the American warships, CIA agents on Chin-men established an elaborate grapevine to keep track of when the Seventh Fleet flagship was in port somewhere in the Far East. This would be the signal for the guerrilla raids to be launched without interference from Seventh Fleet vessels.

In addition to conducting the military and demolitions training of the Chinese guerrillas, the American undercover operatives on the various offshore islands provided logistical support, overflight capabilities for dropping agents and supplies to guerrilla bands on the mainland, and means for spreading propaganda by radio and scattering leaflets by aircraft.

Playing a key role in the accelerated clandestine operations against mainland China was the civilian CAT airline, which actually was owned and operated by the CIA. CAT civilian pilots, flying unmarked, unarmed transport planes, provided "official deniability." That is, if a CAT plane were to be downed over the Chinese mainland, Washington could feign ignorance and claim that it knew nothing about secret operations against Communist China, pointing out that the aircraft had a civilian pilot and crew.

Clandestine CAT flights over the mainland required extensive planning and briefings on Chinese air defenses, coastal penetration points, checkpoints for breaking radio silence, and paths for return flights. Because the Chinese Communists had no night fighters, the secret flights were carried out under cover of darkness.

These intruder missions were risky business. Downed airmen could expect sudden execution as spies or, at best, many years in a bleak Chinese prison. The CIA air crews carried escape-and-evasion kits that included several gold bars to be used as bribes in the event an aircraft were damaged or malfunctioned and forced down. Some of the Americans carried potassium cyanide pills in their kits; others rejected the deadly poison capsules.

Accuracy of the agent drops proved to be a problem. With only old and outmoded maps available to navigators, agents often bailed out up to twenty miles from their designated drop zones. Also, large numbers of young Chinese agents were sometimes dropped "blind" (meaning with no prior knowledge of the situation on the ground) after being instructed to organize guerrilla bands. Few of these "blind drop" agents survived.

Despite the perils, guesswork on occasion, inadequate maps, green agents, and other drawbacks, the operations from Chin-men

and the other offshore islands were thought to be generally successful. Results of covert warfare missions can seldom be measured precisely, but intelligence reports indicated that tens of thousands of
Mao Tse-tung's troops, who might have been shifted to Korea, remained in place along the Chinese mainland because of the threats
posed by the clandestine activities launched from the offshore
islands.

In June 1951, while the undercover warfare against the Chinese mainland was getting into high gear, Airborne Ranger Lieutenant Joseph
R. Ulatoski, who had just been released from a hospital after recuper-
ating from wounds, reported to Colonel John McGee at Taegu. Ulatoski had learned that the six Airborne Ranger companies in Korea
were being deactivated, so he was seeking new employment with
EUSAK Miscellaneous. McGee had a job for him—to go to Nan, an
island six miles off North Korea near Wonsan, halfway up the east
coast, to be executive officer (second in command) of Task Force
Kirkland.

Kirkland was involved in training guerrillas and a hodgepodge of
undercover types for conducting raids and ambushes, collecting intelligence, and directing naval gunfire and air strikes against the Communists in North Korea. Although Kirkland's main base was on Nan,
raids were often mounted from two flyspeck islands only a few hundred yards from shore.[4]

Soon after Joe Ulatoski arrived on Nan, he joined with two other
Airborne Rangers, Corporal Cyril Tritz and Sergeant Bucky Harrison,
and a band of guerrillas in a nighttime incursion onto a small island.
Not long after the intruders got ashore and stacked a large amount of
ammunition, they were pounced on by a much larger Chinese force.
They scrambled into their navy craft and were ready to depart when
Tritz called out, "We can't let those bastards get the ammo!"

Tritz leaped out of the boat and dashed inland. Ulatoski, Harrison, and the guerrillas peppered the foliage with gunfire to keep the
Communists pinned down. Reaching the ammo dump, Tritz activated
a grenade, placed it in the ammo dump, then raced back toward the
beach. Moments later, there was a rocking explosion, and the black
sky burst into iridescence.

Meanwhile, the boat had drifted a short distance from shore.
Tritz walked into the water up to his waist, then halted and called out,
"I can't swim!" In the nearby underbrush sounds of approaching
enemy soldiers could be heard.

Without a word, Ulatoski jumped overboard, swam to where
Tritz was standing in the water, and towed him back to the craft. In
moments, the boat moved off into the night.[5]

Not long after arriving at Nan, Joe Ulatoski was appointed commanding officer of Task Force Kirkland. As the weeks in virtual isolation slipped past, he and the other Rangers on the island radioed Taegu for an airdrop of a precious commodity—a few cases of American beer. Soon a plane winged over Nan and parachuted the shipment right on target. The containers broke open, however, and all the beer bottles exploded on contact with the ground. Airborne Ranger Sergeant First Class William A. Kent, who was involved in air operations and had helped pack the beer shipment, said afterward that "the language Ulatoski used over the radio that day [in reporting on the results of the drop] was not good procedure."

Twenty-four hours later, a similar cargo of beer was parachuted onto Nan. Ulatoski cleaned up his language when radioing Taegu that the "combat cargo" had been received without a drop being spilled.

Bill Kent later became chief of the Air Operations Section of the Far East Liaison Detachment, an undercover warfare unit. Based at several airports in South Korea, its mission was to drop agents by parachute behind Communist lines, resupply individual agents or groups of agents in North Korea, and rescue downed airmen in hostile territory. The type of aircraft used in these missions depended upon the kind of operation and its location.

Kent and other men going on these missions expected trouble; they were seldom disappointed. On one supply drop to agents near the Yalu, the C-47 cargo plane in which Kent was a passenger was rocked by an antiaircraft shell explosion. The elevator in the tail had been hit, and the sturdy old workhorse of World War II vintage began to wobble. When the plane landed in South Korea, Kent saw that there was a hole in the tail large enough for him to stand in.

In the early days of the war, the In Min Gun and the Chinese used primitive weapons, but enemy antiaircraft fire had become far more deadly since then. Kent and others in the Air Operations Section who went on the missions suspected that far more sophisticated radar-controlled guns were being used and manned by Russian troops. Time would prove that assumption to be correct.

On a mission to the far northeastern tip of Korea, Kent and the navigator were perched in the glass nose of a specially equipped B-26 aircraft, a type of plane that had been used as a bomber in World War II. After the supply cargo was dropped, the pilot banked for the return trip over North Korea. A few minutes later, Kent and the pilot spotted a large, brilliantly lit factory. Because the structure was some 250 miles behind the front lines, the Communist authorities apparently felt it would be safe to burn the lights.

There was no doubt in the minds of the Americans in the plane that this factory was churning out war materials, so the pilot fired all eight underwing rockets into the building. Much of the factory burst into flames. Moments later, antiaircraft shells rocked the B-26. The glass in the front of the plane was blown out, the cockpit cover was smashed, a chunk of metal hit the rudder, the radio antenna was demolished, and shrapnel punctured the bomb bay. Miraculously, none of the men on board got a scratch.

On landing at K-16, code name for a secret air base southwest of Seoul, the pilot discovered the plane's brakes were not functioning, but he managed to roll the aircraft to a halt. Later, Kent would learn, the navigator was awarded a Purple Heart for the mission: He cut his shin on a jagged piece of glass while leaving the plane through the nose.[6]

On another mission, four Airborne Rangers and nineteen Korean guerrillas parachuted sixty miles behind UN lines in the Wonsan region to blow up a tunnel through which the Communists were running supply trains from the Yalu River south to the battlefront. A few days after the intruders landed, a supply plane orbited over them and gave away their presence. For three weeks, a running gun battle raged in the mountains between the saboteur band and the pursuing Chinese contingent. All of the guerrillas were killed, and the four Rangers were eventually trapped.

Just when the Rangers seemed to be doomed, they managed to get a radio message through to their base in the South. Hours later, three U.S. Navy helicopters chugged overhead. The first chopper, piloted by Lieutenant John W. Thornton, was circling when it was shot down by antiaircraft fire. Ranger Marty Wilson dashed to the wreckage and pulled the pilot from the debris. Although injured, Thornton survived.

Meanwhile, the second helicopter hovered overhead and winched Edward W. Purcel up and into the cabin. Ray Baker was shot in the face as he was being lifted into the same chopper. A winch on the third craft jammed while William Miles was being hauled up. Gunfire from the nearby Chinese troops became intense, so the pilot had to fly away with Miles dangling under the chopper. Bullets hissed past the helpless Ranger, but he survived the flight.

Lieutenant Thornton, as senior officer, remained on the ground to be lifted last. He never made it. Both he and Marty Wilson were taken prisoners.[7]

Many other Airborne Rangers who parachuted into North Korea on secret missions were involved in harrowing experiences. One of them, Lieutenant William Lewis of the Air Operations Section, was on a reconnaissance flight to pick out a site for a parachute drop far behind Communist lines. His airplane came under heavy antiaircraft fire and was shot down. Only Lewis and the navigator survived, and both were captured. For months, the Ranger resisted brutal efforts by his Communist interrogators to force him to disclose secrets about UN undercover missions in North Korea.[8]

In another episode, Ranger Captain Eugene Perry and a few Korean guerrillas, while on an intelligence-collecting mission behind Chinese lines, were trapped by a Communist patrol. Perry hid in a stack of loose hay in a farmer's wagon. Soon the enemy soldiers arrived and began searching for him. One man thrust a pitchfork into the hay, and Perry could sense the sharp points grazing the top of his head. He eventually escaped to friendly lines.

After a parachute jump with several Korean guerrillas, Ranger Sergeant James N. Kennedy and his band were discovered by a Communist force. Escape routes were blocked by the enemy soldiers, so after five days in hostile territory, the intruders made their way to safety by floating down a river on a makeshift raft.

Still another Ranger, Sergeant Charles Winder, and a team of Korean guerrillas parachuted at night northwest of Pyongyang, Kim Il Sung's capital. They were on an especially perilous secret mission: to free an ROK colonel who had been captured. Spies had pinpointed the structure where he was confined.

Winder's team overpowered the guards and recovered the colonel. Then the intruders and the colonel made their way to a predesignated point on the west coast. There they got aboard two small fishing craft, set sail, and rendezvoused with a speedy crash boat sent by Major Bill Burke, the underwater warfare commander on the west coast islands.

In most cases, undercover agents being dropped into North Korea promptly buried or concealed their parachutes to avoid giving away their presence to Communist patrols. UN intelligence learned that the Chinese and North Koreans were digging up the chutes from their shallow graves or locating their hiding places, then using the chutes to drop their own agents into South Korea.

In the wake of that disclosure, the Air Section hit on a novel scheme to thwart this procedure. Just before a UN agent took off, his chute was treated with a type of acid that would not act on the material for twenty-four to thirty-six hours after it was applied. This would give the agent plenty of time to reach his destination behind Communist lines, bail out, land, and hide or bury his parachute.

Air Section personnel conjectured gleefully about the fate of a Communist agent who would be outfitted with one of these recovered parachutes. There were bets on how far he would fall after jumping from an airplane over South Korea before the chute would disintegrate from the delayed-action acid treatment.

23

Communist High Jinks at a "Peace" Site

I N THE SUMMER OF 1951, the Far East Command's psychological warfare campaign took aim at demoralizing North Korean civilians and turning them against the Kim Il Sung government in Pyongyang. While flying normal missions, B-29 Superfortresses dropped large numbers of "leaflet bombs," each of which held forty-five thousand four-by-five-inch printed pieces. A B-29 carried thirty-two of these bombs and could release a million and a half leaflets on each mission. Weighing 175 pounds when loaded, a leaflet bomb had hinged sides that blew off after plummeting from twenty-five thousand feet to a predesignated height above the earth.

Leaflets scattered over civilian population centers focused on traditional Korean prejudices against both the Chinese and the Soviets. These printed pieces painted the In Min Gun soldiers as brutal men and puppets of the Soviets or Chinese. Russian advisers were depicted as living a life of luxury in Pyongyang while they sent North Korean boys out to die for the greater glory of Josef Stalin.

To undermine the acceptance of the Soviet advisers by the civilian population, racism played a major role. Carefully blending rumors with fact and traditional prejudices, the U.S. propaganda artists reminded the Oriental population that most of the Soviets were Caucasians. Drawn cartoons showed a huge "white" Russian, holding a whip, looking down on tiny "brown" North Koreans.

Other cartoons had themes depicting the Soviets and Chinese as competing strenuously for world leadership. The drawings showed North Korea being bombed and shelled into rubble because the two Communist superpowers had chosen the peninsula as a site to continue their struggle for power.

When spies reported that North Koreans who eked out a meager existence by tilling the soil were angry about the taxes and crop shares they were forced to pay their government, PsyWar conceived Operation Farmer, a stratagem aimed at disrupting the already fragile North Korean agriculture. For centuries, the southern half of the peninsula had been the breadbasket of the Korean people. When war broke out, however, those living in the North could no longer obtain food from the South. Therefore, Kim Il Sung had to rely on the relatively few farms in the North to fill the stomachs of the people and the army.

B-29s sprinkled millions of leaflets offering suggestions about what the North Korean farmer could do about his plight. Why should he turn over the fruits of his labor to Kim Il Sung and other Communist bigwigs living in luxury in Pyongyang? the leaflets asked. He could hide part of his crop so his family could eat better. Or he might sell portions of his harvest on the black market and pocket the money, the leaflets proposed.

Global Communism also was on the propaganda offensive. In late May, Monica Felton and other members of a Communist-front organization calling itself "The Women's International Commission for the Investigation of the Atrocities Committed by the United States and Syngman Rhee Troops in Korea," released a report to the world media. The lengthy document was replete with alleged horror stories of the brutalities of U.S. and ROK troops.[1]

While Felton was compiling the report, North Korean officials showed her investigators bloody baseball bats and clubs that they said had been used to savagely beat civilians. One elderly woman told in vivid detail how red-hot needles had been shoved under her fingernails. Felton and her party were shown a large pit filled with human remains ostensibly dumped by the Americans, the report stated.

Graves were opened to permit Felton's group to inspect bodies that were too mutilated to be identified. "Members could see children's shoes, tufts of women's hair, books, and small personal things," the investigators reported. One witness, Huan Sin-ya, said her mother had been buried alive by the GIs and ROKs but managed to dig herself out. "Then my mother was recaptured and buried alive again with four hundred and fifty other civilians," Huan was reported to have said.

In North Korea, UN aircraft had deliberately set scores of forest fires to burn hundreds of civilians alive, Felton wrote. Those innocents fortunate enough to escape the conflagrations were captured and tortured to death.

Each of Felton's inspectors, representing several Communist nations, signed the report, which concluded: "The people of Korea are subjected by American occupants to a merciless and methodical campaign of extermination which is in contradiction not only with the principles of humanity, but also with the rules of warfare as laid down in the Hague and the Geneva Conventions."[2]

Felton's blockbuster report was accepted as gospel in Communist nations, where it was widely publicized. Those in the Western world, however, knew that the litany of horrors was a propaganda hoax, since the "interviews" and "exhibits" had been set up and produced by the North Korean government.

Throughout late May and early June, James Van Fleet's Eighth Army drove forward along a 140-mile front. A strong Chinese defensive position called the Iron Triangle in the west-center of the line was assaulted by Americans, ROKs, Filipinos, and Turks. The bastion fell on June 13. In the center-east, meanwhile, the U.S. 1st Marine Division and two ROK divisions battled their way into the Punchbowl, a heavily fortified circular depression in the mountains. With its capture on June 16, U.S. and ROK forces were dug into the mountains above the old 38th Parallel border in the east and just below it in the west.

Now Van Fleet drew up a blueprint for victory in Korea. "We had the Chinese whipped," he would state. "They were definitely gone. They were in awful shape. During [one week alone] we captured more than 10,000 Chinese prisoners."[3]

In a year of war in Korea, and especially in April and May of 1951, the Communist armies indeed had taken a frightful beating. In addition to the 163,130 soldiers in Eighth Army POW camps, UN intelligence estimated the North Koreans and Chinese Communists had lost 1,191,422 soldiers through capture, combat, and nonbattle causes.[4]

Sensing a knockout punch against a reeling foe, Van Fleet planned to use the 1st Marine Division and Korean marines to leapfrog up the east coast in a series of amphibious landings. UN spies had reported that the Communists had virtually no defenses there. Van Fleet was confident that the Chinese could not counter the series of ship-to-shore landings. "They're not flexible enough," he told aides. "The Chinese army has no conception of fast moves. They have no communication system. They have no logistical support."[5]

In Washington, Van Fleet's ambitious leapfrog plan was shot down. The Joint Chiefs explained that the Truman administration had already spelled out its policy of limited war. Eighth Army was to remain in place, although Ridgway granted Van Fleet authority to conduct local attacks to seize ground better suited for defense.[6]

Meanwhile, American diplomatic feelers spread around the globe. Neutral officials in Peking informed Mao Tse-tung that President Truman hoped to end the bloodshed in Korea. At the United Nations, Secretary-General Trygve Lie appealed to the Soviets to "say the word the world is waiting for [peace]."

Apparently, it had become clear to Moscow and Peking that no matter how many Chicoms and North Koreans were slaughtered, they could not buy a victory in Korea. In New York on June 23, Yakov Malik, the Soviet representative at the UN, spoke over the United Nations radio station and said that the time had come for a peaceful solution of the "Korean problem."[7]

Washington seized on Malik's overture as a golden opportunity to end the unpopular war, which already had resulted in eighty thousand American casualties, including twelve thousand dead and ten thousand missing in action. Matt Ridgway, therefore, broadcast a suggestion to the Communist forces in Korea that cease-fire negotiations be held aboard a Danish hospital ship, the *Jutlandia*, in Wonsan Harbor.

Within hours, Radio Peking broadcast a reply. In a statement jointly signed by General Peng Teh-huai, leader of the Chinese "volunteers," and Kim Il Sung, commander of the In Min Gun, the Communists said they were willing to halt military action and engage in armistice discussions. Instead of holding talks on the *Jutlandia*, however, it was suggested that the site be Kaesong.

Ridgway sent patrols into Kaesong, which was located less than a mile below the 38th Parallel and ten miles northwest of the UN west flank at Munsan. The patrols reported finding no enemy activity in the town, so Ridgway accepted Kaesong as a neutral site.

On July 8, Air Force Colonel Andrew J. Kinney, chief of the UN liaison party, flew by helicopter to Kaesong to arrange for the armistice talks. Although Kaesong was supposed to be a neutral site, as soon as Kinney climbed from the helicopter he was surrounded by menacing Communist soldiers brandishing submachine guns for the benefit of the large flock of Communist reporters, photographers, and movie cameramen.

With this reception of Colonel Kinney, the Communists had staged a major propaganda event. When these photos and newsreels appeared around the world, they would convey that Kinney and his group represented a beaten UN army and had come to beg the victors for peace.

Kinney was outraged by the media ploy, especially because Matt Ridgway had agreed that Western correspondents would not be allowed in Kaesong. The colonel's first inclination was to fly back to

Seoul. On reflection, however, he concluded that such an act would provide the Communists with a propaganda bonus: They would trumpet to the world that the United States had broken off the peace discussions and wanted to continue the shedding of blood in Korea.

Kinney and his group were "escorted" to the discussion site, an ornate, one-story teahouse, by weapon-wielding Communist soldiers. Again Kinney was angered. Arrayed around the teahouse were more armed soldiers. As the Communist cameras clicked and rolled, Kinney and his group marched into the teahouse, followed by the Communist liaison delegation.

Seated at a long table, the opposing sides glared at each other. Kinney opened proceedings by handing over a list of delegates the UN forces would send to the negotiations and asked for a similar one in return. This request caught the Communists off guard; they apparently had no list and regarded the current exercise as merely a golden opportunity for a propaganda bonanza.

Flustered, the Communist group asked for a three-hour recess, presumably to whip up a delegation list of their own with ranks equal to those of the UN negotiators. During the break, the Communists offered food, whiskey, and cigarettes to Kinney and his party. All were refused. The Americans had no intention of accepting gifts from the supposedly magnanimous conquerors while the Chinese and North Korean cameras and reporters were scrutinizing the scene.

After the recess, the Communists returned and said that the peace-discussion delegation would be headed by Colonel General Nam Il of the North Korean army. Although born in Korea, Nam had spent most of his life in Russia and was a Soviet citizen. As a captain in the Soviet army, he had fought the Germans at Stalingrad and later at Warsaw. After the war, Nam returned to North Korea (probably at the instigation of the Kremlin) and became minister of education in Kim Il Sung's new Josef Stalin–sponsored government. Actually, Nam's education agency was the chief propaganda arm of the North Korean regime.

General Nam would be chief of the Communist negotiation team in name only. The true shot-caller would be Hsieh Fang, a general in Mao Tse-tung's Chinese army. Hsieh's background was cloudy to U.S. intelligence, but he was thought to be regarded as "reliable" by the Kremlin. There was evidence that Hsieh had been a Soviet intelligence agent after World War II.

Chosen by General Matt Ridgway as the UN chief negotiator was Admiral C. Turner Joy, who had served with distinction in combat in World War II. Joy was brainy, tough-minded, and incisive. Above all, he had the composure that would be crucial in absorbing endless hours of Communist verbal abuse without losing his self-control and sabotaging the peace talks with an intemperate remark.

After returning to Seoul, Colonel Kinney told Matt Ridgway that based on his observations, the Chinese and North Koreans intended to convert the peace negotiations into a propaganda extravaganza for worldwide consumption. Ridgway agreed, but his hands were tied. So the peace talks would take place as scheduled.

Aware that the Communists might kidnap the UN negotiators and hold them hostage, Ridgway organized a small, select team of U.S. Airborne Rangers and had it stand alert around the clock. In the event a kidnapping were to occur, the Rangers would parachute in to rescue the hostages.[8]

On July 10, Admiral Joy and his entourage headed for Kaesong in a caravan of vehicles, each of which was flying a white flag, a stipulation agreed to earlier by both sides. Five miles from the negotiation site, Joy's column was intercepted by three "escort" staff cars filled with Chinese and North Korean officers in full-dress uniforms. Although forewarned by Kinney to guard against Communist propaganda tricks, Joy was astonished. Lining the road as the escort cars led Joy's convoy toward Kaesong were a few-score Communist cameramen who filmed the Chinese and North Korean officers giving victory salutes and Joy's vehicles flying the white flags of surrender.[9]

After the two delegations entered the Kaesong teahouse, they took seats along either side of a long table. Earlier, the Communists had arranged the furniture, and when Joy sat down he felt that he was "sinking out of sight." About four inches of his chair legs had been sawed off. Across the table, General Nam Il, puffing on a cigarette, glowered down at the admiral as Communist newsreel cameramen exposed reels of film of the "victor" hovering over the "vanquished."[10]

In the days ahead, the Communists stepped up their propaganda offensive. Outside the teahouse, armed Chinese and North Korean soldiers stalked the premises. During a brief recess, Turner Joy was standing on the lawn when a Communist soldier, no doubt well rehearsed, charged up to the admiral and stuck the muzzle of a submachine gun in the American's stomach. Nearby, a Chinese cameraman was recording the scene on film. Presumably, this scenario within a scenario was intended to demonstrate to viewers around the world that a lowly Communist private was dominating a high-ranking U.S. admiral.

Joy would declare that "in isolation such tactics were childish. [But] it should be borne in mind that a great multitude of these maneuvers can add up to a propaganda total of effective magnitude."[11]

During the first two weeks of the daily talks, General Nam Il, thirty-eight years old, slender, and short in stature, proved to be a clever and implacable foe. He spoke forcefully and seemed to spit out his words. Clearly, he despised Americans. At no time did he ever exhibit a trace of humor. Nam fiddled with pencils, shuffled papers, whispered to his comrades, and chain-smoked endlessly.

At one point in an intense bickering session, Nam vainly tried to light one of his Soviet cigarettes with Chinese matches. Ten or twelve of them were struck, but none fired. Embarrassed and desperate, he reached into his pocket and withdrew an American cigarette lighter. It clicked and ignited brightly. After taking one deep drag, it suddenly occurred to him that the Americans were staring at him with amusement. Aware that he had "lost face," Nam nonchalantly tossed the lighter out the window behind him.

On August 1, Radio Peking launched a series of broadcasts that U.S. intelligence believed was in preparation for the Communists breaking off the gridlocked talks, then blaming the Americans. Radio Peking charged that American and South Korean troops had violated Kaesong's neutral zone on fourteen occasions in an effort to sabotage the talks.

Nam Il, aware that the U.S. negotiators were under heavy pressure from Washington to reach a settlement of the Korea "mess," stalled to gain negotiation concessions. On August 10, when Turner Joy discussed the 38th Parallel as a truce line, Nam's reply was an icy stare. Joy and his team followed suit. For two hours and twelve minutes, the adversarial groups sat facing one another in total silence. Finally, Joy and his men got up and walked out.

In an apparent effort to discredit the United States in the eyes of the world, the Communists hatched new incidents to provide grist for their propaganda mill. On August 19, the Chinese complained bitterly that a UN force had "ambushed" one of their "security patrols" in Kaesong and killed its leader. The Communists labeled it a "wanton attack" and so proclaimed it around the globe.

Investigation disclosed that the assailants had not worn steel helmets or uniforms. Based on this evidence, Turner Joy concluded that there had been an attack on a Chinese patrol, but that it had been the work of anti-Communist guerrillas known to be operating in the Kaesong region.

Three days later, Colonel Andrew Kinney was rousted from bed at midnight by a radio message from Colonel Chang Chun, a member of the Communist liaison team. Highly excited, Chang screamed that an American plane had bombed Kaesong in a deliberate effort to murder the Chinese and North Korean armistice delegation. Chang demanded that Kinney come at once to the site and examine the evidence.

Kinney left the UN delegation's base camp at Munsan and arrived just before 2:00 A.M. A heavy rainstorm was drenching the region. Gathered around a shallow hole in the ground were Colonel Chang and a group of Communist photographers and reporters. Chang pointed to the excavation, which was less than three feet long and four inches deep, where, he said, a U.S. bomb had exploded. Kinney said that the hole had been caused by the explosion of a half-planted grenade.

Chang brought up several Chinese soldiers. They had been well rehearsed. Using almost the same wording, the Chicoms said they had heard an airplane overhead, then a bomb detonation. More evidence was produced in the form of a twisted piece of metal covered with oil. It was part of a napalm bomb dropped by the American plane, Chang said. Nonsense, Kinney scoffed. The metal was the wing tip of an airplane that had crashed long before.

Chang was growing even more agitated. He told Kinney to inspect a small, unexploded rocket. The American was unimpressed. Rockets of that type had become obsolete and had not been issued to the Far East Air Force for a year.

Next, the frustrated Chang turned to another Chinese soldier, who swore that he had seen an American plane "with its lights on" just before the bomb explosion.

"That's absurd!" Kinney snapped. "None of our planes would go on a night mission with their lights on!"

Kinney had debunked each piece of "evidence." There was no napalm jelly, no scorched earth, no deaths or injuries, and no proof of a bomb explosion. Chang continued his harangue until after 3:00 A.M., when Kinney suggested suspending the investigation until after daylight. Chang refused, heatedly demanding that the American confess to U.S. guilt on the spot. When Kinney refused, the Chinese colonel declared that the peace talks were being called off at that moment. Kinney was convinced that Chang, an obscure, middle-level officer, would never have dared to make such a drastic pronouncement had he not been granted this authority when the "bombing" canard was hatched.

This comic-opera propaganda exercise had not been in vain, however. All over the world, Communist newspapers ran blaring headlines and highly creative stories, telling in vivid detail how the Americans had tried to murder the Communist "peace delegation" by bombing Kaesong.

If and when the peace talks resumed, Matt Ridgway had no intention of continuing them in Kaesong, an armed Communist camp. In late August, he radioed General Peng Teh-huai:

> When you decide to terminate the suspension of armistice negotiations, I propose that our liaison officers meet immediately at the bridge at Panmunjom to discuss selection of a new site.

Panmunjom was a deserted hamlet of a handful of mud huts on the road between Kaesong and the UN delegation's base camp at Munsan. The Communist reply to Ridgway was silence.

24

Soviet Troops and Pilots in Disguise

ALTHOUGH THE PEACE TALKS were in recess in September 1951, Operation Strangle, a massive air campaign to cut off the Communist forces from their sources of supply in Manchuria, was going full blast across the width and breadth of North Korea. Major General Edward J. Timberlake, who had succeeded Pat Partridge as commander of the Fifth Air Force, had conceived and was directing the operation.[1]

The plan was to isolate the battlefield by halting or paralyzing movement along the eight highways that snaked through the valleys from Manchuria down to the front lines along the narrow waist of the peninsula. Hundreds of U.S. planes roamed the skies, firing rockets into tunnels, dropping delayed-action and butterfly bombs at road choke points, cratering roadbeds, destroying overpasses and bridges, and shooting up truck convoys and other rolling stock.[2]

During the Operation Strangle blitz, the Polish military attaché, accredited to both the Chinese Communist regime and the North Korean government, was driving along a road near Pyongyang. A U.S. jet fighter-bomber swooped in with machine guns blazing and riddled the vehicle, killing the Pole.

In Warsaw, thirty-two-year-old Colonel Pawel Monat, who had been an officer in the Soviet army in World War II, got word that he was to replace the deceased military attaché in Pyongyang. Drafted into the Russian army after his hometown in east Poland was overrun, Monat fought the Germans at Stalingrad and in the Crimea. After the conflict, Monat transferred to the army of Poland, a puppet state of the Soviets, rose to colonel at a young age, and specialized in military intelligence.

185

In North Korea, Monat's function would be to collect information about the organization, tactics, and fighting ability of the UN forces, especially the Americans. This intelligence was to be sent back to Warsaw, from where it would be shuttled to Soviet commanders in Moscow.[3]

Monat went by rail on the long, arduous trek to Mukden in Manchuria, where he boarded a Chinese train for the ride to the Yalu River. On board were some two hundred men, all dressed in the green uniforms of the Chinese People's Volunteers. But they were not Chinese; they were Russians. And they were not the Soviet advisers that Monat knew were in North Korea. These men were combat engineers, antiaircraft gunners, and other troops who were going to North Korea to fight. With them on the train were jet pilots of the Soviet air force, most of them veterans of World War II combat.

The presence of Soviet combat troops and pilots in the Korean War was a closely guarded secret. But Monat, as a military attaché from a friendly Communist nation, had been able to deftly pry from his companions the true reason for their going to North Korea.

While playing cards with the Soviet officers on the train, Monat was surprised at their attitude toward their secret role. They were boastful. One story told to him by a Soviet colonel (whose Chinese Volunteers' uniform insignia identified him as a lieutenant) involved a Russian antiaircraft unit that had been strafed and bombed on a road by U.S. jets during the colonel's earlier tour of duty in Korea. Sixty Russians had been killed and twice that number wounded.

"It's a pity," the Soviet colonel remarked, "that we have to hide our presence. Otherwise, we could really show the Americans how to fight!"[4]

From the Soviets on the train, Monat learned that Moscow was deeply concerned that the world would find out about the thousands of Russians who had been and were involved in combat in Korea. Great pains were taken to cover their presence, such as wearing Chinese uniforms. To avoid capture, the Soviet combat men stayed a considerable distance from the front. North Korean troops with Soviet units attached to them had orders to immediately evacuate the Russians to the rear in the event of a UN breakthrough.

Soviet MiG pilots had firm instructions never to fly within fifteen miles of the sea to either side of the Korean peninsula. If the MiGs were to be shot down over water and the pilot ejected, he might be picked up by U.S. undercover vessels. The farthest south the Soviet-flown MiGs could venture was to the Chongchon River, which lies some seventy miles south of the Yalu River.

On the train from Mukden, Monat was told that despite the Soviet deception, there had been some close calls. When MacArthur pulled off his audacious landing at Inchon a year earlier, several Soviet officers had been with In Min Gun units cut off deep in South Korea. The Russians managed to escape to the North by disguising themselves as Korean civilians, being careful not to expose their Caucasian faces when working their way through U.S. positions.

The Polish embassy, where Monat would live and work, was located between two tall mountains in a drab compound of huts shared by the diplomats of Hungary, Czechoslovakia, and Outer Mongolia. Eight miles away was bombed-out Pyongyang. Just over the mountain was the Soviet embassy, presided over by a lieutenant general in civilian clothes named Vladimir N. Razuvayev. He was not merely the Soviet ambassador, Monat would soon learn. Razuvayev had been and was the senior Soviet military adviser to the In Min Gun—and the true ruler of North Korea.

In another valley a few miles from the Soviet embassy, housed in another group of huts, was the North Korean high command—the chiefs of the army, air force, and artillery. These military leaders were supervised by a task force of Ambassador Razuvayev's Red Army officers.

The Soviets were painstakingly careful to preserve a facade of diplomatic propriety around their power arrangements. Any Russian embassy staff member who inadvertently addressed Razuvayev as "general" found himself in deep trouble. No Soviet officer ever gave a direct order to the North Koreans in public. The illusion of North Korean sovereignty was studiously protected.

Colonel Monat had to rely heavily on personal contacts with Soviet and North Korean officers for intelligence on the military situation. From majors and colonels up to generals, the Soviets cooperated with their Communist friend from Poland. Among the North Koreans with whom Monat was in contact was General Nam Il, who was acting as front man for Josef Stalin at the peace talks. Monat cemented his relationship with Nam, who was known as a man fond of good booze, by sending him an appropriate gift—thirty-six bottles of fine Polish vodka.

Monat tried to establish a similar rapport with high-ranking Chinese officers—and ran into a stone wall. When the Pole reminded them that he was accredited to their defense ministry in Peking, the Chinese coldly replied that they had no connection with the Chinese Liberation Army. "We are the Chinese People's Volunteers," they insisted.

Making "volunteers" out of two huge Chinese armies having a million professional soldiers had been a simple task, Monat learned. Each unit had been told by its Communist political officer that the greedy and warlike United States, which had been thrown out of mainland China in early 1950, was moving through Korea to invade China again. At the end of the emotional lecture, every soldier willing to fight patriotically against the invasion of China by the United States was asked to take one step forward. Those who did not have a love for their country and were afraid to fight against the aggressor Americans could stand still. Not surprisingly, each soldier "volunteered."[5]

Pawel Monat was not the only one in Korea given the cold shoulder by the Chinese leaders of the "volunteers." Even the Soviets could not penetrate their aloofness. For months, a group of Russian officers in Peking had badgered the Chinese for permission to visit some Chinese units in Korea. Finally, Mao Tse-tung's generals granted approval. The Soviet delegation from Peking was met at the Yalu River by several stone-faced Chinese officers, who escorted the Soviet visitors on a wild ride over mountains, across rivers, and along back roads throughout the night. At dawn, the convoy reached the visitors' quarters, a damp cave equipped with electricity and running water.

After sleeping a few hours, the Soviets tried to go out for a walk. Armed Chinese sentries gruffly ordered them back into the cave. It was for their own protection against marauding U.S. planes, the visitors were told. They neither saw nor heard any aircraft.

Angry and baffled by this treatment at the hands of their Chinese comrades, the Soviets remained virtual prisoners in the cave for several days. Then a group of high-ranking Chinese officers appeared and admitted that they needed advice on a military problem. "Fine," the Soviets replied. "Take us to the area."

"No! No!" the Chinese responded. "We brought maps. We can discuss it right here."[6]

The Chinese officers' military problem was a minor one that any competent captain could have solved. But in order not to cause the Chinese to "lose face," the Soviets dragged out the discussion for two days. Satisfied, the Chinese left.

For forty-eight more hours, the Soviets, penned up in the cave by Chinese guards and suffering from boredom and claustrophobia, decided to head back for their post in Peking. The Chinese immediately agreed. They hustled the Soviets into several cars and took them back to the Yalu. This time the all-night trip took less than an hour.

Despite thousands of sorties and a deluge of bombs, rockets, and bullets, Operation Strangle, the air plan to isolate the battlefield, fizzled. It had failed mainly because of the tenacity and ingenuity of Chinese General Tao Chu, chief of logistics in Korea. Proving to be a master of covert warfare, Tao thwarted Strangle through ingenious cat-and-mouse games with UN intelligence officers.

Tao had organized fifty thousand troops into road-repair battalions of five hundred men. Each battalion was assigned to a specific locale in North Korea. As soon as a road or overpass was damaged or destroyed by air attacks, repair crews stationed nearby would rush to the site. Using only simple tools like picks, axes, and shovels, they would clear the road within a matter of hours.

The Chinese deception artists proved to be ingenious. Badly damaged and useless trucks, often brightly painted to attract the eye of UN pilots, were left in plain view. Airplanes often pounced on these inviting targets, wasting precious ammunition, fuel, and time. Truck drivers carried oily rags. When under attack from the air, they set fire to the rags to give the impression that their unscathed vehicle had been hit and was ablaze, prompting the pilot to fly off in search of other prey.

When a Chinese truck was caught out in the open in daylight and there was no place to hide, the driver would remove the wheels and lift the hood, thereby conveying to marauding jet pilots that the truck was crippled and not worth attacking. During the day, trucks were parked alongside churches, hospitals, and schools, the drivers knowing that UN pilots would not attack for fear of hitting these structures. Chinese convoys often had UN flags on their vehicles, and they painted red crosses on the cabin roofs of ammunition trucks.

When UN spies reported that the Chinese were depending far more heavily on railroads than Ridgway's intelligence officers had thought, Operation Strangle was expanded to include the North Korean railroad network. Chinese General Tao was ready to meet that threat, too. Cranes, construction materials, surveying gear, welding torches, and other special equipment were hidden near railroad bridges and switching yards. Within minutes after a bombing attack, railroad-repair troops, already in the area, were at work. Using horses and wagons for hauling rails and wooden ties, they would have trains rolling again in six hours or less.

Clever techniques were used to make railroad bridges that were operable at night appear from the air to be damaged and unusable in the daytime. Shortly before dawn, a huge crane would lift out a span from a serviceable bridge and place it in a nearby tunnel. To enhance the impression that the bridge was under repair, large piles of construction materials were left visible nearby. When darkness fell, the span would be removed from the tunnel and put back in place, thereby permitting trains to pass over the bridge again.

Slickly conceived railroad deception schemes included leaving worn-out or otherwise inoperable locomotives out in the open. Deliberately sloppy means were used to partially conceal them, thereby drawing attacks from UN warplanes. Operable locomotives were placed in the center of a rolling string of freight cars, rather than in the front or back, to escape being rocketed or machine-gunned by aircraft. To convey to reconnaissance planes that a rail line had been badly damaged by bombs and was impassable, large sections of track were strewn with debris. Dummy trains made of straw and cardboard were placed in a valley to lure UN pilots into the range of antiaircraft guns positioned on the mountains to either side.

With the peace talks in limbo, General Matt Ridgway had only one recourse: to keep up the battlefield pressure to force the Communists back to the negotiation table. Therefore, Jim Van Fleet launched a series of heavy assaults all along the front. The Communists, dug in on the high ground and resupplied with artillery, mortars, and machine guns, resisted fiercely.

During the savage fighting, Brigadier General Haydon L. "Bull" Boatner, assistant commander of the U.S. 2nd Infantry Division, was at a command post two miles behind the front. Boatner had taken only five days to reach Korea from the presidency of Texas A & M University. He had a short temper, and his icy stare and high-pitched voice could cut like a scalpel.

While Boatner was conferring with the command post officers, an American airplane swooped in and showered the men with Psy-War leaflets. Written in Chinese, they called for surrender and promised humane treatment and adequate food.

After returning to his headquarters, Boatner telephoned the Eighth Army PsyWar branch and barked at the commander, "The U.S. 2nd Infantry Division has no intention of surrendering to the Eighth Army!"

"What are you talking about?" the puzzled officer asked.

Boatner ticked off map coordinates to tell the PsyWar man where the Chinese front lines were located. "What's more," Boatner snapped, "your leaflets are no damned good!"

Boatner had spent many years in China before and during World War II and held a master's degree in Chinese from the Evangelical Missionary Language School in Peking. Now he explained that the surrender leaflets had been written in high literary Chinese. "They wouldn't motivate a common Chink soldier with a full gizzard to take a crap!" the general declared.[7]

A few days later, a PsyWar officer called on Boatner and said that he had drawn up the surrender leaflet, explaining that his knowledge of Chinese had been gained from studying only high literary Chinese in college. Boatner said that he would help, and gave him the address of Sung Shih, a general in Chiang Kai-shek's Nationalist Army, who was posted to Tokyo at that time.

When Sung arrived in Korea in response to the PsyWar officer's plea, his presence angered several Allied staff officers, mainly the British, in Eighth Army. They loved to hate Chiang Kai-shek. Sung was of enormous help, however, and when surrender leaflets later were dropped over Chinese positions, the common soldier could read and understand the contents.

With the war evolving into a static slugfest, PsyWar greatly accelerated its leaflet campaign aimed at the surrender of Communist soldiers. Most of the leaflets were designed in Tokyo, printed in Yokohama, and flown to air bases in Korea for distribution. Often the leaflets had photographs of genuine Communist soldiers enjoying the relative comforts of POW camps. To hide the identity of those in the pictures and thereby avoid savage reprisals in the Koje compounds, black bars were airbrushed across their faces. Chinese political commissars attached to each combat unit sought to turn around the impact of these photos. The black bars, they explained, were there to conceal horrible scars from disfiguring chemical warfare experiments inflicted on the helpless POWs by the Americans.

In September and October, Jim Van Fleet's sledgehammer assaults, backed by airpower and thunderous artillery barrages, inflicted horrendous casualties on the Communists. During those two months, the Chinese and North Korean losses were set at about 235,000 by Eighth Army intelligence. But war is never totally one-sided. Eighth Army suffered some 60,000 casualties, 22,000 of which were Americans, in the battles for a series of seemingly obscure ridges and peaks. Total U.S. casualties in the war had now reached approximately 100,000.[8]

Even by the standards of Communist leaders for accepting enormous casualties on the battlefield to obtain a goal, the bloodbath inflicted on their armies by Van Fleet's fall offensive was too much for their ample appetites. So on October 25, the Communists broke their self-imposed silence, and peace talks resumed at a table set in the middle of a tent in Panmunjom.

For a week, the two sides haggled over a truce line pending an armistice agreement. The Communist delegation insisted that the present battlefront be the permanent demarcation line. Admiral Turner Joy held that the truce line should be the battlefront at the time the armistice was signed.

Joy had seen through the Communist ploy. If the UN agreed to the present battlefront as the permanent demarcation line, it would mean that Van Fleet's Eighth Army could no longer attack, thereby providing the Chinese and North Koreans with an unmolested sanctuary to build up their forces for another offensive. If the truce line designated by the Communists were made permanent, it would result in a de facto cease-fire, because neither side would want to suffer casualties to capture a peak or ridge it would have to give back.

In Washington, the staggering UN casualties greatly accelerated the search for peace and an end to the "Korea mess." In October, polls disclosed that two-thirds of the American people had soured on what they perceived to be the senseless shedding of blood in far-off Korea for some vague cause whose purpose eluded them. So, in November, Admiral Joy was ordered by the Truman administration to give the Communists' de facto cease-fire a thirty-day trial.

At Panmunjom, staff officers on both sides struggled for weeks to reach an agreement on where the truce line lay for what would become known as the Little Armistice. After seemingly interminable quibbling by the Communists, a truce line, mile by tortured mile, was finally marked out on a huge map of Korea. Both sides agreed to it.

Then the Communists began welshing. Chinese Colonel Tsai Chen Wen pointed to a section of the line that he himself had marked in with a red pencil and declared that it was unacceptable. Colonel Ray Murray, a hard-nosed officer who had led the 5th Marines in heavy fighting, slammed down his fist on the conference table and barked at the Chinese colonel: "Why, you goddamned buffoon! You deny agreements you entered into not an hour ago, in fact one you yourself offered!"[9]

Tsai was visibly shaken by Murray's unexpected outburst and retired to the far corner of the tent, muttering that he could not be bullied.

Despite the incessant bickering, by November 27, the disputed points were resolved and the Little Armistice was in effect. Once more, the GIs and marines on the front lines began talking of being home for Christmas.

25

A Cable-Cutting Caper

REAR ADMIRAL ARLEIGH A. "31-KNOT" BURKE, who had gained his sobriquet in World War II when his destroyer division was chasing Japanese warships around the Pacific at full throttle, had become disgusted and frustrated from dealing with the recalcitrant Communists as a member of the peace-talk delegation and asked for relief. It was granted, and in early December 1951, he was in Washington on a new assignment.[1]

Learning of Burke's presence in the capital, Harry Truman sent for him. On his arrival at the White House, the admiral, who was known for his outspokenness as well as for his daring in battle, was given fifteen minutes to brief the president on the peace talks in Korea. It was a time frame akin to giving a historian ten pages to tell the story of Western civilization.

Truman, always a pleasant and courteous man when talking with military brass, asked questions and listened attentively to Burke's replies. The allotted fifteen minutes had almost expired when Burke suddenly blurted out: "Mr. President, who in the hell is—are *you* giving these orders?"

"No," replied the president, presumably startled by such a blunt question from one of his admirals. "I accept what the Joint Chiefs agree to."

Burke continued to bore in. "Then who originates them?" he asked.

"The State Department."

"Who in the State Department?"

"I don't know exactly."

There were a few moments of awkward silence. Then Burke said, "Mr. President, somebody in this government is leaking information [to the Communist negotiators] because I know that the Communists were getting our orders before we did. I can't prove it, but I know it!"[2]

The implication was clear: One or more parties in the State Department were traitors, in Burke's opinion, a view shared by most high-ranking officers in Korea.

Halfway around the world in Korea, the political and propaganda extravaganza billed in the media as peace talks disintegrated into a test of wills, a showdown between obstinate Asian Communism and a fragile alliance of Western powers. No longer was the thorniest issue one of real estate and truce lines but rather one of ideology. With the arrival of New Year's Day 1952, the sharpest focus was on the difficult matter of exchanging POWs. There were a few thousand UN prisoners in Chinese camps, and the UN had nearly 150,000 Chinese and North Korean POWs behind barbed wire, most of them at Koje.

The UN commanders knew that a large percentage of the Communist POWs had been drafted involuntarily, and, if given a choice, would prefer to remain in South Korea. Also knowing that fact, the Chinese negotiators refused to accept any permanent cease-fire until all Communist POWs had been exchanged. This situation resulted in peace-talks gridlock. The United States and its allies refused to return these hapless Communist pawns against their will. The Chinese and North Koreans could not admit to the world that a huge percentage of their soldiers preferred enslavement by capitalist nations rather than the paradise of life in the Communist countries.

Koje had turned into a semi-armed Communist camp. Kangaroo courts were established, and "deviationists" were sentenced and killed on the spot. Suspected spies had their tongues cut out and were left to bleed to death. POWs charged with lesser "crimes" were severely beaten. Others were stoned. While American guards outside the barbed wire looked on, the POWs openly trained in combat tactics. The Communist flag flew from the tops of most buildings, and huge posters of Mao Tse-tung and Josef Stalin mysteriously appeared in the camp and were erected at many places. Koje was a ticking time bomb ready to explode. And the American camp administration did nothing about it for fear of condemnation from Washington or the United Nations in New York.

Inside the compounds, a newly arrived North Korean POW, Private Jeon Moon-il, was introduced to a few key Communist officers as Brigadier General Pak Sang-hyon, the chief of North Korea's Political Committee and the new "commandant" of Koje. Back in 1945, Pak had been a major in the Soviet army; a few years later, he was one of the thirty-six Korean natives Josef Stalin had dispatched to Pyongyang to create a puppet nation. In early 1952, Pak donned an In Min Gun private's uniform, went to the front lines, and surrendered in an intricate scheme to foment an organized breakout at Koje and stir up a major uproar and confusion deep behind UN lines.

Inside the barbed wire, Pak set up his organization along military lines. His command, called the General Leading Headquarters, was divided into four sections: Agitation and Propaganda, Political Security, Guard Unit, and Planning. Political Security planted trusted Communists in each of the compounds to be on the lookout for "spies." Agitation devised schemes for provoking the American guards into violent confrontation. Propaganda continued to grind out leaflets on the mimeograph machines provided by U.S. taxpayers. Planning drew up detailed instructions for a breakout when the time was appropriate. The plan stated:

> The members dispatched to the outside will assist the basic fighting units to get out of the compound by occupying stationary firing and guard posts by surprise attack. [They will then] light signal fires on the hills, capture weapons, and destroy United Nations ammunition and arms warehouses. . . . On completion of this duty, they will go to the mainland and join the guerrillas.[3]

One day early in February 1952, a North Korean private arrived at Koje and promptly sought out General Pak. In hushed tones, the newcomer disclosed his true identity: He was a major in the In Min Gun, and he had made his way to Koje with direct orders from Premier Kim Il Sung to launch a POW uprising.

A month earlier, intelligence officers in Pyongyang had called in the major and informed him that he was going on a secret mission of the highest importance. It would be a dangerous venture, he was told, but there would be promotions, decorations, and other benefits for him once the war was concluded. If he were killed while on the mission, the North Korean government would pay his widow a handsome pension for the next forty years.

Then the major was briefed on his task. Wearing a dirty, torn private's uniform with American surrender leaflets in his pocket, he was to go to the battlefront. There he would take the first opportunity to surrender. He was to explain to his American captors that he had surrendered because he was secretly anti-Communist and that his wife and children had been murdered by Kim's secret police. This cover story, along with his lowly rank, would result in his receiving only nominal interrogation before being shipped to Koje.

Now Premier Kim's secret instructions were handed over to Pak. They called for him to organize the violent uprising to provoke the Americans into perpetrating a bloodbath on the POWs in an effort to squelch the revolt. That deadly action would permit Kim to prove to the world that his repeated charges of U.S. atrocities in Korea were true. The result would be an enormous propaganda victory for the Communists.

By mid-February, UN repatriation teams had entered each compound and naively asked for a show of hands from those who did not want to be sent back to China or North Korea after their release. Under the icy stare of hard-core Communist *hanchos* (leaders), no POW raised his hand.

If individual screening were to be conducted out of range of the hanchos, the Koje camp would have to be brought under control, Eighth Army officers decided. On February 28, a battalion of the U.S. 24th "Wolfhound" Infantry Regiment slipped into the camp just before daylight. Suddenly, the POW lookouts shouted, "Yankees! Yankees!" Within moments, the GIs were peppered with stones, bricks, and bottles. Then a horde of POWs charged forward with spears, flails, knives, and homemade grenades. Rifle fire and a bayonet charge by the Americans drove the prisoners back to their huts. In the melee, one GI had been killed and thirty-nine were wounded. The Communist attackers had seventy-eight men killed and one hundred thirty-nine wounded.

As planned at Pyongyang, the riot triggered a flood of anti-American propaganda around the globe. A banner headline in New York's Communist *Daily Worker* screamed: "GIs Butcher Helpless POWs."

While the disorders and POW agitations were growing more intense at Koje, Major Jack Singlaub reported to CIA headquarters near Pusan after a flight from Washington. Singlaub had organized and directed a spy network in North Korea for the CIA and had been called back to the United States just before war broke out in mid-1950. Since that time, he had been training new Rangers at Fort Benning, Georgia. Now he was on a second tour of duty with the clandestine agency.

Singlaub found that the CIA station had its own bland cover name—Joint Advisory Commission, Korea, or JACK. A short time after he arrived, its station moved to the Traymore Hotel in Seoul. There Singlaub discovered that JACK's neighbor and rival for funding, aircraft, ships, and missions was the Combined Command for Reconnaissance Activities, Korea, or CCRAK. Its agents quipped that CCRAK stood for Crazy Communists Running Around Korea.

In Japan, Captain Robert Channon, the Airborne Ranger who had conducted the secret missions to the islands off Yellow Sea Province a few months earlier for Colonel John McGee's EUSAK Miscellaneous, was on duty with the 187th Airborne Regimental Combat

Team as plans officer. Soon after Jack Singlaub reached the Far East, he called on Channon. He probably had a list of the Airborne Rangers who had joined the 187th after their companies had been deactivated and wanted to recruit them for JACK's unconventional warfare operations, Channon deduced.

Singlaub was seated by Channon's desk when the telephone rang. It was Brigadier General Trap Trapnell, the hard-nosed leader of the 187th combat team, who apparently had learned of Singlaub's visit.

"Is that *man* there?" Trapnell barked.

"Yes, sir," Channon replied.

"Is he offering you a job?"

"Yes, sir."

"Then you tell him *no!*"

"Yes, sir."

That terse exchange ended the discussion between Channon and Singlaub.[4]

If the enterprising Singlaub had intended to shanghai Airborne Rangers (many of whom he had trained back at Fort Benning) from the 187th, he was undaunted by his lack of success. Soon he was planning and launching undercover operations. One of his most successful and intriguing secret missions involved a hardy free spirit, a U.S. Air Force sergeant, who operated a junk from an island off the west coast of North Korea. He lived on the junk with his crew and his "wife," an attractive young Korean woman.

Singlaub and other CIA men learned that there was an underwater telephone-telegraph cable connecting the Shangtung peninsula on mainland China with Darien, Manchuria. This cable was a key communications link between the Chinese military hierarchy in Peking and its army commanders in Korea. Further probing revealed that the plot of the cable's route was across the Yellow Sea, where the water was generally shallow.

In early May, the sergeant set sail in his junk, which was disguised as a fisherman's boat. Three days later, the craft was anchored above the cable. Grappling hooks hauled up the cable onto the deck, where the sergeant hacked the thick wire in two with a large axe. One end of the cable was towed for a considerable distance before it was dropped into the water, a tactic that would make it even more difficult for the Chinese to repair the communications link, even after the long search it would take to locate the break.[5]

The sabotage proved to be an intelligence bonanza for the super-secret U.S. National Security Agency (NSA), which had been established by law in 1947, and whose existence was seldom publicly mentioned. A primary duty of the NSA was to protect the security of government communications by the creation of elaborate encrypting machines and devices for monitoring the radio messages of other nations—including friendly ones.

The main mission of the NSA monitoring station in the Far East, located at Atsugi Air Force Base outside Tokyo, was eavesdropping on Chinese military and diplomatic traffic. But pickings had been slim because the security-conscious Chinese Communists, aware of America's sophisticated monitoring devices, mainly used telephone and cable to exchange high-level messages.

NSA specialists doing the intercepts and decoding of messages did not attempt to analyze what they had "heard." Rather, transcripts were passed along to a tight bureaucratic circle, first to the NSA headquarters in a collection of rundown, unmarked buildings at Arlington Hill outside Washington, D.C. There the message was analyzed and passed along to President Truman, three of his top advisers, and a few key officials in the State Department and the Pentagon. So confidential were the intercepts that they were disguised as coming from some other source to shield their true origin.

Now, as a result of the CIA cable-cutting caper in the Yellow Sea, the Chinese had their main source of communication cut off (literally) and were forced to use radio to transmit orders and other information back and forth between Peking and the military high command in Mukden. Almost at once, the NSA monitoring apparatus, already in place, began "reading" the Communists' radio traffic, an action that provided an enormous bonus for both UN battle commanders and peace-talks negotiators.

In the meantime, the Koje POW camp time bomb was ticking faster. CIA agents had informed the UN high command that the hard-core Communist hanchos there were scheming to kidnap Brigadier General Francis T. Dodd, who had taken over as camp commandant. Despite this stern warning, Lieutenant Colonel Wilbur Raven, Dodd's aide, responded when he was summoned by POW leaders to report to Compound 76, which held 6,500 of the most militant Communists.

Amazingly, Raven strode alone into Compound 76. In a carefully conceived and executed operation, the POWs, loudly chanting slogans, surrounded the American and whisked him into a hut. When the mob dispersed, GI guards outside the barbed wire noticed that Raven had vanished.

Perhaps through a radio link between Pusan and Pyongyang, Premier Kim Il Sung learned that his "army" in Koje had kidnapped an American lieutenant colonel. After holding Raven for three hours, while the U.S. camp administration wrung its hands over how to recover the hostage, Raven was released. He was covered with bruises from being hit repeatedly, and his uniform was stained with the soup that had been poured over him.

Unbeknownst to the Americans, the seizing of a lieutenant colonel had been so easy that the POW leadership set its sights on kidnapping an even bigger target—General Dodd himself.

26

The Big Bug Bonanza

WHILE THE POW LEADERS AT KOJE were plotting to pull off a major coup, the Communists launched a global propaganda campaign accusing the United States of conducting germ warfare in North Korea and China. The cacophony of strident claims was trumpeted mainly by Communist China, but North Korea, the Soviet Union and its satellites, and sympathetic parties in the free world joined in the chorus.

In late February 1952, Mao Tse-tung's delegates at an Oslo, Norway, conference of the World Peace Committee, a Communist front, denounced the United States for the germ warfare "atrocity." Forty-eight hours later, Dr. Istvann Florian, head of the Communist-controlled Hungarian Red Cross, sent a cable to the headquarters of the International Red Cross in Switzerland. "Americans have hurled from their airplanes sickened insects upon the Korean People's Army, the Chinese Volunteers, and the rear areas," Florian declared. "The International Red Cross must raise its voice against these American atrocities."

Within hours, the Red Cross of Communist Poland and the Red Cross of Communist Russia leaped into the act, demanding that the United States be stopped from "inflicting this bacteriological war of mass extermination."

In New York, Soviet Ambassador to the United Nations Yakov Malik, in a long harangue, charged that U.S. soldiers in Korea were using bullets filled with toxic gases. In Peking on March 8, Chou En-lai, the Chinese foreign minister, announced that downed American airmen using bacteriological weapons would be tried as war criminals.

A week later, Chou claimed that the U.S. Air Force had flown 448 sorties to spread millions of germ-carrying beetles, lice, ticks, rats, fleas, and spiders over Manchuria as a prelude to an invasion of that Chinese province by American troops.

Communist propagandists charged that the United States was bent on wiping out the North Korean people. In an effort to infect the crops in that country, it was claimed, the Americans were dropping diseased grasshoppers, human and animal excrement, and dead birds. These infected items, carried in containers that looked like bombs, were scattered from special bacteria-proof planes, the Communists stated.

To back up their accusations that the United States had targeted the North Korean food crops, "scientific" papers were released to the world press by the ministry of agriculture in Pyongyang. Photos of wilted farm crops were provided as "proof" that diseased bugs and birds, along with excrement, were being sown by U.S. planes with the goal of starving women and children to death.

In China, Mao Tse-tung whipped the civilian population into a frenzy with an all-out "Hate America" campaign. Millions of people were mobilized to take preventive measures against America's germ warfare by killing bugs and insects. Later, Peking announced that this massive program had destroyed 120,000,000 rats and 1,500,000 pounds weight of flies, mosquitoes, fleas, and ticks. There was no mention of how this astronomical number of insects and rodents had been collected, sorted, counted and weighed.[1]

Carefully selected media reporters from around the world were invited to Peking to view an elaborate germ warfare exhibit featuring large glass containers said to contain germs that had been sown over North Korea. It was not explained how germs could be collected and placed in bottles.

Another highlight of the Peking exhibit was a hundred pounds of clams said to have been dropped on North Korea by U.S. airplanes. The clams were inspected by members of the International Scientific Commission, a group from Communist nations and a few Westerners, including Joseph Needham, a Cambridge University biochemist from London. The visiting delegation announced that the Americans had been clam-bombing North Korea. The mouths of clams, they declared, are perfect breeding places for cholera organisms.

In North Korea, reporters from Communist countries were taken on escorted tours to certain locales where largely illiterate, frightened, and confused civilians told how the American germs had destroyed their crops and infected their families with diseases.

In East Berlin, the World Peace Council, a Communist front, charged that Americans were not only raining infected organisms on North Korea, but had poisoned the fishing waters off the east and west coasts.

Dr. Hewlett Johnson, the dean of Canterbury Cathedral (widely known as the Red Dean), returned to England after a visit to Manchuria and told the British-China Friendship Association that he had been shown a test tube containing insects dropped on a North Korean village. "Facts about germ warfare are conclusive and irrefutable," Johnson declared.

In Moscow, *Pravda* labeled U.S. generals as "butchers in white gloves, the bloody bigots and traders in death who have unleashed the most inhuman carnage of history, warfare with the assistance of microbes, fleas, lice, and spiders."

Peking and Pyongyang repeatedly refused to allow on-site inspections by the International Red Cross and the World Health Organization, both of which the Communists branded as "tools and lackeys of the American imperialists."

In New York, Communist members of the UN General Assembly took to the floor to bitterly denounce the U.S. germ warfare offensive against the "innocent old men, women, and children of North Korea." The delegates demanded that these "inhuman atrocities" cease at once.

In Europe, tens of thousands of persons took part in Communist-sponsored protest rallies in Paris, Rome, London, Brussels, Madrid, and other major cities. Huge banners called for halting the killing of innocents by bacteria dropped by U.S. planes. Throngs cheered as effigies of Uncle Sam were hanged. Hundreds of American flags were burned. So convincing had been the global propaganda barrage that these rancorous rallies attracted large numbers of well-meaning peace activists who had no connection to Communist groups.

What the Chinese propagandists needed most to substantiate their germ warfare charges were confessions by the "culprits"—captured American pilots. So for many weeks, the captors subjected the pilot POWs to a brutal technique calculated to bring a man to the point where a dry crust of bread or a few hours' uninterrupted sleep was a great event in his life. The airmen were methodically reduced to a status lower than that of animals—filthy, lice-infested, with festering wounds full of maggots, unshaven, denied baths and haircuts, clad in rags, exposed to the harsh elements. Their water was served in rusty cans, and they were fed carefully measured quantities to allow them to exist just short of death.

Rotating squads of trained interrogators hammered at the American pilots night and day, browbeating them and depriving them of sleep. Selected POWs were "tried" as war criminals before a Communist court, convicted, and sentenced to death. Then the "war criminal" was put up against a wall and the firing squad squeezed triggers. All that was heard were clicks: The rifles were empty.

Finally, their spirit broken by brutality and threats, two U.S. pilots "confessed" that they had dropped diseased insects on North Korea as a part of a campaign to wipe out the population.

Most of the "confessions" were written for the pilots by Alan Winnington of the *Daily Worker*, London's Communist newspaper, and

Wilfred Burchett of Paris's pro-Communist *Ce Soir*. Incredibly, both reporters were accredited to the U.S. Eighth Army, where they, along with other Western correspondents, received regular briefings.

Burchett had been regarded, naively perhaps, by Marguerite Higgins of the New York *Herald Tribune* and a few other Western reporters as a misguided idealist. Winnington, however, had been despised because of his arrogant and haughty personality. On the occasion of Winnington's birthday, the American correspondents had presented the Briton with a cake, topped by a penis in pink icing. The wording read: "Happy Birthday, You Prick!"[2]

Now that Winnington and Burchett had switched from covering the war from the Eighth Army camp to the Communist side of the battle lines, they were of enormous help in coercing the American pilots into "confessing." Colonel Walker Mahurin, who had shot down twenty-one German planes in World War II and was one of the last American POWs to be coerced, would recall:

"Burchett and Winnington were writing the confessions and making us copy them and sign them. And, of course, in their [Communist] society, those confessions were going to jibe with each other because by that time they had all kinds of information so they could make them interrelate."[3]

Alone or in pairs, the American pilots were paraded before movie cameras to "confess" their involvement in the germ warfare. On hand were Winnington and Burchett, who always had with them an entourage of Chinese cameramen and reporters, a stark indicator of their importance to the Communists. These films were distributed throughout the world. Even scores of theaters in the United States showed them to astonished audiences.

Even though the Communist germ warfare propaganda included a slew of absurdities (such as photos of "special germ-hunting teams" picking bacteria off the ground with chopsticks), a huge amount of anti-American sentiment had been generated, not only in North Korea and China, but around the world. A few newspapers branded Americans as the "New Nazis." Cartoons of U.S. generals in Korea showed them in caps shaped like the exaggerated military headgear the Nazi generals had worn. The FBI was the "Gestapo," and the U.S. was ruled by "Chicago gangsters" who were stooges of "Wall Street." American bombardiers deliberately aimed at hospitals and schools and reveled in the bloodshed and destruction of innocents. Harry Truman was "a second Hitler" who was trying to conquer the entire world.

Washington's official reaction to the outlandish germ-warfare charge was to maintain a discreet silence. Presumably, this stance was intended to convey that the United States refused to dignify the accusation with a reply. However, much of the world interpreted the

Truman administration's muteness to mean that the United States had been caught red-handed and was too embarrassed to respond.[4]

For many months, the germ-warfare canard reverberated around the globe, and it would prove to be one of history's most successful propaganda hoaxes. In the meantime, Premier Kim Il Sung was ready to launch a carefully orchestrated scheme designed to give the Communists another gargantuan propaganda bonus—a major riot at the Koje POW camp.

Early on the morning of May 7, General Francis Dodd, the camp commandant, received a written "demand" from Colonel Lee Hak-ku, who the Americans thought was the senior officer, to report to him in Compound 76, the same stockade in which Lieutenant Colonel Raven had been kidnapped a few days earlier. Incredibly, Dodd decided to answer the summons of the North Korean colonel who was his prisoner.

At 2:00 P.M., Dodd and his aide, Colonel Raven, by now a veteran of kidnapping by enemy prisoners, arrived at the Compound 76 gate. Both Americans were unarmed. The gate was opened and Colonel Lee and a few other POWs stepped just outside the swinging barrier.

When the discussion got under way, Lee lodged the customary complaints about a need for more food, clothing, medical supplies, and other items. He "demanded" that the Soviet Union be accepted as a neutral nation to oversee the eventual exchange of POWs. All the while, other POWs were drifting up to the gate to listen to the discussion, which droned on until 3:15 P.M.

When Dodd turned to leave, perhaps twenty POWs rushed forward, seized the general, and hustled him off. Raven managed to elude a second kidnapping by clinging to the gate post until GI guards rescued him. It had been a closely timed operation. Within minutes, the jubilant POWs hoisted signs that they had painted on blankets earlier. The signs stated: "We capture General Dodd. If there is brutal act or shooting his life in danger."

That night, by coincidence, Lieutenant General Mark W. Clark arrived in Tokyo to replace Matt Ridgway as UN commander. Ridgway would take charge of the North Atlantic Treaty Organization (NATO) from General Dwight Eisenhower, who was retiring from the army, reportedly to seek the Republican nomination for president of the United States.

During World War I, Mark Clark had been wounded in France while serving as an infantry captain. At age forty-seven in the Second World War, he had been one of the youngest three-star generals in the army when he commanded the Fifth Army in Italy. One of his boosters had been Winston Churchill, who called Clark the "American

Eagle." Like his predecessors, MacArthur and Ridgway, Clark was bright and tough, and spoke his mind when required.[5]

Clark learned that General Van Fleet had reacted swiftly, dispatching tanks to Koje and appointing Brigadier General Charles F. Colson to succeed Dodd with orders to use military power if necessary to free the kidnapped officer.

Inside the barbed wire, the POWs "tried" Dodd as a war criminal and sentenced him to death. Hoping to save his life, Colson signed a document written for him by the POWs, agreeing to "cease immediately the barbarous behavior, insults, torture, [and] mass murdering of prisoners by UN guns, germs, poison gas, and atomic weapons."[6]

On the morning of May 10, General Colson received an ultimatum from the POW leaders. If he wanted to see his close friend Francis Dodd alive, he was ordered to sign another document stating, in part: "I do admit that there have been instances . . . in which POWs have been killed and wounded by UN forces. . . . I will do all I can to eliminate further violence and bloodshed."[7]

In Tokyo, Mark Clark was furious at Colson and promptly released a statement repudiating Colson's document-signing as being made "under duress."[8]

Dodd was released the next day, but the Communists exploited the two signed documents as "further proof of UN atrocities." This had been the goal of Premier Kim Il Sung when he had dispatched General Pak Sang-hyon (masquerading as Private Jeon) to Koje a few months earlier to organize a mass breakout.[9]

Replacing Colson as camp commander was the hard-nosed, battle-tested General Haydon "Bull" Boatner. His orders were to break the Communist control of the camps by moving the hard-core POWs to smaller, more secure compounds. As an initial test, Boatner ordered the Chinese POWs to remove a Communist flag and statue of Josef Stalin from their compound and gave them until noon the next day to do so. Boatner was told the Chinese equivalent of "Go to hell!"

Boatner intended to dramatize to the POWs that he meant business. At noon, a platoon of infantrymen and two tanks entered the compound, removed the flag and statue, and withdrew from the camp, all within five minutes.[10]

When Boatner was ready to move the tens of thousands of POWs to new compounds, he gave written orders with a specific date for them to comply voluntarily. The Chinese wanted to negotiate. "POWs don't negotiate!" Boatner replied sharply.

Just before dawn on June 10, precisely one month after the release of General Dodd, loudspeakers outside Compound 76 ordered the POWs there to form into groups of one hundred so they could be marched to a new compound in thirty minutes. Silence. Standing on a low hill overlooking the sprawling camp, Boatner gave a signal. A flare shot into the sky. Elements of the 187th Airborne Regimental Combat Team, with bayonets fixed, pitched tear-gas grenades into Compound 76 as Patton tanks crunched forward, knocked down fence posts, and crushed the barbed wire into the dust. Wearing gas masks, the paratroopers moved in behind the tanks.

A few thousand frenzied POWs, chanting and hurling stones, homemade grenades, spears, and Molotov cocktails, charged into the paratroopers. A hand-to-hand battle ensued. Some Americans were felled by clubs, spears, and barbed-wire flails. When six Patton tanks entered the compound, the wild melee ended and the POWs were subdued. Not a shot had been fired by the keenly disciplined paratroopers. One airborne man had been killed and fourteen were wounded.

Boatner, armed to the teeth, strode into the smoke-filled Compound 76 to take charge of the sixty-five hundred die-hard Communists who meekly marched off to their new, smaller enclosure. Strewn about the premises were the bodies of forty-one POWs who had been killed in the two-hour-long battle. Two hundred seventy-four POWs were wounded.[11]

A huge cache of POW weapons was found: a thousand Molotov cocktails, forty-five hundred knives, three thousand tent-pole spears, and hundreds of clubs, hatchets, flails, and hammers. Paratroopers found Colonel Lee Hak-ku hiding in a ditch and hauled him out roughly. They also discovered two detailed sets of plans, one for the defense of the POW camp if the Americans tried to take it over and the other for a mass breakout set for June 20.[12]

In the wake of the Koje violence, a torrential burst of indignation erupted in the Communist media around the world. The orchestrated propaganda theme, planned long in advance, focused on the "massacre of helpless POWs by bloodthirsty American warmongers." *Pravda* screamed: "Koje Island! Again the gloomy shadow of Maidenek [a Nazi concentration camp] has come upon the world. Again the stench of corpses. We have learned that 'civilized' Americans can be yet more inhuman, more infamous, than the bloody Hitlerites. . . . The American hangmen are torturing, tormenting, and killing unarmed people. . . . The Koje butchers will not escape."[13]

General Mark Clark tried vigorously to counter the Communist propaganda barrage by explaining the true circumstances of events at Koje. His voice was drowned out by the Communists, who had the world's ear and were shouting too noisily for anyone else to be heard.

By May 22, 1952, Admiral Turner Joy, who had suppressed his true emotions no matter how bitterly he and the United States were attacked through ten months and twelve days of almost constant bickering at the on-again, off-again Panmunjom peace talks, finally became convinced that it was hopeless to try to deal in good faith with the Communists. At the close of negotiations that day, he told the Communist delegation:

"From the very start, you have caviled over procedural details; you have manufactured spurious issues and placed them in controversy for bargaining purposes; you have denied the existence of agreements made between us; you have made false charges based on crimes invented for your purposes; and you indulged in abuse and invective when all other tactics proved ineffective. . . . You impute to the United Nations Command the same suspicion, greed, and deviousness which are your stock in trade. You search every word for a hidden meaning and every agreement for a hidden trap."

Joy then introduced his replacement, U.S. Major General William K. Harrison, and said, "May God be with him!"

Despite his discouragement over failure to reach an armistice agreement, Joy had achieved much at the bargaining table. He had successfully negotiated all major issues except the one apparently insoluble one—the repatriation of POWs. Doggedly, the Communists insisted that all prisoners be returned to each side.

General Harrison was a descendant of a famous family that included a signer of the Declaration of Independence and two presidents. He was blessed with two attributes that would hold him in good stead at the bargaining table—a happy disposition and a tough mind. He would brook no nonsense from the Communist delegation.

After several days of incessant wrangling over inconsequential points, Harrison got to his feet, looked General Nam Il directly in the eye, and calmly said: "Apparently the only way I can convince you that I mean what I say is to get up and go out."

Harrison and his staff filed out of the tent as Nam Il, who was not prepared for the likes of the American general, stared after them in confusion and bewilderment.

27

An Intricate Invasion Hoax

ACROSS THE NARROW WAIST OF KOREA in the summer of 1952, the UN and Communist forces were locked in a stalemate in the vicinity of the 38th Parallel. Soldiers on each side dug deep bunkers along the crests of peaks and ridges. Miles of barbed-wire entanglements were erected. Almost nightly patrols clashed in sharp, brief fights in no-man's-land.

Although "stalemate" meant to those in the United States that nothing was happening at the front, casualties were heavy and fighting was bitter as the Chinese and North Korean forces tried to seize high ground overlooking the UN main defensive line. Correspondents changed landlords frequently, and mountain peaks were given fanciful names by the GIs.

In these bloody battles, the U.S. 1st Marine Division fought for Bunker Hill; the U.S. 7th Infantry Division was on Triangle Hill; the U.S. 25th Infantry Division and the Turkish Brigade were on Heartbreak Ridge; the ROK 8th Division was in the Punchbowl region; the U.S. 3rd Infantry Division, with attached Greek and Belgian battalions, defended Kelly Hill and Big Nori; and the U.S. 2nd Infantry Division and its French battalion were clinging to Old Baldy and Arrowhead Hill.

In Washington, the Joint Chiefs, hoping to exert pressure on the Communists to force them into a settlement at Panmunjom, issued instructions to Mark Clark: "Maintain unrelenting military pressure on the enemy, particularly through air action. No major ground action should be contemplated at this time."[1]

Orders from the Joint Chiefs directed that leaflets warning North Korean civilians to evacuate were to be dropped on towns two or three days before a bomber force arrived to plaster supply depots, railroad yards, and other military targets. Code-named Plan Blast, this leaflet-dropping technique was intended to reduce civilian casualties. A sidebar was that masses of fleeing civilians would clog the narrow roads and hamper Chinese and North Korean military traffic.

Lieutenant General Glenn O. Barcus, who had taken command of the Fifth Air Force at about the same time Mark Clark was ordered to step up the heat on the Communists, took note of the "partial paralysis" that had settled over UN forces in Korea and resolved that Fifth Air Force would attack the Communists with "increasing vigor and efficiency."[2]

In an effort to supplement the leaflet-dropping, Barcus released to media reporters the identity of eighty targeted towns. That humanitarian action ignited nervous tics in the State Department, which was concerned that Communist propagandists would flip-flop Barcus's true intention and howl to the world that the Americans had a "hit list" for bombing North Korea back to the Stone Age.

Based on the State Department protest, the leaflet warnings were discontinued. However, Communists leaped on the eighty-town target list as a propaganda theme. In Moscow, *Pravda* trumpeted that the "hit list" was a devious American scheme to demolish North Korean factories, thereby depriving that country of a chance to join the modern world. Radio Peking complained loudly that the B-29 raids were designed to annihilate the civilian population under the guise of bombing military targets.

Propagandists at the Far East headquarters in Tokyo tried to blunt the considerable impact of the Communist charges. But it proved to be a losing battle. Civilians are bound to be killed in any bombing raid. So it was impossible to counter the photos of demolished schools and houses and wounded and dead children that the Communists were sending to media around the world.

In Washington, President Truman was growing more frustrated by the failure of the Panmunjom negotiators to reach a settlement that would end the shooting war. So he gave the green light to a plan of the Far East Air Force to bomb the major hydroelectric system—Suiho, Pusen, Chosin, Kyosen, Funei, and Kongosan—on the North Korean side of the Yalu River. These facilities provided power for much of North Korea and southern Manchuria. "If [these plants] were suddenly destroyed, it would deny electrical power to many war factories and might impress the North Koreans with the price they are paying for their continued recalcitrance," General Otto P. "Opie" Weyland, leader of the Fifth Air Force, declared.[3]

Almost from the outbreak of the war, General MacArthur had made numerous requests to wipe out the hydroelectric system, but his plan always had been rejected. Now, Truman's approval reflected the growing desperation in Washington to seek a cease-fire or an armistice.

On June 23, the previously untouchable power facilities were heavily bombed by five hundred UN aircraft, most of them American. Twenty-four hours later, two hundred bombers returned to finish the job.

During the war, the North Koreans had carved out the center of the Moranbong, a historic old mountain in the heart of Pyongyang, and converted it into a lavish, bombproof theater that was used by Kim Il Sung and other Communist officials for parties and receptions. The walls leading down into the big salon were decorated with portraits of Josef Stalin and Mao Tse-tung, posters showing how the Americans were practicing germ warfare in North Korea, and rousing slogans of Communist brotherhood like "Long Live the Friendship of the Korean and Soviet Peoples."

On the night of August 29, Pawel Monat, the young Polish military attaché who had ridden on the train from Mukden with Soviet pilots and combat troops dressed in Chinese Volunteers' uniforms, was driving toward Moranbong to celebrate a Bulgarian holiday. He hated the idea of going there and having to watch the bosses of Korean Communism—along with their local Chinese, Soviet, Hungarian, Mongolian, Rumanian, Bulgarian, and Polish comrades—spend seven or eight hours gorging themselves on fine food and vodka in the midst of a war in which the ordinary people were suffering and starving. The big shots danced with the Korean nurses and women soldiers and made long-winded speeches about how the American barbarians were killing their wives and children.

As Colonel Monat tooled along the road from the Polish embassy to Pyongyang, he had no way of knowing that spies had informed the UN high command of this night's social gathering in the Moranbong and the Far East Air Force was going to celebrate the occasion with a massive attack called the "All United Nations Air Effort." Carrier-based aircraft would join in the strike, which would include 1,403 sorties. While paying their respects to Kim Il Sung and his cronies in the Moranbong, the bombers also would drop explosives on Pyongyang's government buildings, Radio Pyongyang, and the Ministry of Rail Transportation headquarters.

As Monat and his driver neared the city, he heard the loud gongs sounding an air-raid alert. Bombs—hundreds of them—were falling. Fires were raging, and the people were screaming and running for shelter. Monat and his driver took shelter in a shallow hole near the road. Then, when the sound of powerful aircraft engines and bomb explosions ended, the two men drove on to the Moranbong. The mountain was pockmarked with bomb craters, but the celebrants inside were untouched.

Monat walked down the 150 steps into the shelter. There, with Pyongyang burning and virtually a pile of rubble, Monat had to listen while Kim Il Sung proposed a toast to the brotherhood of Communism and to "final victory." How, the Pole asked himself, could there be any "final victory" for the people of North Korea, so ruthlessly sacrificed by their own leaders?[4]

Mindful that his current mission was to keep heavy pressure on the Chinese and North Korean armed forces without getting his foot soldiers and tankers involved in bloody slugfests, Mark Clark hatched an intricate hoax. It would be the most extensive deception operation since Plan Bodyguard, the scheme that hoodwinked Adolf Hitler on the date and location of the Normandy invasion during World War II.

Most of the Chicoms and In Min Gun units had gone to ground after the stalemate set in, but Clark hoped to lure them into the open where the UN's monstrous airpower and big naval guns could wreak havoc on them. He wanted to alarm the Communist generals, to keep them off balance, to cause them to shift troops around, and to divert manpower and effort to construct defenses along both coasts of North Korea.[5]

On October 3, 1952, Clark set the wheels in motion for the hoax by issuing a letter of instructions. D-day would be October 15, and the target for the phony airborne-amphibious landing would be near the east coast port of Kojo, about fifty miles north of the battlefront.

Spearheading the seaborne assault would be the U.S. 1st Cavalry Division, which was garrisoned in Japan after months of heavy fighting in Korea. The cavalrymen were put through rigorous amphibious training, including a full-scale landing rehearsal. As intended, word of the 1st Cav's activities was bound to get back to Communist intelligence, because there was no shortage of spies in Japan.

Clark's operational order called for the 187th Airborne Regimental Combat Team to bail out inland from Kojo prior to H-hour and link up with the 1st Cav coming in over the beach. Only high-ranking UN commanders were aware that the entire scenario would be called off at virtually the last minute.

As D-day neared, preparations reached a feverish pitch—mainly for the eyes and ears of Communist spies. Air force and navy pilots launched heavy strikes ostensibly intended to soften up the east coast of North Korea for an amphibious assault. Communist army barracks, antiaircraft batteries, railroad junctions, headquarters, and supply dumps were pounded.

Minesweeping vessels—war's unsung heroes—chugged along the coastline in the Kojo region. In the Naktong valley of South Korea, a region infested with Communist guerrillas and secret agents, battalion-sized paratroop and heavy equipment drops were made, presumably in preparation for a combat operation. Then, the 187th Airborne Regimental Combat Team was confined to its camp. On D-day minus 1, the paratroopers climbed into transport planes. Then, much to the men's astonishment, instead of heading for Kojo, they were flown back to Japan.[6]

The phony scenario continued to unfold. At 3:00 A.M. on D-day, crews of the 403d Troop Carrier Wing, based at Ashiya Air Force Base in Japan, were rousted from bed and informed that they had been ordered to fly a feint toward the North Korean coast. That was the first they knew about the Kojo hoax. There was heavy grumbling. Generals were roundly castigated for dreaming up silly schemes to get men out of their beds in the middle of the night.

Two hours later, just before dawn, thirty-two C-119 Flying Boxcars, presumably loaded with American paratroopers but actually carrying only air crews, lifted off from Ashiya and headed westward in tight formation across the Sea of Japan. Near Kojo, the huge transports dropped to eight hundred feet (the paratroop-drop altitude), then wheeled abruptly southward and flew to an airfield at Taegu.

That morning, the mightiest naval task force assembled since the end of World War II bore down on the Kojo coast and dropped anchor offshore. At 2:00 P.M., men of the 8th Cavalry Regiment scrambled down rope nets tossed over the side of transport ships, jumped into assault boats, and headed for the beach. When the first wave was within four thousand yards of shore, the landing craft suddenly reversed direction and returned to the transports, which then sailed southward to Pusan.

High-level evaluation of the Communists' reaction to the elaborate false-alarm spoof indicated that the enemy generals had been "genuinely afraid of the amphibious threat" deep in their rear and had rushed troops and artillery to the Kojo locale. Because the movements were made at night, however, the Chinese and North Korean forces did not present the juicy targets for UN air and naval-gun power that had been hoped.[7]

One stark factor indicated that the hoax had achieved a second desired result—forcing the Communists back to the negotiating table, which they had abandoned in one of their periodic piques. Within twenty-four hours of the Kojo high jinks Kim Il Sung and General Peng Teh-huai, the Chinese commander in Korea, fired off a strongly worded protest to Clark about the recess in the peace talks, blaming the Americans for the lull, and indicating they were eager to get back to the bargaining table.

At the same time that the Kojo operation was in progress, intelligence officers of the Fifth Air Force were informed, through reports from CIA spies, that the North Koreans had established the "Kumgang Political School" at Odong-ni. The secret facility was actually an espionage-training institution where one thousand men were undergoing six months of intensive instructions. After graduation, nearly all of the new agents were to infiltrate South Korea on the ground, by parachute, or by sea. This would result in a massive penetration of Communist agents, who would blend in with the civilian population and be relatively safe from detection by UN counterintelligence units.

U.S. reconnaissance planes were sent over Odong-ni, and photos confirmed the existence of the spy installation. Fifth Air Force laid on an attack for October 25. In the first wave, B-26s dropped general-purpose and fragmentation bombs, and eighty-four fighter-bombers finished demolishing the spy school with explosives and napalm.

In Tokyo, General Mark Clark was so frustrated by the gridlock in the Panmunjom peace talks that he cabled the Joint Chiefs to authorize the bombing of Manchuria, which Douglas MacArthur had described as the Communist armed forces "privileged sanctuary." Clark added: "I consider it necessary that plans be made for the use of atomic weapons."

Harry Truman promptly rejected the proposal even though he himself had threatened to use this ultimate weapon. Perhaps Truman's response was influenced by the fact that he was a lame-duck president. He had chosen not to seek reelection, so any use of atomic bombs or shells in Korea would be left to his successor in the White House.

By now, most Americans were fed up with the seemingly endless war in Korea and the often fruitless peace negotiations that the Communists had strung out for nearly fifteen months to provide them with a propaganda forum to rant about germ warfare and U.S. "atrocities." The initial burst of home-front patriotism largely had evaporated, hastened along by the heavy American casualty toll.

In late October 1952, the presidential campaign was heating up. Up to now, the Republican candidate, Dwight Eisenhower, had been promising vaguely to work for a just and lasting peace. Most of this rhetoric fell on deaf ears. Then the retired five-star general and World War II hero electrified voters with a political blockbuster: "If elected, I shall go to Korea!"

That verbal stroke of genius caused the Eisenhower campaign to take off like a greased rocket. Good old Ike was going to go to Korea, wave his magic wand, and bring an end to the war. When the votes were counted, Eisenhower had swamped his opponent, former Illinois Governor Adlai Stevenson, 442 electoral votes to 89.

Keeping his campaign promise, President-elect Eisenhower went to Korea, arriving on December 2, for a three-day tour that included a reunion with his son, Lieutenant John Eisenhower, then serving as a battalion operations officer in the 15th Infantry Regiment.

Mark Clark and Jim Van Fleet huddled with Eisenhower and tried to sell him on a plan to win the war militarily, including the use of Chiang Kai-shek's Nationalist Chinese troops and dropping atomic bombs.[8]

Clark and Van Fleet no doubt had a deep emotional interest in winning the conflict. The Eighth Army commander's son, James Van Fleet Jr., had been killed in action, and Clark's son, William, had been wounded three times while fighting with the 9th Infantry Regiment. Eisenhower, however, displayed little if any interest in these proposals, leaving Clark and Van Fleet to conclude that the president-elect would continue the Truman policy of seeking a negotiated peace.[9]

28

Disaster on a CIA Mission

BY EARLY WINTER OF 1952, Operation Tropic, a CIA project that was parachuting spies and supporting guerrilla bands in Communist China, had been functioning for a year and now was getting into high gear. Much of Tropic's focus was on Liaoning and Kirin, the Manchurian provinces through which the Communists were sending Chinese troops over the Yalu into North Korea by rail and by road, and where they were basing their large numbers of modern jet aircraft and stockpiling huge caches of weapons, shells, and ammunition.

Recruitment of agents by the CIA for Tropic was centered on Hong Kong, the British crown colony, which has a primarily Chinese population. These recruits were hired by the Far East Development Company, a CIA front, ostensibly to work in a civilian capacity on Guam, a large island in the mid-Pacific and the scene of a bitter battle in World War II. Guam was still in need of extensive rebuilding, the recruits were told.

In batches, the agent recruits were flown, instead, to Saipan, another Pacific island, which was being managed by the Navy Technical Unit, also a fake organization. There they were given parachute training, instructed on operating a radio, taught the rudiments of handling explosives, and given lessons in the use of small arms. Then the Chinese recruits were formed into teams and taught how to set up secure bases, establish radio networks, and memorize simple codes—all the basic skills needed for guerrilla and espionage missions.[1]

Tropic involved double deceit by the CIA. Its existence would have to be concealed from the Chinese Communists and North Koreans. And Chiang Kai-shek, who was supposed to be a close ally of the United States, also would have to be kept in the dark. The reason for not informing him about Tropic was that most of the guerrillas in Kirin and Liaoning provinces were not necessarily loyal to the Chinese Nationalist leader. Rather, they were opposed to the Communists.

Tropic operational missions began in April 1952. Briefings were held at the Joint Technical Advisory Group (Jay-Tag) base, the CIA complex that Hans Tofte had built near Atsugi Airport in Japan. From there, a C-47 assigned to a mission flew to either Pusan or Seoul, picked up its spies or guerrilla leaders, and then headed northward in the direction of Manchuria. En route, the pilots made wide swings on occasion to avoid detection by U.S. radar, whose technicians knew nothing about the covert operation.

Nearing the Manchuria drop zone, the C-47 would zoom in low and watch for a visual signal from the ground, usually a blinking flashlight. On word from the pilot, the two CIA agents in the cabin would line up the Chinese agents and have each recheck his parachute. Then, when a green light flashed on, the spies would leap out into the black unknown.

Typical of the derring-do Tropic pilots who flew the night skies over North Korea and Manchuria was twenty-two-year-old John T. Downey, a native of New Britain, Connecticut, and the son of a prominent judge. In the spring of 1951, young Downey had just completed his senior year at Yale University, where he was a 195-pound guard on the football team and wrestled on the varsity squad.[2]

Downey was regarded as among Yale's best and brightest, and he looked forward to entering law school in the fall. Then, a CIA recruiter, masquerading as a business executive seeking young talent for his firm, visited the Yale campus and spoke at length with Downey about the excitement of parachuting and operating behind enemy lines. Downey was hooked; law school could wait.

"During the Korean War there was a big mix of idealism and self-interest," he would explain. "I certainly had no doubt we were the good guys—Communist North Korea had invaded South Korea. CIA was a new outfit, rumored to be red-hot."[3]

Downey was not alone in sensing excitement. "Hey, that was as glamorous as anything we could hope for," he would say. "A large number of the outstanding people in my class applied."[4]

Downey's first CIA assignment was at Fort Benning, Georgia, an infantry center, although he retained a civilian status. After three months of intensive and rigorous training, he became a GS-7, which was equivalent to a second lieutenant in the army, and drew the first increments of his $3,100 annual salary. After going to the Jay-Tag base at Atsugi for briefings and more training, Downey was told that his first secret mission would be to organize a guerrilla and espionage network in Kirin Province.

In April 1952, he flew to the recruit training base on Saipan and picked Chinese agents to form a four-man team, led by Chang Tsai-wen, a twenty-eight-year-old native of Kirin. Known as Team Wen, the intruders dropped in his home province three months later.

It soon became clear to the CIA planners at Atsugi that dropping agents over Manchuria was not nearly as difficult or hazardous as spiriting them back out. So an ingenious technique, worthy of Rube Goldberg, was developed. A pair of long, sturdy poles were driven firmly into the ground and a strong wire was stretched tautly between the uprights. Connected to the wire was a heavy line that led to a harness worn by the man to be picked up. Then a C-47 would fly just above ground level toward the contraption at about sixty miles an hour (just fast enough to keep from stalling) and hook onto the wire, snatching the man into the air. As the aircraft resumed speed, the agent would be reeled into the C-47, much like a large catch being hauled into a fishing boat.[5]

Repeated practice runs were made. The clay pigeons (Chinese agent recruits) stood a chance of getting their heads jerked loose from torsos if the technique failed. However, the procedure seemed to work, and the first snatching of a CIA agent in Manchuria was set for the night of November 29.

After darkness, four CIA men boarded a C-47 at the Seoul airport to make the pickup: John Downey; Richard G. Fecteau, who had been with the CIA only a few months; Captain Norman A. Schwartz, a gifted athlete who had flown marine fighter planes in World War II; and Captain Robert C. Snoddy, who had been involved in the ill-fated Li Mi project in Burma.

For three hours, the C-47 flew northward in routine fashion. Then, just as the craft neared the designated site where the Rube Goldberg–like apparatus had been set up, a torrent of fire erupted from the dark ground. Riddled with bullets, the lumbering, unarmed transport plane spun sideways and crashed. Snoddy and Schwartz were killed; Downey and Fecteau, although shaken and cut up, survived and were taken prisoners by a Chicom patrol that had been lurking nearby. Only later would Downey learn that Communist intelligence earlier had captured members of Team Wen, the four CIA agents that Downey had dropped the previous April. Under torture, one or more of them disclosed Downey's mission to snatch the spy from the ground.[6]

When Downey's C-47 failed to return, John H. Mason, a highly decorated infantry combat leader in World War II who was now in charge of operations at the CIA complex at Atsugi, was deeply worried. No doubt a catastrophe of some sort had occurred. Yet the existence of the clandestine operations in which spies were being dropped in Kirin and Liaoning provinces had to be concealed. So a cover story was put out on radio and in newspapers that a civilian C-47 had vanished while on a routine flight from Seoul to Japan. An extensive air-sea rescue search was launched to inject credence to the cover story.

Unbeknownst to the CIA, Jack Downey and Dick Fecteau were alive and being held in a Chinese prison. For months, the two men were grilled relentlessly in an effort to obtain detailed information about the CIA. Neither American would admit he belonged to the covert agency.[7]

Then Radio Peking announced that Downey, who was described as "an arch-criminal," had been tried as a spy and sentenced to life in prison. Fecteau, for some reason, was judged to be less culpable, and he was given a twenty-year term.[8]

Early in February 1953, a vast number of CIA agents in Korea, Japan, and China had a new boss in Washington. Beetle Smith, who had energized and greatly expanded the clandestine agency since taking the helm in late 1950, was shifted to the State Department as undersecretary. Replacing him as CIA director was the veteran cloak-and-dagger operative Allen Dulles, the pipe-smoking minister's son who had made a big name for himself as OSS station chief in Switzerland in World War II.[9]

Dulles relished cooking up undercover schemes but, like many persons blessed with creative talent, he detested the administrative part of his job. So Lieutenant General Charles P. Cabell, his deputy director, assumed the task of handling internal management. During World War II, Cabell commanded a wing of the Eighth Air Force in Europe and later was director of intelligence for the Allied Air Forces in the Mediterranean. After the conflict, he rose to director of Air Force intelligence before being assigned to the CIA.

At about the same time that Allen Dulles took the CIA reins, there was a major command change in South Korea. On February 11, Lieutenant General Maxwell Taylor, who had gained fame in World War II as leader of the crack 101st Airborne Division in Europe, was sent by President Eisenhower to relieve Jim Van Fleet as commander of Eighth Army.

Taylor was aware of Eisenhower's goal of holding down casualties and obtaining a rapid but honorable peace. Only hours after Taylor arrived, the Chinese launched a heavy assault that kicked the U.S. 7th Infantry Division off the hill Old Baldy. Chagrined, the division commander asked for permission to take back the peak, but Taylor refused, dismissing the Chinese assault as a "face-saving propaganda maneuver."[10]

Jim Van Fleet returned to the United States a bitter and frustrated man. In *Life* magazine, he loosed a blast at Truman and the State Department. "We could have beaten the [Communists] in the spring of 1951," he declared. "Our offensive caught the Chinese by complete surprise. We could have followed up our success, but that was not the intention of Washington. Our State Department had already let the Reds know that we were willing to settle on the 38th Parallel."

Less than three weeks after Max Taylor reached South Korea, Radio Moscow made an announcement: "The heart of the comrade and inspired continuer of Lenin's will, the beloved leader and teacher of the Communist Party and the Soviet people—Josef Vissarionovich Stalin—has stopped beating."

Much of the Communist world was stunned. Death had removed the leader who had probably ordered, or at least encouraged, the invasion of South Korea. Taking his place would be Georgi M. Malenkov, another hard-liner. Ten days later, the new dictator made a speech in which he declared that there was no existing dispute between Moscow and Washington that "cannot be decided by peaceful means." Soviet propagandists highly touted the oration.

Eisenhower's hawkish secretary of state, John Foster Dulles (brother of the CIA chief), brushed off Malenkov's speech as "more Communist trickery." Over Dulles's objections, Eisenhower responded with a speech in which he challenged Malenkov to match his words with specific deeds, including "an honorable armistice" in Korea.[11]

Meanwhile, a revolutionary new battlefield weapon developed by U.S. scientists on an isolated range in New Mexico triggered serious reevaluation of the deadlocked situation in Korea. The new mass destruction device was an atomic warhead small enough to be used in field artillery shells.

In a blockbuster study finalized on March 27, the Joint Chiefs declared:

> The timely use of atomic weapons [in Korea] should be considered against military targets affecting operations, [including] any possible military course of direct action against Communist China and Manchuria.[12]

Another Pentagon study suggested launching a wide-ranging offensive if the recessed Panmunjom peace talks were not resumed and an armistice successfully negotiated. Naval and air attacks would hit China and Manchuria, including "extensive strategical and tactical use of atomic bombs." Twenty-four hours later, the National Security Council put its stamp of approval on these Joint Chiefs recommendations.[13]

Dwight Eisenhower's challenge to the Communist leaders to replace their words of peace with deeds had fallen on deaf ears. So now the president turned hawkish. In a dramatic move, he announced that the U.S. Seventh Fleet would be withdrawn from patrolling the Strait of Formosa. "We certainly have no obligation to protect a nation [Communist China] fighting us in Korea," Eisenhower declared. At the same time, a green light was flashed by the White House for the CIA to accelerate guerrilla raids against the Chinese mainland.

Because the Chinese Nationalist guerrillas had been trained and were already in place on the string of islands offshore from the mainland, stepping up the raids was a simple matter. Soon Radio Peking was howling loudly about "adventurous American imperialists supporting the running dogs of the tyrant Chiang." Those running dogs were the CIA agents, such as James Smith, the World War II combat marine veteran on Chin-men, and the other Americans who had organized and armed the guerrillas.[14]

Up to now, Smith and the other CIA men on Chin-men had had to snoop out the location of the patrolling Seventh Fleet before sending guerrillas in junks across the Formosa Strait to raid installations on the mainland. Now, in light of Eisenhower's edict, the presence (or lack of presence) of the Seventh Fleet was no longer a factor. Therefore, by the Chinese Communists' own count as related over Radio Peking, more than two hundred raids and incursions hit the mainland during a four-month period.

By coincidence, or so it was made to appear, hard-line Secretary of State John Foster Dulles was on a diplomatic trip to the Far East and Asia in late May 1953. During his tour, he called on Prime Minister Jawaharlal Nehru in New Delhi, India. Nehru, who had graduated from Harrow School and Cambridge University in England, had played a leading role in gaining his country's independence from Great Britain, and he had become the first prime minister in 1947. He had often spoken out against atomic bomb tests of the United States and the Soviet Union.

Although India was neutral in the Korean War, U.S. leaders felt that the Nehru government was "more neutral" toward the North Korean and Chinese Communists. Much of the U.S. suspicion had been generated by the actions of K. M. Panikkar, the Indian ambassador to Peking, who was believed to be pro-Communist and anti-American. One factor was clear in Washington: Panikkar had a cozy relationship with Chou En-lai, the Chinese Communists' foreign minister.

Now, in New Delhi, Dulles pulled no punches in laying out America's new hard-line stance. Unless a settlement of the Korean War was not reached soon, he told Nehru, the United State would not hesitate to use both atomic bombs and atomic artillery shells against Manchuria and mainland China. Dulles urged Nehru to make known this position to Mao Tse-tung in Peking.

During the late winter of 1952 and spring of 1953 on the static Korean battlefront, "loudspeaker warfare" broke out. The Americans had developed tactical propaganda over loudspeakers to a fine science. Not only did success in loudspeaker operations depend on knowing the identity of the Communist unit across the front line, but the message had to be as personal as possible and in the targeted soldiers' own dialect. It was shattering to a Communist unit's morale to be secretly inserted into the front line, then have an American loudspeaker blare out the unit's designation and even mention by name one or two of its men.

Where possible, South Korean soldiers or Chinese POWs spoke over the loudspeakers, thereby eliminating the accents of American voices and making the message seem more personal because it was being spoken by a fellow Chinese or Korean. A typical loudspeaker message might begin with: "Hello there, soldiers of the 6th Regiment! Welcome back to the war! Sergeant Pang and Corporal Chai, what are your loved ones back home doing tonight? They miss you and will grieve when you fail to return."

U.S. intelligence learned that these loudspeaker propaganda broadsides were having considerable impact on enemy morale. Communist officers began to order their men to shoot weapons, ring bells, shout, and bang on empty containers to drown out the loudspeakers.

Especially during Chinese and Korean holidays, nostalgic music, intended to make soldiers homesick, blared out across no-man's-land from UN positions. To play on the Oriental superstitions that were widely prevalent among the enlisted men, eerie sounds were sent out over the loudspeakers on dark and windy nights.

Two C-47 aircraft of the U.S. 21st Troop Carrier Squadron were equipped with loudspeakers mounted on their bellies. Designated "the Speaker" and "the Voice," the C-47s flew five thousand feet above Communist lines and blared propaganda messages about surrendering and empty stomachs and certain death. Flying loudspeakers often used South Korean WACs to gain propaganda mileage from an Oriental prejudice. It was humiliating to the Chinese and North Korean soldiers to have a *woman* fly back and forth over their front lines without being shot down.

On one occasion, "the Voice" called on a large Chinese group to surrender. Then the speaker said a smoke screen would be laid in front of its position by UN artillery and urged them to run through it to safety. The smoke screen was needed to protect surrendering soldiers from being shot by their own officers. Several Communist soldiers did bolt through the smoke to UN lines.

"Talking tanks"—loudspeakers mounted on Patton tanks—closely followed GI infantrymen. At an appropriate time, the Patton halted and a North Korean POW inside called over the loudspeaker to his fellow countrymen: "Cease fighting now and save your life for your family!" In an effort to create friction between North Korean and Chinese soldiers, the talking tank referred to Mao Tse-tung's troops as *foreign* Communists.

GIs and marines, living like moles in bunkers that honeycombed the mountainsides, found Communist loudspeaker propaganda a welcome relief from the monotony and fear of impending death that is the lot of a front-line soldier. Just past 1:00 A.M. on a dark night in April, Marine rifleman Martin Russ left with several comrades for a patrol into no-man's-land. After stealing ahead for several hundred yards, the patrol heard a Chinese loudspeaker begin blaring from a hill the Americans called Siberia. The program seemed interesting, so Russ and his comrades lay down to listen. Many of the phrases were comic opera in tone. A voice in cracked English declared: "Ike is one of the leaders who could bring about peace in Korea. But, like the rest of the big-money boys, he is not interested in peace."[15]

Eisenhower, who had come from a hardworking but poor Kansas farm family and had earned only an army officer's pay during his adult life, no doubt would have been intrigued to learn that the Communists regarded him as a "big-money boy."

29

Operation Moolah: A $100,000 Bribe

ON THE NIGHT OF APRIL 26, 1953, two B-29 Superfortresses winged along the North Korean side of the Yalu River and scattered more than one million leaflets written in Chinese, North Korean, and Russian. A few days later, a half-million similar leaflets were dropped on Communist airfields above the 38th Parallel. The dramatic message may have been the most bizarre in the history of warfare: Any Communist pilot who would fly his MiG-15 jet to Kimpo airfield (near Seoul) would be awarded $50,000 and political asylum in a country of his choosing. The first pilot to accept the offer would receive an additional $50,000.[1]

A footnote on the leaflets stated: "This is a message from the Americans to any jet pilot who can *read* Russian. If you know such a person, please give it to him." For whatever reason, U.S. PsyWar specialists, who had created the message, had chosen not to allude directly to what most American pilots already felt was the case: Soviet pilots were flying combat missions over North Korea.

Two days after the tons of leaflets were sprinkled around North Korea, General Mark Clark repeated the message in a broadcast over the UN radio in Tokyo. After he spoke, his words were translated into Chinese, Korean, and Russian.[2]

UN suspicions that the Soviets were secretly involved in the shooting war intensified shortly after the broadcasts began. An unlocated but powerful jammer blocked the Russian language translation. Curiously, it did not jam the Chinese or Korean language airings.

There were ample clues that Soviet pilots had been and were flying the swift and highly maneuverable MiG-15s, which outclassed all the warplanes in the UN arsenal. For one, the solid red star of the

Soviet air force was painted on fuselages and wings, rather than Chinese or North Korean markings. Also, for nearly two years, UN pilots had reported hearing Russian voices on the radios when engaged in dogfights, and, periodically, they saw "Caucasian faces" under billowing parachutes after a MiG-15 pilot leaped from his damaged plane. Moreover, many of the enemy pilots were so skilled that the U.S. flyers felt they had to be Russian.

A few months earlier, American aviation and design experts had their first opportunity to inspect a MiG when a pilot ejected near the North Korean coast and landed safely on firm ground. His aircraft went into a shallow glide, ditched into the sea, and came to rest on a sandbar. The UN command promptly launched a secret operation to recover the wreckage before the North Koreans destroyed it or it floated off into the sea.

A task force of two British ships, the aircraft carrier *Eagle* and the cruiser *Birmingham*, along with a large Japanese barge and several small South Korean navy craft, managed to bring the MiG wreckage back to Pusan. There it was dismantled and shipped to Wright-Patterson Air Force Base in Ohio. The wreckage provided scientists with much valuable information, but only American test pilots flying a MiG could produce the wealth of technical data so urgently needed to design tactics to counter the Communist plane's superior performance.

Code-named Operation Moolah (GI slang for money), the $100,000 bribe concept had two goals. One was to obtain an intact MiG for exhaustive testing by aviation experts, and the other was to infect Communist air commanders with doubts about the loyalty of their pilots. Any defection would provide a propaganda bonus: The pilot would be portrayed to the world as fleeing the brutal society of the Soviet Union, Communist China, or North Korea in favor of freedom in a democracy.

Moolah had been hatched a year earlier when an American war correspondent in Tokyo was mulling over schemes for obtaining an intact MiG. Why not dangle a big chunk of hard U.S. cash in front of Communist pilots as a reward for flying one of the sleek craft to South Korea? he reflected.

For the amusement of his media colleagues, the reporter put his thoughts on paper in the form of a fictitious interview with a U.S. Air Force general. Never in his wildest dreams did he envision that his plot would evolve into the most productive psychological machination of the war, one that would cause the Communist air force to take drastic countermeasures.

Later, the satirical interview found its way to the Far East Air Force, whose intelligence officers felt it was a unique approach that just might pay off. The document was sent to Washington, where it made the rounds of the Pentagon and the State Department. On March 30, 1953, after thorough study, the plot that would become known as Moolah was approved by the Joint Chiefs.

Then it was shuttled back to Tokyo, where it was given the stamp of approval by the Joint Psychological Command and forwarded to Mark Clark, who bestowed his enthusiastic blessing. He was especially eager to lure a Soviet pilot into defecting, an act that would unmask Moscow's claim that the Soviet Union was neutral in the war.

Timing of Moolah was carefully conceived. After a six-month adjournment, the peace talks at Panmunjom had recently reconvened and the two sides had agreed to exchange sick and wounded prisoners, a procedure the UN dubbed Operation Little Switch. The swap began on April 20, 1953, and continued for a week, during which the UN handed over 6,670 North Koreans and Chinese Communists. Released to the UN command were 684 POWs mostly South Koreans, but including 149 Americans.

Despite the glimmer of hope generated by the small POW exchange, General Nam Il and his team at Panmunjom dug in their heels and were tough-minded and inflexible. They continued to play psychological games, seemingly intent on antagonizing the U.S. negotiators to trigger a verbal outburst that the Communists could convert into global propaganda. At this point, the embarrassment of a defecting pilot might cause the Communist negotiators to soften their resistance to every U.S. armistice proposal, the Far East Command's Joint Psychological Committee believed.

At the time when Mark Clark made his Moolah broadcast, General Glen Barcus, commander of the Fifth Air Force, was ready to launch an air mission to coincide with May Day, the traditional Communist holiday on which "working people" around the world demonstrate their joy at living under totalitarian rule. Deducing that Premier Kim Il Sung and foreign Communist functionaries would be gathered that day in the bombproof theater deep inside Moranborg mountain in Pyongyang, Barcus planned to cause them to lose great face by knocking out Kim's propaganda mouthpiece, Radio Pyongyang. Its facilities were underground and had withstood previous B-29 bombings, but now Barcus was going to have his fighter-bombers cut the power lines to the station by pounding a nearby communications center.

On May Day, a large formation of Fifth Air Force fighter-bombers flew northward over Pyongyang as if heading for a routine patrol along the Yalu River. Suddenly, the warplanes wheeled and, one after the other, peeled off and bombed the radio station's power source. Taken by surprise, gunners at the scores of antiaircraft weapons in and around the capital reacted belatedly. Only one fighter-bomber was damaged, and its pilot managed to return to South Korea safely. The target was demolished and Radio Pyongyang fell silent.

Knowing that North Korean wireless monitors in Pyongyang were tuned to the radio frequency he was deliberately using, Glen Barcus, whose jet was circling the target to direct the attack, taunted the eavesdroppers below. "This is General Barcus, commander of the United States Fifth Air Force," he said into his microphone. "We will be back every time you bastards broadcast filthy lies about us!"[3]

In the days after Moolah was announced, no Communist pilot flew into Kimpo to claim his $100,000 reward, but peculiar changes in the enemy air force were evident to U.S. pilots as they winged over North Korea. The red star of the Soviet air force had been replaced on the MiGs by Chinese Communist and North Korean markings. Most of the MiGs were handled erratically and in hesitant fashion when involved in dogfights, and numerous pilots were bailing out as soon as they were engaged by U.S. planes.[4]

Based on these telltale clues, U.S. air intelligence was convinced that the Soviets had grounded their pilots rather than take the chance that one or more of them might defect. This view was reinforced after Premier Kim Il Sung issued an exhortation to North Korean pilots. He said that they would now have a much greater responsibility in the air war and would have to "strengthen your military discipline."

Far East Air Force intelligence interpreted Kim's reference to military discipline to mean that North Korean pilots should cease bailing out so soon when encountering U.S. Sabre jets and other high-performance fighter-bombers.

Mark Clark also felt that Soviet pilots had gone back home or else were serving as advisers in the Manchurian sanctuary. MiG pilots encountered after the Moolah bribe was broadcast were "the worst of the whole war," he said.[5]

With the decline in the quality of Communist pilots after the Soviets suddenly vanished from the skies over North Korea, U.S. jet pilots shot down a phenomenal number of enemy aircraft during the months of May and June 1953. To American air veterans of World War II in the Pacific, the situation was reminiscent of the famed "Marianas Turkey Shoot," in which scores of Japanese naval planes had been blasted from the sky in a brief period of time.

Sabre pilots learned that the MiG, although superior in performance to U.S. jets, could be unstable in the hands of the less experienced North Korean pilots now flying them. In several instances, MiGs went into inadvertent spins at high altitudes and the pilots had to bail out. In other instances, Communist pilots ejected when a Sabre fired its first rounds.

"A new, inexpensive, highly efficient 'MiG killer' technique has been found," stated a whimsical Far East Air Force intelligence report. "If a MiG pilot sees you, he bails out; if he doesn't see you, you shoot him down. What could be more effective?"[6]

At the same time, Eighth Army's PsyWar branch studied means for demoralizing Chinese and In Min Gun soldiers who no doubt were aware that it was mainly UN warplanes that now roamed the skies. Hundreds of thousands of leaflets were sprinkled onto Communist positions. There were but five words: "Where is your air force?"

30

A Scheme to Kidnap Syngman Rhee

WHILE THE KOREAN WAR VERSION of the Marianas Turkey Shoot was raging over North Korea in the spring of 1953, the Panmunjom peace talks, which had resumed after a hiatus of six months, soon bogged down in a morass of incessant bickering. Bitter name-calling erupted. One Communist officer shouted to Major General Henry I. "Hammering Hank" Hodes, an old combat cavalryman, "You are a turtle egg!" That was one of the most insulting epithets in the Chinese language.

Focus of the hot dispute was the Communist delegates' fierce resistance to the UN demand that all repatriated POWs be allowed to go to the country of their choice, not be forced to return to their own homelands against their will.

During the wrangling, Mark Clark was shocked by a cable from President Eisenhower. The UN commander was instructed to go along with many of the Communist negotiators' demands.[1]

It was the lot of Clark and Ellis O. Briggs, a veteran diplomat who had replaced John Muccio as U.S. ambassador to South Korea the previous November, to call on Syngman Rhee and advise him of Eisenhower's order. Predictably, the veteran Korean statesman flew into a rage.

For many months, Rhee repeatedly had made it clear that he never would agree to an armistice that did not require the withdrawal of Chinese troops from Korea, the disarming of North Korean forces, and the reunification of the two Koreas under Rhee's government.

Heatedly Rhee told Clark and Briggs: "You can withdraw all UN forces, all economic aid. We will decide our own fate. We do not ask anyone to fight for us!"[2]

When Clark tried to reason with Rhee, the Old Patriot snapped, "Your country is making a great mistake in adopting these appeasement tactics. We will never accept the armistice terms. We will fight on, even if it means suicide!"

Menacingly Rhee added: "Now I feel free to take such steps as seem appropriate."

Clark and Briggs interpreted Rhee's threat to mean that he would pull out his ROK troops, who manned two-thirds of the battlefront, an action that could create a disaster for the UN command.

After the tension-racked session, Clark returned to Tokyo and called Maxwell Taylor, the Eighth Army commander, giving him instructions to develop a plan of action to prevent Rhee from sabotaging a looming armistice. By May 27, the scheme, code-named Plan Everready, was completed. It detailed various responses to possible Rhee actions.

That same day, Clark cabled Everready to the Pentagon. If all other efforts to rein in the angry Rhee failed, the plan stated, he would be invited under some pretext to visit Seoul. The idea was to get him away from Pusan, his temporary seat of government. As soon as Rhee left for Seoul, Taylor would rush U.S. troops into Pusan, seize ten top ROK government officials, and take control of South Korea by martial law called by the ROK army chief of staff. If the Korean general balked, Taylor himself would declare martial law.

If, after these steps have been taken, Rhee did not agree to accept UN armistice terms, he would be kidnapped by American troops in Seoul—"held in protective custody and incommunicado," was the diplomatic wording. Then Clark would try to establish a government under ROK Prime Minister Chang Taek Sang. If Chang declined, a UN military government would be set up.

In Washington, the Joint Chiefs approved Everready, then sent the plan to Secretary of Defense Charles Wilson and Secretary of State John Foster Dulles. Both officials gave the scheme the green light, but they hedged to keep the heat off themselves in the event Everready should go awry. To skirt the matter of kidnapping Rhee, Wilson and Dulles would only state that in the event of a "dire emergency," Clark was authorized to "act as necessary." It was a classic example of passing the buck to the field commander.

In the truce tent at Panmunjom on June 8, 1953, an agreement was reached on the mechanics of exchanging the main bodies of POWs. Within sixty days of an armistice, prisoners who wished to do so could return to their homelands. Those who did not want to go back to their own country would be handed over to a Neutral Nations

Repatriation Committee for a period of ninety days. During that time frame, representatives of their own governments, described vaguely as "explainers," would discuss their decision with them. After thirty more days, if the POWs still did not want to return home, they would be declared civilians.

One thorny issue remained—the creation of the Neutral Nations Repatriation Committee. The UN selected Sweden and Switzerland, countries with a tradition of neutrality in armed conflicts, while the Communists chose Poland and Czechoslovakia, both satellites of the Soviet Union and hardly "neutral" by any yardstick. However, to push along negotiations, the UN agreed to Poland and Czechoslovakia. Then the Communists demanded that a fifth nation, India, be a member of the committee. Although India had close ties to Mao Tse-tung, the UN delegates approved its selection.

After two years of bitter squabbling, peace in Korea seemed to be at hand.

Syngman Rhee was dismayed and irate. His dream of a unified Korea under his control seemed to be dissolving like wisps of smoke in a hurricane. On June 8, he called in Lieutenant General Won Yong-duk, one of the handful of ROK generals he trusted. Rhee told Won that the North Korean POWs choosing not to return to their country of origin should be released. Won got the point.

Secretly Won went to work on an intricate plot to release the thirty-six thousand anti-Communist North Koreans who were being held in several compounds at the southern end of the peninsula. Forty-eight hours later, his plan was approved by Rhee, the ROK delegate at the Panmunjom talks, and the home minister. Only these three men knew about the conspiracy.

A few days later, General Won summoned several key officers, including his operations chief, Colonel Song Hyo-soon, swore them to secrecy, and disclosed the plot to free the POWs. Song was given the most demanding task: He was to make secret arrangements with North Korean POW leaders inside the camps and coordinate tactics with the ROK military police guarding the facilities.

At midnight on June 18, all was quiet at Camp 9, which held 7,097 North Koreans. Stealthily, a contingent of ROK MPs led by Lieutenant Colonel Sun Yong-chang entered the camp and cut twenty-four large breaks in the barbed-wire fences. At the same time, six MPs disarmed two GI guards who were lolling about inside a nearby house.

Fifteen minutes after midnight, there was a heavy shuffling of feet and hordes of POWs streamed through the breaks in the barbed wire. Outside the fence, ROK soldiers and military police gave the escapees civilian clothes, food, and directions to private homes in which they could safely hide.

Identical scenarios were unfolding at other camps. Altogether, some twenty-seven thousand North Koreans fled from compounds and found refuge in friendly homes. The mass escape had been a masterpiece of planning and execution.

Syngman Rhee and his co-conspirators made no effort to conceal the fact that they had pulled off the audacious caper. At 7:00 A.M., only a few hours after the final POW had fled, General Won disclosed over Radio Pusan that he had ordered the ROK guards to free the North Koreans. He exhorted South Korean civilians to "help protect these patriotic youths."

Two hours later, Rhee took to the airwaves, explaining that according to the Geneva Convention and the principle of human rights, the POWs should have been freed much earlier. "The reason why I did this, without full consultation with the United Nations Command, is too obvious," he declared. By "too obvious," the Old Patriot apparently meant that the UN had sold him out.

Rhee's bold action hit Washington with all the delicacy of a blockbuster bomb. Eisenhower was furious. But he believed that Mao Tse-tung still desired an armistice and that the situation could be salvaged. So the president dispatched an envoy, Assistant Secretary of State Walter Robertson, to Seoul to both read the riot act to Rhee and get him to cease his rebellious antics.

Meanwhile, American generals in the Far East were secretly applauding Rhee's brash maneuver. It was not only a slap in the face of the Communists, but it would spare the UN command an enormous amount of time and aggravation in administering their release when the armistice was signed.[3]

Meeting with Rhee in the presidential palace in Seoul, Walter Robertson, a suave, gray-haired Virginian with a rich, soothing voice, provided a shoulder for the Korean leader to weep on for two days. Then, using his most persuasive skills, the envoy coerced Rhee into promising not to obstruct the implementation of an armistice. In return, Rhee was promised long-term economic assistance and a mutual security pact in which the United States would help the Republic of Korea repel any post-armistice attack by Communist North Korea.[4]

With peace or war hanging in the balance at Panmunjom on July 13, three Chinese armies, totaling a hundred thousand men, struck furiously at five ROK divisions along a thirty-mile sector in the center of Eighth Army lines. The heaviest Communist offensive in two years, it was apparently designed to impress on Rhee that he would be foolish to continue the war alone if the UN pulled out. No doubt a spy planted in the ROK hierarchy had informed General Peng Teh-huai, commander of the Chinese "volunteers," that a violent dispute was raging in the UN family.

In Tokyo, Mark Clark said of the sledgehammer blow: "There is no doubt in my mind that the principal reason . . . for the Communist offensive is to give the ROKs a bloody nose, to show them and the world that *puk chin* (go north) is easier said than done."[5]

Typically, General Peng pressed his assault with total disregard for the lives of his soldiers. In savage fighting, the ROKs were driven back for nearly two miles before a gargantuan cascade of UN artillery shells slaughtered the Chinese and halted their advance. Casualties were enormous on both sides.

Meanwhile, Rhee's effort to sabotage the peace talks failed. William Harrison, the chief U.S. negotiator, handed the Communist delegation a written apology for the mass escape of North Korean POWs. In the statement, Rhee was singled out as the mastermind of the maneuver. Grudgingly, the Communists accepted the apology and the peace talks resumed.

Now there was but one sticky point to be resolved—a demarcation line. After three days of hassling and horse trading, a map of the demarcation line (which would become known as the Demilitarized Zone, or DMZ) was initialed by both sides. By July 25, all details of an armistice agreement had been hammered out. The document would be signed two days later.

In anticipation of an armistice signing, the Communists at Panmunjom had constructed a special building for the ceremonies. It came to Mark Clark's attention that the Chinese and North Koreans intended to gain global propaganda mileage out of the signing by portraying it as a Communist victory. This became starkly evident when two giant blue and white "peace doves," copied from Picasso's famous painting, were painted over the entrance to the building. The doves were symbols of international Communist propaganda, and similar ones appeared in all "peace" demonstrations around the world.

Clark was angry and contacted General Harrison, instructing him to notify the Communist delegation that the UN would not take part in any meeting inside the building unless the doves were removed. Already Communist newsreel cameras had been set up at the entrance to record the "defeated" UN generals walking into the building under the "peace doves." The symbols were removed.

Some dickering remained: How and where should the armistice documents be signed? It was finally agreed that the papers first would be signed in what the Communists now called the Peace Pagoda (the dove-less building) by the principal negotiators, Harrison and Nam Il.

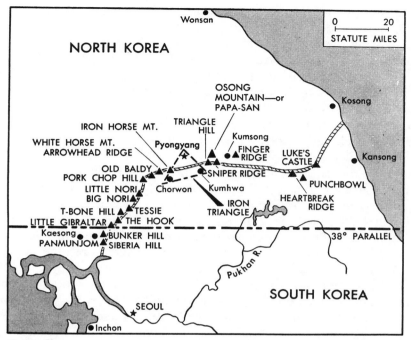

Truce line

A few hours later, the three supreme commanders—Mark Clark for the UN, Peng Teh-huai for the Chinese, and Kim Il Sung for the North Koreans—would affix their signatures independently at their respective headquarters.

At precisely 10:00 A.M. on July 27, Generals Harrison and Nam strode into the Peace Pagoda from opposite sides and sat down at a table covered with green baize. Neither man spoke a word, nodded, or gave any indication that he had ever seen the other previously. Each negotiator signed his name nine times on the armistice documents. Then the ritual was over. Like wooden actors, Harrison and Nam, still without speaking, rose and walked out of the building.

After thirty-seven months of one of history's most bizarre wars, the guns fell silent in Korea. The UN's enormous cost in blood and treasure would never be accurately calculated. Pentagon figures had 996,937 men killed, wounded, or missing, 850,000 of them ROKs. America's sons and daughters paid a high price for President Truman's decision to draw the line against Communist aggression: 54,246 dead and 103,284 wounded.[6]

During the two years of the "talking war" at Panmunjom, there had been 63,200 U.S. casualties alone, 12,300 killed in combat.[7]

Pentagon analysts estimated that the Communists also had paid a frightening toll in their effort to seize South Korea and drive the UN forces into the sea: 1,420,000 men killed, wounded, or missing. North Korea and South Korea were utterly smashed, and it would take decades for each nation to rise from the rubble.[8]

Three hours after the armistice signing at Panmunjom, Mark Clark strolled briskly into a building at the UN delegation's camp in an apple orchard near Munsan. The large room was packed with people. Klieg lights flooded the scene for the benefit of newsreel cameramen, still photographers, and cameras for a new fad known as television. Grim-faced, Clark took a seat and affixed his signature nine times to the armistice papers.

The Korean War had not been just a professional matter to Mark Clark. Three times during the conflict he had known a father's anguish when advised that his son had been wounded in action and eventually would be invalided out of the army. Although thankful that the bloodshed had ended, he remained convinced that the Korean War had been only a deadly skirmish fought on the perimeter of the free world, and that the struggle against global Communism would not end in his lifetime.

After laying down his pen, Clark solemnly declared: "I cannot find it in me to exult in this hour. Rather, it is a time for prayer that we may succeed in our difficult endeavor to turn this armistice to the advantage of mankind. If we extract hope from this occasion, it must be diluted with recognition that our salvation requires unrelaxing vigilance and effort."[9]

In Washington, there were no celebrations or lofty pronouncements about how the democracies had hurled back the Communist aggression in Korea. President Eisenhower simply said, "We have won an armistice on a single battlefield, not peace in the world."[10]

His words would prove to be prophetic.

Aftermath

ALTHOUGH DWIGHT EISENHOWER had carried out his presidential campaign pledge to end the unpopular conflict in Korea, criticism was heaped on him, even by fellow Republicans, for his "no-win" war policy. Speaker of the House Joe Martin declared, "You cannot go into a military operation with any hope of success without victory as its objective." Senator William Jenner called the armistice "a tribute to appeasement."

A Democrat senator from Texas, Lyndon B. Johnson, was blunt in his condemnation of Eisenhower. The Korean armistice "merely releases aggressive [Communist] armies to attack elsewhere . . . and is a fraud," he asserted.[1]

Harry Truman, in retirement at his home in Independence, Missouri, made no public criticism of Eisenhower's action. Privately, he was furious. He told cronies that the Republicans had hammered him for two years for his "no-win" stance; then the GOP's "glamour boy" had agreed to the same armistice terms that Truman had proposed in mid-1951.

General Douglas MacArthur was at his home in the plush penthouse of New York's Waldorf Towers when he learned of the armistice signing. He said: "This is the death warrant for Indochina [Vietnam, Cambodia, Laos]."

No sooner had the sound of the final shot of the Korean War faded than Mao Tse-tung began pouring tanks, guns, artillery, trucks, and supplies across the border of mainland China to a Communist firebrand, Ho Chi Minh, in French Indochina (later Vietnam). After World War II, Ho had proclaimed himself the head of the Republic of Vietnam and started a war to drive out the French, who had controlled the country since 1893.

Alarmed by this latest Communist threat to world peace, Eisenhower received the approval of Congress to send $785 million in military aid to the French forces battling Ho's Vietminh, as he called his army. Seeking to reassure nervous critics, the president declared, "This country has no intention of getting bogged down in another major conflict in the Far East."

Soon, a force of ten thousand French paratroopers and men of the Foreign Legion were surrounded by forty thousand Vietminh under a skilled and savvy general, Vo Nguyen Giap, near an obscure town called Dienbienphu. A major disaster loomed for the French.

In a secret meeting in Washington, Eisenhower approved CIA Director Allen Dulles's urgent request to use the clandestine agency's Civil Air Transport (CAT) planes and crews, which had performed with great distinction in the Korean War, to parachute thousands of tons of supplies, ammunition, and dismantled artillery pieces to the French trapped at Dienbienphu. CAT's planes were marked with the insignia of the French Air Force.

The CIA aircraft flew through flak curtains on scores of drops over Dienbienphu, but the massive effort, code-named Squaw II, only prolonged the French agony. Dienbienphu fell in May 1954. At the time, few, if any, of the power barons in Washington realized that the Korean War confrontation between global Communism and the democracies would shift inexorably in the years ahead to the killing grounds of Vietnam.

Although the shooting war had ended in Korea, the covert war and Communist double-dealing continued. When the armistice was signed at Panmunjom, its terms included a specific ban against the importation, by either adversary, of any more warplanes, tanks, guns, or troops than were present when the firing stopped at 10:00 P.M. on July 27, 1953. Events would disclose that the Communists had never intended to observe this ban.

Established by the Panmunjom negotiators, the Neutral Nations Supervisory Commission's task was to conduct on-site inspections in both South and North Korea to ensure compliance with the ban. Hundreds of Communist Polish and Czechoslovakian army men came to Korea to work as "neutral" inspectors, but most of them were actually intelligence officers.[2]

When four-member inspection teams of Poles, Czechs, Swedes, and Swiss went into South Korea, the Poles and Czechs slipped away from the others to collect and photograph all the classified information they could on U.S. planes, airfields, port facilities, logistics, and training.

Conversely, when the teams went to North Korea, the Poles and Czechs tried to keep the Swedes and Swiss from seeing anything of military significance. At Sinuiju and Manpojin, the two border cities on the Yalu where the Swiss and Swedes wanted to check reports that war materials were coming into North Korea by train from China, the Poles and Czechs worked directly with the Communist generals they were supposed to be policing to thwart an inspection. Chinese and North Korean officers informed the Czechs and Poles whenever a train loaded with forbidden weapons was coming through. Then the Poles and Czechs lured the Swiss and Swedes away, often by producing a phony train schedule showing that the conveyance carrying the weapons was only a passenger train. When the inspectors' backs were turned, the guns and tanks went rolling through into North Korea.

In Tokyo, UN intelligence officers learned from spies that the North Koreans, in a stark violation of armistice terms, were constructing a large new military airfield sixty miles north of Pyongyang and had already stocked it with new jets from the Soviet Union. A team from the Neutral Nations was asked to take a look. At first, the Poles and Czechs argued vehemently that the trip was unnecessary. Failing to block the inspection, the Poles and Czechs then stretched out the journey for two days, giving the North Koreans time to move the new jets and hide other evidence.

No doubt the Swiss and Swedes suspected foul play, but with a team pitting two nations against two, there was nothing they could do to speed up the inspection trip. It was late afternoon when the team finally arrived near the targeted airfield, so it was decided that the inspection would be postponed until morning.

This respite gave a Pole the opportunity to make certain that the new jets had been moved as ordered. Dusk was gathering when he climbed a hill and looked down on the airfield. Much to his astonishment, he discerned some twenty new MiGs parked alongside the runways.

Infuriated and worried, the Pole rushed to the airfield and upbraided the North Korean commander. "But the planes are not on the strip," the officer explained to the Pole. "We moved them just as we were told."

"You merely moved them around on the field, you idiot!" the Pole shouted. "You were supposed to move them away from the field! What in the hell do you expect will happen if the Swede and Swiss climb the same hill I did?"

"Well," replied the North Korean, "just don't let them climb it!"

Angered at the other man's indifference, the Pole managed to get him to rapidly move the MiGs away from the field to hiding places where they could not be seen. Then he literally stood over North Korean work crews while they cleared away new spare parts that would have given away the fact that MiGs were based at the field. All the while, the Pole was periodically mumbling about stupid Koreans and the lengths to which he had to go to be "neutral."[3]

As time passed, the Communists grew even more flagrant in their violation of armistice terms. Without even bothering to hatch an excuse for their noncompliance, they simply refused to permit UN observers to visit the ten ports of entry in North Korea.

On September 23, 1953, two months after the armistice signing, Operation Moolah had a dramatic development. As U.S. ground crews looked on in amazement, Captain Ro Kum Suk of the North Korean Air Force landed a MiG-15 at Kimpo airfield and asked for political asylum.[4]

Captain Ro, who apparently had been hibernating in a North Korean cave when the Moolah announcements were made, claimed that he had never heard of the $100,000 reward and had been motivated solely by his hatred of the Chinese and Soviet "advisers."

It was publicly announced that Ro had rejected the $100,000. Actually, the CIA had hatched an intricate maneuver whereby the North Korean would quietly receive the financial equivalent in educational benefits and other financial considerations. Later, Ro would be given a job with a CIA-front organization called the Committee for Free Asia.

Captain Ro's defection brought howls of outrage from Soviet propagandists. Moolah was branded a "cheap, dirty trick" and in violation of international law. Moscow and Peking labeled it "an unethical stunt."

Meanwhile, Mark Clark had a propaganda field day. Piously, he offered to return Ro's plane to "its rightful owner" as a gesture of good will. Actually, he knew that he had put the Communists in a quandary. For weeks during the Panmunjom talks, the North Koreans had been insisting that the Soviet Union had been neutral in the war, a stance that Moscow also had strictly maintained. So if the "rightful owner" (the Soviet Union) stepped forward to claim the aircraft, the Communists would be confessing to the world that they had been lying and that Moscow was directly involved in the conflict. So no one ever claimed Ro's MiG.[5]

A shaky truce was in effect in Korea, one that could burst at any moment, and America's top jet fighter, the F-86 Sabre, might again be engaged in dogfights with the MiG. So Ro's plane was shipped in secrecy to Kadena Air Force Base in Okinawa for exhaustive flights by a crack test pilot, Major Charles E. "Chuck" Yeager.[6]

Yeager flew the MiG in mock dogfights against U.S. jet fighters and plotted its speed, power, climb rate, and range. He wrote in his diary:

"I'm beat and grim. I've come to bust my ass during the past few days. I'm flying [the MiG-15] every which way but loose in a tropical storm that's been sitting over this damn island for nearly a week—flying on gauges with a strange metric system, in a strange airplane, flying it higher and faster than any Russian pilot had ever dared. Those bastards know better."[7]

As a result of the Okinawa test flights, a wealth of valuable scientific intelligence was collected on the MiG, information that would be of enormous value to U.S. pilots in the event hostilities were to erupt again in Korea—or elsewhere in the world. Once more, Moolah had paid off handsomely.

Kim Philby, the Soviet masterspy, continued to lead a charmed life, even though his two comrades in the espionage conspiracy had long ago fled to Moscow. In 1955, Philby was named publicly in England as one of those high in the government being investigated as possible spies for the Communists. However, he was cleared of any disloyalty by Prime Minister Harold Macmillan.

The notoriety forced him to resign from the British Foreign Office, but, oddly, this was not the end of Philby's role as a spy. He then worked as a journalist in the Middle East for another nine years, sending a flood of secret information to his masters in Moscow. On January 27, 1963, when he felt that MI-5's bloodhounds were closing in on him, he slipped onto a Soviet ship and surfaced in Moscow.

Had this unholy triumvirate of Philby, Maclean, and Burgess been able to dramatically aid the Communist armies in Korea? Much evidence concludes that their treachery had been vast. On February 16, 1956, U.S. Secretary of the Army Wilbur M. Brucker issued a shocking report (before Philby had been unmasked) in which he asserted: "Burgess and Maclean had secrets of priceless value to the Communist conspiracy [in Korea]."

Lieutenant General James M. Gavin, who had access to top-secret files in the Pentagon, declared: "I have no doubt whatsoever that the Chinese Communists moved confidently and skillfully into North Korea. . . . I believe that they were able to do this because they were well informed not only of the moves [General Johnnie] Walker would make but the limitations on what he might do."[8]

Gavin, a World War II paratroop legend and one of the Pentagon's brightest minds, concluded: "[I am] quite sure that all of MacArthur's plans flowed into the hands of the Communists through the British Foreign Office."[9]

MacArthur himself cited an "official leaflet" published in China after the war by General Lin Piao, commander of the Chinese Communist army that assaulted U.S. forces in late 1950. Lin was quoted as stating: "I would never have made the attack and risked my men and military reputation if I had not been assured that Washington would restrain General MacArthur from taking adequate retaliatory measures against my lines of supply and communications."[10]

Much to its consternation, the British government learned ten years after the armistice that another high-ranking "insider," who had been assigned to the embassy in Seoul, also had been a spy for the Communists.

Syngman Rhee, the Old Patriot who had sought to unify the two Koreas (under his rule), remained president in the South until 1960. His regime had become steadily more repressive. Periodically, he had spoken out loudly about resuming the war. Seven years after the armistice, when even his boosters considered him senile, street protests and student riots drove him into exile in Hawaii. There he blustered about returning to South Korea one day and launching an army into the North.

In North Korea, Kim Il Sung continued as the unchallenged strongman. On occasion over the years, he blustered about "uniting Korea in my lifetime" under his dictatorship. Under the aging ruler, North Korea continued its belligerency. In 1968, Kim nearly touched off a widespread war (or nuclear conflagration) when his armed forces seized the U.S. intelligence ship *Pueblo*, killing a crew member in the process, and then jailed eighty-two officers and men in brutal conditions for ten months.

Kim Il Sung died on July 8, 1994, more than four decades after the Panmunjom armistice talks had opened. His son, Kim Jong Il, ascended to the premiership. The elder Kim apparently had intended to "live on" in North Korea, because Soviet experts were reportedly paid $5 million to use a secret process to mummify the body. Kim Il Sung was put on public display in July 1995—and presumably on occasion for decades to come.

General Peng Teh-huai, commander of Chinese Communist forces in Korea and signer of the armistice document, met an ignoble fate. In one of Mao Tse-tung's periodic "culture cleansings" in 1959, Peng was arrested, tortured fiendishly, and executed.

In early 1972, President Richard M. Nixon arrived in Peking on a much ballyhooed jaunt that was described as a goodwill gesture by the United States. While there, he discussed the situation of John T. Downey, the then youthful CIA agent who had been shot down and captured while on Operation Tropic, a secret mission over Manchuria in late 1952. Downey had been held in a Chinese prison for nearly twenty years.

On his return to the United States, Nixon, presumably as part of a deal cut with the Communist leaders in Peking, admitted at a press conference that Downey had been a CIA agent. Satisfied that Uncle Sam had "lost face," the Chinese released Downey on March 12, 1972. Richard Fecteau, who had been captured with Downey, had been freed by the Chinese several months earlier.

After returning to his home in Connecticut, Downey obtained a law degree at Yale University, a course he had planned to follow at the time he joined the CIA two decades earlier. In 1995, he was a judge in a large New England city.

It took forty years for the Communists to publicly admit that Josef Stalin had played a leading role in the invasion of South Korea. In July 1990, Li San-cho, North Korea's ambassador to Moscow in the 1950s, told Reuters, the British news agency, that Stalin had approved Kim Il Sung's invasion plans and had provided weapons, advisers, and other military support.[11]

Korea had not been a monumental victory for the United States and the democracies, if victory means the total destruction of an enemy's capacity to wage war. Nor had Korea been a humiliating defeat for the forces of freedom, as a few American revisionist historians have tried to portray it. In retrospect, the brutal war had been a landmark conflict, and America's 54,246 dead and 103,284 wounded fighting men had not died and suffered in vain. For the first time, global Communist armed aggression had been repelled, and the Red tide that threatened to engulf the free world began to ebb and eventually nearly vanished.

Forty-two years after the Korean War, in late July 1995, the millions of American veterans of that era found their rightful place in history. At that time in Washington, the Korean War Veterans Memorial was dedicated on the National Mall in the shadow of the Lincoln Memorial.

Among the thousands of Korea-era veterans attending the stirring ceremonies were large numbers of unsung heroes—men who had risked their lives as warriors in the covert war. Their little-known and largely unrecorded achievements, along with those of the other participants in the conflict, were summed up in the statement set into an eight-ton granite slab at the Korean War Veterans Memorial:

Our Nation Honors Her Sons and
Daughters Who Answered the Call
to Defend a Country They Never
Knew and a People They Never Met.

Notes and Sources

Chapter 1. "Terminating" a Communist General

1. After the Korean War, Milt Von Mann played football at and graduated from Virginia Tech. In late 1994, he was inducted into the Alabama High School Football Hall of Fame.
2. Because of the secret nature of the mission, Harry Branson and Miles Gibbons are not their real names.
3. Author interview with Milt Von Mann, 1995.
4. Ibid.
5. Ibid.
6. Ibid.
7. Milt Von Mann earned a Ph.D. at the University of Georgia and later coached college football teams for many years. In 1995 he was a scout for the Indianapolis Colts and Pittsburgh Steelers professional football teams.

Chapter 2. A Tangled Web of Politics

1. A short time later, Hirohito shocked his people once more by announcing that he was not a god.
2. Dorris James, *The Years of MacArthur* (Boston: Houghton Mifflin, 1975), vol. II, p. 390.
3. Bruce G. Cummings, *The Origins of the Korean War* (Princeton, N.J.: Princeton University Press, 1987), pp. 122–29.
4. John Gunther, *The Riddle of MacArthur* (New York: Norton, 1951), p. 178.
5. Dean Acheson, *Present at the Creation* (New York: Norton, 1969), p. 449.
6. A. Wigfall Green, *The Epic of Korea* (Washington, D.C.: Public Affairs Press, 1950), p. 106.
7. T. R. Fehrenbach, *This Kind of War* (New York: Macmillan, 1963), p. 38.
8. As with all Communist leaders of that era, Kim Il Sung's detailed background and precise dates are impossible to track.
9. *Foreign Relations of the United States* (hereafter FRUS), U.S.–Korea, 1950–53, Government Printing Office, Modern Military Records Branch, National Archives, Washington, D.C.
10. Max Hastings, *The Korean War* (New York: Simon & Schuster, 1991), p. 33.
11. FRUS, U.S.–Korea, 1950–53, National Archives, Washington, D.C.
12. Frazier Hunt, *The Untold Story of Douglas MacArthur* (New York: Devin-Adair, 1954), p. 427.
13. Ibid, p. 428.

Chapter 3. A Conspiracy in Moscow

1. Joseph C. Goulden, *Korea* (New York: Times Books, 1982), p. 29.
2. Trumbull Higgins, *Korea and the Fall of MacArthur* (New York: Harper, 1960), p. 9.
3. Goulden, *Korea*, p. 23.
4. Modern Military Records Branch, Group 319, National Archives, Washington, D.C.
5. Daily Intelligence Summary, Far East Commander, 1949–50, National Archives, Washington, D.C.
6. Ibid.
7. Ibid.
8. Author interview with Major General John K. Singlaub (Ret.), 1995.
9. Ibid.
10. Ibid.

11. Hastings, *Korean War*, p. 47.
12. Nikita Khrushchev, *Krushchev Remembers*, translated by Strobe Talbott (Boston: Little, Brown, 1970), pp. 367–68. Several American experts on the Soviet Union have stated they believe Khrushchev's account of the Moscow meetings is accurate.
13. Ibid., p. 369.
14. Ibid.
15. Ibid., p. 370.
16. Harold J. Noble. *Embassy at War* (Seattle: University of Washington Press, 1975), p. 235.

Chapter 4. A Ruse to Mask an Invasion

1. Harold J. Noble writing in the *Saturday Evening Post*, August 5, 1952.
2. Ibid.
3. Ibid.
4. Ibid.
5. Author was unable to determine the eventual destiny of the three Fatherland Front men, but presumably they were freed when the North Koreans quickly captured Seoul.
6. Noble, *Saturday Evening Post*, August 5, 1952.
7. John Toland, *In Mortal Combat* (New York: Morrow, 1991), p. 19.

Chapter 5. Search for a Scapegoat

1. Douglas MacArthur, *Reminiscences* (New York: Norton, 1964), p. 327.
2. Ibid., p. 328.
3. Ibid.
4. Robert T. Oliver, *Syngman Rhee* (New York: Dodd, Mead, 1955), pp. 300-301.
5. *Saturday Evening Post*, July 24, 1950.
6. John J. Muccio, oral history, Harry S. Truman Library, Abilene, Kans.
7. Margaret Truman. *Harry S. Truman* (New York: Morrow, 1973), p. 217.
8. Ibid.
9. John D. Hickerson, oral history, Harry S. Truman Library, Independence, Mo.
10. Noble, *Embassy*, p. 47.
11. Cabell Phillips, *The Truman Presidency* (New York: Macmillan, 1966), p. 296.
12. George F. Kennan, *Memoirs* (Boston: Atlantic Monthly Press, 1967), p. 256.
13. Ray S. Cline. *Secrets, Spies, and Scholars* (Washington, D.C.: Acropolis Books, 1976), p. 106.
14. Author interview with Major General John K. Singlaub (Ret.), 1995.
15. Harold P. Ford, *Estimative Intelligence* (Washington, D.C.: School of Strategic Intelligence, 1989), pp. 60–65.
16. Author interview with Major General John K. Singlaub (Ret.), 1995.

Chapter 6. Reign of Terror in Seoul

1. A commissar is a political officer in the Soviet military or government.
2. "United States Policy in the Korean Crisis" (Washington, D.C., Government Printing Office, 1951), pp. 63-64.
3. Ibid.
4. Kennan, *Memoirs*, p. 336.
5. Phillips, *Truman*, p. 304.
6. *Washington Post*, June 28, 1950.
7. Toland, *Mortal*, pp. 58–59.
8. Ibid.
9. Courtney Whitney, *MacArthur* (New York: Knopf, 1956), p. 319.
10. Gunther, *Riddle*, p. 73.
11. Frank Kelley and Cornelius Ryan, *MacArthur: Man of Action* (New York: Morrow, 1950), p. 139.
12. Whitney, *MacArthur*, p. 331.
13. MacArthur, *Reminiscences*, p. 333.
14. Ibid., p. 215.

15. Merle Miller. *Plain Speaking* (New York: Norton, 1973), p. 303.
16. White House press release, June 30, 1950.
17. CIA Daily Intelligence Reports, Korea, July 1–14, 1950, National Archives, Washington, D.C.
18. Father Philip Crosbie, *Pencilling Prisoners* (Melbourne: Hawthorn, 1954), pp. 67–81.
19. Ibid.

Chapter 7. A Deception to Confuse the Invaders

1. Transcript of testimony by General Douglas MacArthur before Senate Armed Services Committee, 1951, pp. 231–32.
2. *Saturday Evening Post*, October 23, 1950.
3. Toland, *Mortal*, p. 82.
4. Dunkirk (or Dunkerque) is a French port on the English Channel coast. In May 1940, a fleet of 1,000 British ships carried nearly 350,000 trapped Allied soldiers from Dunkirk to England during World War II. Since that time any looming military withdrawal by sea has been called "a Dunkirk."
5. *New York Herald Tribune*, July 16, 1950.
6. Admiral Roscoe Hillenkoetter report to President Harry Truman, July 8, 1950, National Archives, Washington, D.C.
7. Goulden, *Korea*, p.134.
8. William J. Sebald and Russell Brines, *With MacArthur in Japan* (New York: Norton, 1965), p. 199.

Chapter 8. A Clandestine Organization Is Born

1. For a complete account of the Allied Intelligence Bureau (AIB) in World War II, see William B. Breuer, *MacArthur's Undercover War* (New York: John Wiley & Sons, 1995).
2. As a brigadier general, Holmes K. Dager led a combat command of the U.S. 4th Armored Division that helped spearhead the Allied breakout from Normandy in August 1944 during World War II. Later Dager was seriously wounded.
3. Drawn from "History of the Central Intelligence Agency," Select Committee to Study Governmental Operations with Respect to Military Intelligence, 94th Congress, 1976, National Archives, Washington, D.C.
4. Author interview with William A. Colby, former director of the CIA. An OSS agent, Colby had jumped behind German lines in France and Norway in World War II.
5. After World War II, William Stephenson, gained wide renown in a book and Hollywood movie, both entitled *The Man Called Intrepid* (his code name).
6. Goulden, *Korea*, p. 466.
7. Ibid., p. 205.
8. Carl Berger, *An Introduction to Wartime Leaflets* (Washington, D.C.: Special Operations Research Office, American University, 1959), pp. 27-29.
9. Hastings, *Korean War*, p. 84.
10. Ibid., p. 89.
11. Background from "History of the Counterintelligence Corps," compiled by the U.S. Army Intelligence Center, Fort Holabird, Maryland, 1959.

Chapter 9. Spying on the Enemy

1. Whitney, *MacArthur*, p. 346.
2. Robert D. Heinl. *Victory at High Tide* (New York: Lippincott, 1958), pp. 20, 24, 32.
3. Whitney, *MacArthur*, p. 347.
4. MacArthur, *Reminiscences*, p. 349.
5. Ibid., p. 350.
6. Ibid.
7. Roy Appleman, *South to the Naktong, North to the Yalu* (Washington, D.C.: Center of Military History, 1986), p. 490.
8. General Oliver P. Smith, oral history, U.S. Marine Corps History Division and Museum, Washington, D.C.

9. Ibid.
10. Appleman, *South*, p. 509.
11. Heinl, *Victory*, pp. 67–69.
12. Goulden, *Korea*, p. 466.
13. Toland, *Mortal*, pp. 183–84.

Chapter 10. Machinations to "Hide" a Landing

1. *New York Times*, September 14, 1950.
2. Walter Karig, *War in Korea* (New York: Rinehart, 1952) pp. 176–182.
3. Heinl, *Victory*, p. 276.
4. Summary Report, "Operation Trudy Jackson," Far East Division, CIA, Tokyo, September 23, 1950. National Archives, Washington, D.C.
5. Ibid.
6. Letter from Commander, Mine Squadron 3, to Chief of Naval Operations, March 10, 1951. Office of Naval History, Washington, D.C.
7. Heinl, *Victory*, p. 313.
8. Toland, *Mortal*, p. 186.
9. Ibid., p. 187.
10. Ibid.
11. James A. Field Jr., *History of U.S. Naval Operation, Korea* (Washington, D.C.: Government Printing Office, 1962) pp. 183–85.

Chapter 11. Guiding In a Fleet

1. Malcolm W. Cagle and Frank A. Manson, *The Sea War in Korea* (Annapolis, Md: U.S. Naval Institute, 1957), p. 93.
2. Lieutenant Commander Eugene F. Clark was awarded the Navy Cross, America's second highest award for valor, for his role in Operation Trudy Jackson.
3. General Lemuel Shepherd, oral history, U.S. Marine Corps History Division and Museum, Washington, D.C.
4. Ibid.
5. Heinl, *Victory*, p. 96.
6. Cagle and Manson, *Sea*, p. 95.
7. Ibid., pp. 99–100.
8. General Lemuel Shepherd, oral history, U.S. Marine Corps History Division and Museum, Washington, D.C.
9. Carl Mydans writing in *Life* magazine, October 2, 1950.
10. George C. McNaughton, oral history, U.S. Marine Corps History Division and Museum, Washington, D.C.
11. *Pravda*, September 23, 1950.
12. Ibid.
13. A predecessor of L Troop, 7th Cavalry, was wiped out by Chief Crazy Horse and his Indian warriors at the Little Bighorn River in 1876.
14. Stephen E. Pease, *PsyWar* (Harrisburg, Pa: Stackpole, 1992), p. 90.
15. Heinl, *Victory*, p. 262.
16. Author interview with Lieutenant General James M. Gavin (Ret.), 1987.
17. Ibid.
18. Ibid.
19. MacArthur, *Reminiscences*, p. 358.
20. Sebald and Brines, *MacArthur*, p. 200.
21. Harry S. Truman. *Years of Trial and Hope* (Garden City, N.Y.: Doubleday, 1956), p. 362.

Chapter 12. A Secret Trek to the Yalu

1. Clay Blair, *The Forgotten War* (New York: Times Books, 1987), p. 337.
2. FRUS VII, U.S.–Korea, 1950–53, pp. 935–36.
3. Walter Karig, Malcolm Cagle, and Frank A. Manson, *Battle Report* (New York: Rinehart, 1952), p. 348.

4. Ibid., p. 349.
5. Toland, *Mortal*, p. 253.
6. Ibid., p. 255.
7. After the United States became involved in World War II, the Flying Tigers were absorbed into the U.S. Army Air Corps.
8. William M. Leary, *Perilous Missions* (Tuscaloosa: University of Alabama Press, 1984), p. 41.
9. Ibid., p. 110.
10. "Escape and Evasion Organization and Guerrilla Operations in Korea," report by Hans Tofte, February 23, 1980, National Archives, Washington, D.C.
11. Goulden, *Korea*, p. 469.
12. Truman, *Years*, p. 362.
13. Cline, *Secrets*, p. 108.

Chapter 13. Three Communist Masterspies

1. Such a large number of mines had been sown in Wonsan Harbor that the devices were still being detected long after the war.
2. *New York Times*, Oct. 26, 1950.
3. Jim G. Lucas interview with Douglas MacArthur in January 1954, but not published until after the general's death, *U.S. News and World Report*, Apr. 20, 1964.
4. Robert Considine interview with Douglas MacArthur in 1954, but not published until after the general's death, *Washington Post*, Apr. 9, 1964.
5. Bruce Page, David Leitch, and Phillip Knightley, *The Philby Conspiracy* (New York: Doubleday, 1968), p. 196.
6. Ibid., p. 197.
7. U.S. Vice Admiral A. E. Jarrell (Ret.) writing in U.S. Naval Institute *Proceedings*, Annapolis, January 1974.
8. Ibid.
9. Page et al., *Philby*, p. 237.

Chapter 14. A Colossal Intelligence Swoon

1. Carl Mydans writing in *Life* magazine, March 17, 1964.
2. Appleman, *South*, pp. 661–63.
3. Ibid., pp. 757–58.
4. Lieutenant General Alpha A. Bowser, former G-3, 1st Marine Division, oral history, U.S. Marine Corps History Division and Museum, Washington, D.C.
5. Appleman, *South*, p. 761.
6. FRUS, U.S.–Korea, 1950–53, p. 1013.
7. Richard H. Rovere and Arthur M. Schlesinger, *The General and the President* (New York: Random House, 1952), pp. 142–43.
8. Sidney Huff, *My Fifteen Years with MacArthur* (New York: Paperback Library, 1964), p. 133.
9. Martin Blumenson report, "Combat Actions in Korea," Chap. 7, p. 96, Chief of Military History, Washington, D.C.

Chapter 15. CIA Target: Douglas MacArthur

1. Sebald and Brines, *MacArthur*, p. 205.
2. *New York Times*, December 1, 1950.
3. *Chicago Tribune*, December 2, 1950.
4. Dean Acheson papers, Harry S. Truman Library, Independence, Mo.
5. In the late 1950s, Hollywood made a movie, *Retreat Hell!*, that focused on the marine withdrawal from the Chosin Reservoir region.
6. Acheson, *Present*, p. 481.
7. Lieutenant General Pedro A. del Valle, USMC (Ret.), transcript of interview with Captain Miles Duval, April 30, 1969. MacArthur Memorial, Norfolk, Va.
8. Ibid.

9. Ibid.
10. Pedro Del Valle letter to Douglas MacArthur, MacArthur Memorial, Norfolk, Va.
11. MacArthur, *Reminiscences*, p. 383.
12. Robert Leckie, *Conflict* (New York: Putnam, 1962), p. 243.
13. *Time* magazine, March 5, 1951.

Chapter 16. Top Secret: The Li Mi Project

1. FRUS, U.S.–Korea, 1950–53, W. Stuart Symington, report to the National Security Council, "Recommended Policies and Actions in Light of the Grave World Situation," January 11, 1951. National Archives, Washington, D.C.
2. Ibid.
3. Monthly report of Counterintelligence Corps Activities, signed by Lieutenant Colonel Arthur Slattery, December 1950, U.S. Intelligence and Security Command, Fort Belvoir, Va.
4. Ibid., January 1951, signed by Major Millard F. Dougherty.
5. Ibid.
6. Transcript of conference at Eighth Army headquarters, Jan. 8, 1951, General Matthew B. Ridgway papers, U.S. Army Military History Institute, Carlisle Barracks, Pa.
7. Thomas Powers, *The Man Who Kept the Secrets* (New York: Norton, 1979), p. 81.
8. Leary, *Perilous*, p. 247.
9. Richard Dunlop, *Behind Japanese Lines* (Chicago: Regnery, 1974), p. 315.
10. FRUS, U.S.–Korea, 1950–53, cable to Secretary of State, Aug. 15, 1951, pp. 288–89, National Archives, Washington, D.C.
11. FRUS, U.S.–Korea, 1950–53, cable from Assistant Secretary of State Dean Rusk to Ambassador David M. Key, pp. 287–88, National Archives, Washington, D.C.
12. Elizabeth P. MacDonald, *Undercover Girl* (New York: Norton, 1947), pp. 147–48.
13. In an interview with Hans Tofte, historian Joseph C. Goulden was told that the CIA had earmarked $1,000,000 for Operation Stole. However, not one penny of it was spent, because Chiang Kai-shek footed the entire bill.
14. MacArthur, *Reminiscences*, p. 384.
15. Acheson, *Present*, p. 517.

Chapter 17. A Raid to "Kidnap" a Corpse

1. Far East Command Intelligence Report, Tokyo, March 10, 1951, National Archives, Washington, D.C.
2. Ibid.
3. Toland, *Mortal*, pp. 416–17.
4. A whaleboat is a long, narrow craft with both ends sharp.
5. Toland, *Mortal*, p. 418.
6. Far East Command Intelligence Report, Tokyo, March 10, 1951, National Archives, Washington, D.C.
7. Ibid.
8. Ibid.
9. Brigadier General Crawford Sams was awarded the Distinguished Service Cross, America's second highest award, for the secret mission.
10. Charles A. Willoughby, *MacArthur* (New York: McGraw-Hill, 1954), p. 384.
11. Ibid., p. 385.
12. Matthew B. Ridgway, *The Korean War* (New York: Doubleday, 1967), pp. 109–110.
13. General Matthew B. Ridgway, oral history, U.S. Army Military History Institute, Carlisle Barracks, Pa.
14. Ibid.

Chapter 18. Father Sam and the Soviet Agent

1. When the German soldiers had been about to execute Father Sam, he quickly said an Act of Contrition. Only later would he reflect that in his nervousness, he had recited the Prayer Before Meals instead.

2. Korea was not Father Sampson's final war. While stationed at the Pentagon in the late 1960s and early 1970s, he made numerous trips to Vietnam, visiting GIs at the front countless times.
3. Author interview with Monsignor Francis L. Sampson, 1995.
4. Ibid.
5. Ibid.
6. Father Sam rose to major general and was chief of chaplains when he retired in 1971. His lengthy, impressive list of combat decorations includes the Distinguished Service Cross, the Purple Heart, and Master Parachutist Badge with three combat jump stars.
7. Pease, *PsyWar*, p. 78.
8. General Douglas MacArthur memorandum to the Joint Chiefs of Staff, February 15, 1951, National Archives, Washington, D.C.
9. Ibid., February 26, 1951.
10. MacArthur, *Reminiscences*, p. 393.
11. Whitney, *MacArthur*, pp. 464–65.
12. Rovere and Schlesinger, *General and President*, pp. 168–69.
13. Ibid.

Chapter 19. An Espionage Conspiracy Unmasked

1. General Earle Partridge report to General George Stratemeyer, April 15, 1951, National Archives, Washington, D.C.
2. Report of 3d Bombardment Wing, "Tactics and Weapons of Aerial Night Attack," to General George Stratemeyer, Feb. 20, 1951, National Archives, Washington, D.C.
3. The workhorse C-47s (known to the British as Dakotas) were used extensively in World War II to carry paratroopers, tow gliders, and rush supplies to armored spearheads.
4. Far East Air Force report, pp. 7–9, April 1, 1951, National Archives, Washington, D.C.
5. Sidney L. Mayer. *MacArthur in Japan* (New York: Morrow, 1973), pp. 123–25. Acheson, *Present*, p. 520.
6. *New York Times*, April 6, 1951.
7. *Life* magazine, April 23, 1951.
8. James Van Fleet, at age fifty-four, was a colonel on D-day in Normandy. Earlier, his name had been submitted numerous times for promotion to brigadier general, but each time, Army Chief of Staff George Marshall rejected it. Finally, Marshall realized that he had thought Van Fleet was another colonel with a similar name who had an alcohol problem.
9. Far East Command report, pp. 44-45, April 1951, National Archives, Washington, DC.
10. CIC booklet on counterintelligence operations in Korea. U.S. Intelligence and Security Command, Fort Belvoir, Va.
11. Page et al., *Philby*, p. 232.
12. This account of the luncheon at the RAC Club was given by Donald Maclean years later to three British reporters, *Times of London*, May 2, 1961.
13. Many years later, British Prime Minister Edward Heath told the House of Commons that Kim Philby was the one who had tipped off Donald Maclean about his looming interrogation.
14. Curiously, neither the FBI, the CIA, nor MI-5 interviewed Kim Philby after Maclean and Burgess fled to the Soviet Union, although it was known that Burgess had once lived in Philby's home in Washington.

Chapter 20. A POW Camp Propaganda Machine

1. Ridgway, *Korean*, p.121.
2. After the war, Premier Kim Il Sung appointed Colonel Lee Hak Ku to a high post in the North Korean government, apparently in payment for Lee's agreeing to surrender and gain entry into a POW camp.
3. Fehrenbach, *This Kind*, pp. 472–73.
4. Ibid., p. 476.
5. *Washington Post*, May 22, 1951.
6. Acheson, *Present*, p. 529.
7. Ibid., p. 532.
8. Goulden, *Korea*, p. 550.

Chapter 21. The Donkeys of Yellow Sea Province

1. Throughout the war, EUSAK Miscellaneous and its successors underwent a number of name changes. For clarity's sake, the name EUSAK Miscellaneous is used throughout the book.
2. John H. McGee eventually retired as a brigadier general.
3. *Columbus Ledger-Inquirer*, November 12, 1950.
4. William A. Burke eventually retired as a major general.
5. Major Shaun M. Darragh writing in *Army* magazine, November 1984.
6. Author interview with Colonel Robert I. Channon (Ret.), 1995.
7. The raft was painted bright yellow so it could be spotted from the air in a rescue mission.
8. A sailing junk sometimes had an engine in it.
9. Author interview with Colonel Robert I. Channon (Ret.), 1995.
10. Ibid.
11. Robert I. Channon, *The Cold Steel Third* (Franklin, N.C.: Genealogy Publishing Service, 1991), p. 501.

Chapter 22. Widening the Unconventional Warfare

1. Whitney, *MacArthur*, p. 369.
2. Author interview with James Smith, 1995.
3. Ibid.
4. Channon, *Cold Steel*, p. 405.
5. Cyril Tritz received the Silver Star and Joseph Ulatoski the Bronze Star for this action. Ulatoski eventually retired as a brigadier general.
6. Channon, *Cold Steel*, p. 484.
7. Ibid., p. 52. John Thornton and Marty Watson survived the war in a POW camp.
8. Lieutenant William Lewis survived the war after spending many months as a POW.

Chapter 23. Communist High Jinks at a "Peace" Site

1. "Report of the Women's International Commission for the Investigation of the Atrocities Committed by U.S. and Syngman Rhee troops in Korea" (Monica Felton), Harry S. Truman Library, Independence, Mo.
2. Ibid.
3. Cagle and Manson, *Sea War*, p. 308.
4. Robert F. Futrell. *The U.S. Air Force in Korea* (Washington, D.C.: U.S. Government Printing Office, 1983), p. 370.
5. General Matthew Ridgway apparently did not agree with General James Van Fleet's plan to end the war. In his memoirs, Ridgway said that the Eighth Army could have reached the Yalu if the U.S. had been willing to pay the heavy price in dead and wounded. But he did not believe it would have been worth the cost.
6. *New York Times*, May 24, 1951.
7. Author interview with Colonel Robert I. Channon (Ret.), 1995.
8. Admiral C. Turner Joy, *How Communists Negotiate* (New York: Macmillan, 1953), p. 4.
9. Ibid., p. 5.
10. Ibid., p. 6.
11. Leckie, *Conflict*, p. 314.

Chapter 24. Soviet Troops and Pilots in Disguise

1. Futrell, *Air Force*, p. 324.
2. On release from an airplane, a butterfly bomb breaks into a number of small clusters that flutter to the ground and lie inert until disturbed. Then they explode.
3. After the war, Colonel Pawel Monat had a three-year tour of duty as Polish military attaché in Washington, and in 1958, he returned to Warsaw to head the military attaché branch of Polish intelligence. In 1959, he defected to the United States with his wife and young son. A year later, Communist Poland sentenced him to death in absentia.
4. *Life* magazine, June 27, 1960.
5. Among the Chinese "volunteers" was Colonel Mao An-ying, the eldest son of Mao Tse-tung. Soon after arriving in Korea, Colonel Mao was killed in a bombing raid on Pyongyang.

6. *Life* magazine, June 27, 1960.
7. Pease, *PsyWar*, p. 147.
8. Modern Military Records Branch, National Archives, Washington, D.C.
9. Joy, *Negotiate*, p. 131.

Chapter 25. A Cable-Cutting Caper

1. Arleigh A. Burke eventually rose to four-star admiral and chief of naval operations, the service's top post.
2. Admiral Arleigh A. Burke, oral history, U.S. Naval Institute, Annapolis, Md.
3. Leckie, *Conflict*, p. 340.
4. Author interview with Colonel Robert I. Channon (Ret.), 1995.
5. Author interview with Major General John K. Singlaub (Ret.), 1995.

Chapter 26. The Big Bug Bonanza

1. Denis Warner, *Hurricane from China* (New York: Harper, 1954), p. 27.
2. Toland, *Mortal*, p. 586.
3. *New York Times*, September 12, 1953.
4. As a result of the Communist propaganda blitz, many around the world still believe, in 1995, that the U.S. engaged in germ warfare in Korea and China.
5. After Mark W. Clark retired from the army, he spent many years as president of The Citadel, a military college in South Carolina. He is buried on the campus.
6. Walter G. Hermes, *Truce Tent and Fighting Front* (Washington: Office Chief of Military History, 1966), p. 247.
7. Ibid., p. 249.
8. After the Koje affair, Brigadier Generals Francis Dodd and Charles Colson were reduced in rank to colonel.
9. North Korean General Pak Sang-hyon, the true Communist leader at Koje, apparently escaped detection by the Americans because he was listed on the camp rolls as Private Jeon.
10. Major General Haydon L. Boatner writing in *Army* magazine, August 1963.
11. Ibid.
12. Ibid.
13. Leckie, *Conflict*, p. 348.

Chapter 27. An Intricate Invasion Hoax

1. Joint Chiefs to General Mark Clark, September 28, 1952, National Archives, Washington, D.C.
2. Futrell, *Air Force*, p. 483.
3. Ibid., p. 482.
4. *Life* magazine, June 27, 1960.
5. The U.S. Navy credits Vice Admiral Robert P. Briscoe, commander, Far East Naval Forces, with suggesting the landing hoax.
6. Anis G. Thompson. *The Greatest Airlift* (Tokyo: Dai-Nippon Printing Company, 1954), pp. 251–56.
7. Clark, *Danube*, pp. 98–99.
8. Ibid., pp. 232–237.
9. Dwight D. Eisenhower, *The White House Years* (Garden City, N.Y.: Doubleday, 1963), pp. 130–34.

Chapter 28. Disaster on a CIA Mission

1. E. J. Kahn Jr., *A Reporter in Micronesia* (New York: Norton, 1966), pp. 39-40.
2. John T. Downey's grandfather was an Irish saloonkeeper and politician.
3. *People* magazine, December 18, 1978.
4. Ibid.
5. Leary, *Perilous*, p. 140.
6. *People* magazine, December 18, 1978.

7. Captain Robert C. Snoddy and Captain Norman A. Schwartz carried nothing that would have identified them as CIA agents. To this day, they are apparently buried in some unmarked grave in Manchuria.
8. John Downey and Richard Fecteau, although kept in the same prison, rarely were able to see each other.
9. Walter "Beetle" Smith served as undersecretary of state for about a year. Then he went into private business as chairman of A.M.F. Atomic, Inc.
10. Hermes, *Truce Tent*, pp. 393–95.
11. Stephen E. Ambrose, *Eisenhower* (New York: Doubleday, 1984), pp. 94-97.
12. Memorandum, "Future Course of Action in Connection with the Situation in Korea," Joint Chiefs of Staff to Defense Secretary Charles E. Wilson, March 27, 1952, National Archives, Washington, D.C.
13. Ibid., May 19, 1953.
14. Author interview with James Smith, 1995.
15. Martin Russ, *The Last Parallel* (New York: Rinehart, 1957), pp. 238–39.

Chapter 29. Operation Moolah: A $100,000 Bribe

1. The $100,000 reward would be the equivalent of about $1,000,000 in 1995.
2. *Saturday Evening Post*, May 8, 1954.
3. Futrell, *Air Force*, p. 653.
4. Ibid., p. 652.
5. Clark, *Danube*, p. 208.
6. Futrell, *Air Force*, p. 654.

Chapter 30. A Scheme to Kidnap Syngman Rhee

1. Clark, *Danube*, p. 260.
2. Ellis O. Briggs, *Farewell to Foggy Bottom* (New York: McKay, 1964), p. 231.
3. Hermes, *Truce Tent*, pp. 449–51.
4. In 1995, forty-two years after the armistice, no peace treaty has been signed. The United States still maintains a large military presence in South Korea to discourage an invasion from North Korea.
5. Clark, *Danube*, p. 271.
6. Acheson, *Present*, p. 652.
7. Ibid.
8. Korean War casualty figures vary considerably according to a variety of sources.
9. Clark, *Danube*, p. 264.
10. *New York Times*, July 28, 1953.

Aftermath

1. *New York Times*, July 28, 1953.
2. Colonel Pawel Monat writing in *Life* magazine, June 27, 1960.
3. Ibid.
4. Futrell, *Air Force*, p. 652.
5. Captain Ro's MiG eventually found a home in the Air Force Museum, Dayton, Ohio.
6. Charles E. "Chuck" Yeager gained wide renown as the first pilot to break the sound barrier.
7. Charles E. Yeager and Leo Janos, *Yeager* (New York: Bantam Books, 1985), p. 205.
8. William Manchester, *American Caesar* (Boston: Little, Brown, 1978), p. 597.
9. Author interview with Lieutenant General James M. Gavin (Ret.), 1987.
10. MacArthur, *Reminiscences*, p. 378.
11. *Washington Times*, July 5, 1990.

Index